FAT AND
FURIOUS

FAT AND FURIOUS

IGNITING RADICAL FAT RESISTANCE

BREANNE FAHS

BEACON PRESS, BOSTON

BEACON PRESS
24 Farnsworth Street
Boston, Massachusetts
www.beacon.org

Beacon Press books
are published under the auspices of
the Unitarian Universalist Association of Congregations.

28 27 26 25   8 7 6 5 4 3 2 1

This book is printed on acid-free paper that meets the uncoated paper
ANSI/NISO specifications for permanence as revised in 1992.

Text design and composition by Kim Arney

*Library of Congress Cataloging-in-Publication
Data is available for this title.*
ISBN: 978-0-8070-1091-4; e-book: 978-0-8070-1092-1;
audiobook: 978-0-8070-2098-2

The authorized representative in the EU for product safety and compliance
is Easy Access System Europe 16879218, Mustamäe tee 50,
10621 Tallinn, Estonia: http://beacon.org/eu-contact

For Eric Swank

CONTENTS

ON BECOMING FAT AND FURIOUS

A friend of mine likes to say, "No one is born a radical. You have to *become* radical by living in the world and suffering from its logics." The fury that I feel about fatness—when I think about the everyday traumas and oppressions fat people endure, the possibilities that are limited and foreclosed by virtue of living in a fat body—is not some kind of inevitability. I did not start my life as radical, fat, or a feminist. Fury is also a kind of becoming. It requires ignition. It is underlaid by loss and grief, recognition of injustice, and a rejection of self-loathing. It comes from an instinct to survive and protect but also to expand, to push outward. Fury transforms and breaks, shakes and disturbs. It works against alienation, isolation, and depression and toward humanity, collectivity, and justice.

People grow into fatness, sometimes slowly, sometimes not, but always against the current of a culture that is painfully anxious about that growth. For those who live in fat bodies, the becoming of their fatness has many different trajectories and paths, set against a backdrop of subtle and not-so-subtle metrics for what is "too much" and "too big." For some, this becoming arrives in childhood, with parents and doctors and peers undermining a sense of bodily freedom and autonomy. Some become fat during adolescence, fatness arriving in tandem with burgeoning desire and sexuality. Others grow into fatness during their adulthood, no longer bolstered by the metabolism of their youth. This becoming, at any age, suggests that we emerge as fat and then make sense of it, that we have to shape our understanding of the world around our changing bodies. We are often ill-equipped to do so, with very little (if any) structural or social support to conceptualize or care for ourselves. Instead, we are inundated by anti-fat messaging, institutionalized sizeism, and complicated, multilayered stories of gender, race, class, sexuality, and ability. Some of us live an entire life in denial of that becoming, taking up the common tropes of "battling" or "defeating" our own fatness. To live as fat is often a state of eternal becoming, laced with messages of failure, deviance, risk, and violation.

And yet, fatness also carries with it so many narratives outside the typical stories that link fatness and deviance. Fatness is love, affinity, affection, strength, similarity, humor, work, and life; this collision has produced in me a relentless defiance about the "ideal" shape of bodies. The dread and terror that people impose upon fat bodies still feels strange and abhorrent to me. I feel disoriented by the ire directed toward fat women, even though I know all too well I am reduced by it. I find it impossible to see anti-fatness as an inevitability or a default setting. Fury is a refusal to accept "what is" at the expense of what could be. I want this book, and the voices within it, to establish a chorus of permanent opposition to that which denigrates fat bodies, even as we all sort out the stakes and possibilities of complicity and resistance. I want to understand what we carry.

If there is to be any joy in fatness, any course correction for the linking of fat bodies with dread and fear, any rectifying the connections between anti-fatness and abjection, it will require a closer consideration of fat bodies as identities of resistance and spaces of fury. In this book, I approach fatness on multiple levels, within the context of feminist politics, activism, and body politics. I argue that fatness operates as an imaginary fear, as lived experience, as a projection screen for political battles about bodies, and as a site of possibilities for resistance. As such, I work to not delineate fat and thin as a dichotomy but as a continuum, a fantasy and a projection, and, of course, as material conditions. The popular story we see today in nearly every aspect of rhetoric around gender and fatness is that the best and most radical thing one can do about fatness is to either accept one's own fatness (see Jennifer Weiner's memoirs), talk openly about fatness as an outgrowth of trauma (see Roxane Gay's *Hunger*), or use fatness to "inspire" exercise and dieting regimens. Self-love and self-acceptance dominate the landscape of individualistic solutions to the problem of fat negativity. If only people practiced body positivity and body acceptance, they could, within these frameworks, escape the problems of fat shame and fat negativity.

The obvious omission at the center of these mainstream discourses is the social and structural critique of anti-fat rhetoric and the material consequences of fat misogyny (economic, romantic, social, and more). This is driven by an even broader failure to understand how women in particular feel terrorized by fatness and how fatness is used not only as a weapon to perpetuate sexism but as a tool to exacerbate tensions about race, class, and sexual identity. Anti-fatness and fat-shaming are used most often as a way to inspire fear in others (by degrading fat bodies and modeling hatred of fatness widely and publicly), to terrorize the self (by inducing a profound fear of fatness), and to silence the obvious links between misogyny and the control of bodies. In doing so, the hatred of fatness comes to feel inevitable, real, and immutable.

Anti-fat rhetoric relies on deeply felt emotions and affect to sustain itself and grow. The intense fear of fatness pushed on fat bodies, and maintained rigorously in thin bodies, works in tandem with structural forms of fat oppression, manifested in a wide variety of institutions that pervade daily life. From schools and workplaces that do not accommodate fat bodies (with their small chairs and improperly sized desks) to forms of transport that exclude or limit fat bodies (air travel and commuter rail) to reductionistic and offensive media representations (see *The Whale*) to failures in the medical field to provide even the most basic accommodation for fat bodies (MRI machines that aren't big enough, blood pressure cuffs meant for smaller bodies, improperly dosed vaccines, and incorrectly sized speculums), structural forms of oppression limit and disempower fat bodies relentlessly.

The COVID-19 pandemic illustrated the pervasive negative affect surrounding fat bodies, revealing the fusion of structural and affective responses to fatness. Many pandemic narratives either ignored the link between higher body weight and COVID mortality rates or blamed fat people for making themselves more vulnerable to COVID, neither of which helped protect fat people in any meaningful way. The near-catastrophic level of fat death during the pandemic, and the refusal to take seriously what this means for fat vulnerability and risk, put in stark terms the disdain placed on fat bodies and fat lives. In essence, messaging around fat death is nothing new, but the pandemic ratcheted up those fears in painful ways.

In this book, I seek to better understand how, and why, this terror of fatness exists as an accepted reality for so many people and how we can work to unpack and undo some of that damage. In particular, I direct energy toward foregrounding the experiences of fat women, recognizing the cultural baggage they face that links their value and their appearance in insidious ways. When looking for stories that counter the invisibility of fat lives or that work against the fearmongering and body-shaming tactics so often present in body politics, there is a notable lack of content outside of fat activist spaces that seeks any real radical and structural critique of sizeism directed toward women. Instead, there are untold numbers of images of women seeking out thinness alongside occasional images of fat women on TV (the grotesquely stereotyped Chrissy Metz character in *This Is Us*), some fat memoirs that describe the trauma of living as a fat person and/or getting gastric bypass surgery, occasional stories in mainstream magazines about fat celebrities (Adele's weight loss), a claiming of space for fat Black women as empowered and, at times, heroic (Lizzo as feminist hero, the frenzy around Oprah and her body), and the occasionally refreshing take on fat women learning to love themselves (Lindy West's *Shrill*).

Missing in these representations is the larger analysis that *all* of the structures we inhabit—the institutions we participate in or are subjected to, the imagery we see, the professions we work in, the medical options we have—work to criticize, exploit, and discriminate against fat people, especially fat women. To be fat, particularly for women, is to experience an extreme form of vulnerability on a daily basis. Outside of fat activist voices, almost no one else is visibly concerned about the aggressive anti-fat biases that permeate American life and often go unchecked. Painfully, progressives and the Left have mostly ignored this as a moral and ethical problem, academia has perversely marginalized fat studies (and allowed the abuse of fat professors and graduate students[1]), Marxists have largely failed to provide class-based critiques about the roots of fat phobia, and radical feminists have shouted into an empty void since Judy Freespirit and Aldebaran wrote about fat liberation in the 1970s. What this means on the ground is that fat women often feel weighed down by oppressive narratives of their own failure without the protections offered by widespread, mainstream, collective structural critiques and analyses of fat oppression. They are, in essence, going it alone.

Ultimately, this book isn't merely about the gaps in representation, the omissions on the Left, the problematically neoliberal framing of fatness in the public sphere, and the painful irony of "woke" people worrying about flabby underarms. This book is about *making space for fat fury*, better understanding and valuing the nuances of fat lives, and giving a platform to voices who engage in structural critiques that link anti-fatness to the politics of misogyny, classism, racism, homophobia, and ableism. Through analysis of popular culture, academic research, and individual interviews with fat women and activists, I explore how people think about, imagine, and dread fatness in order to understand how fatness functions not only as something that many people live with and through but as something thinner people inadvertently terrorize themselves and others with. I work to unpack the lived conditions of fatness and to better understand the nuances of fat life: workplace culture, media representations, feelings about food, and even fat death. I push back against the regressive medical framings of fatness and ask questions about the possibility of healing, the ubiquity of fat fearmongering, and, fundamentally, how fat lives can be recognized as valuable rather than disposable.

This book takes as a key part of its intervention the problems of how women are terrorized about fatness and then argues that rage—or fat fury—becomes the necessary antidote to that resignation and powerlessness. I argue that a new kind of fat fury can, and perhaps must, emerge in this moment, one that elevates fat activist voices above the cacophony of dread, terror, and fear projected onto fat bodies. The fat fury in this book confronts and challenges, reworks and repositions, and seeks to take down structures and systems that degrade, humiliate, and fixate on fat women and their always failing bodies.

By making these anti-fat frameworks more visible—by showing how women have been terrorized about fatness as a means to control them—the interplay between capitalism and the control of women's bodies is laid bare. I work in this book to show how fear, silence, and shame around fatness have constructed women's bodies as "projects" and capitalistic interventions as "tools," ultimately portraying fat bodies as always failing and thinner bodies as always having the potential to fail. These moralistic narratives serve as a means to reduce the complexity of what it means to live as a fat person while also limiting possibilities for linking fat oppression to other kinds of injustices. I am interested in looking closely at how the weaponization of fatness becomes a disguise for misogyny and racism and how the accommodation of stigma (bariatric surgery as a "solution" to the "problem" of fatness) rather than the challenging of stigma (exploring a multitude of avenues that do not equate "fat" with "unhealthy") keeps anti-fatness secure and firmly in place.

Finally, I grapple with how fatness must be reoriented into a mundane experience rather than something extreme or extraordinary, as the continued assumptions that fat bodies are exceptional or deviant rather than normative diminish the political power of fatness. Much like abortion is framed as an exceptional rather than a normative experience of living as a woman, fatness and sizeable weight gain are commonplace experiences too often marginalized and othered. Framing fat bodies as exceptional rather than normative allows for an intensified vilification of fat bodies because people do not read themselves into the story of fatness and do not see their own lives reflected in it.

I want this book to serve as a political and emotional reframing of fatness, shifting instead toward the political project of sabotaging and undoing oppressive systems that scapegoat and degrade fat bodies. I simultaneously criticize the far right for weaponizing fatness in service of patriarchy and misogyny and tackle the Left's overwhelming embrace of neoliberal stories like body positivity and girl power without fundamentally dislodging the central notion of health and anti-fatness. I express skepticism about the superficial solutions of modest size-based accommodations, and I worry aloud about the depth of fat oppression and the silencing and sidelining of fat activist work. Further, because gender is so deeply tied to the body and because liberation politics have long looked to the body as a space to understand revolt and revolution, particularly within feminism, I want this book to upend which bodies are seen and which are not, which bodies are understood as politically charged and which are not. To simultaneously look at fat bodies from these multiple perspectives—emotional, structural, ideological, embodied—is indeed a crucial form of political work, particularly when done with fat activists at the helm.

THE FEAR OF FATNESS

A key argument that I trace throughout this book posits that fatness operates as a kind of conceptual outer limit, particularly for women. Fatness is, most pointedly, an identity that women are terrified of becoming, or a self that women are disgusted at being. Consequently, fatness ends up circulating as a weapon between and among women, as the negative emotions associated with fatness stick to women of all sizes. This means that the terror associated with fatness is not localized to particular bodies or particular people, but operates quite robustly at the level of emotion itself. Anti-fatness—both internalized and externalized—is driven and fortified by emotions. Fat phobia then—the derogatory framing of fatness as something that produces fear, and the claiming of fear in relation to fat bodies—is *actual fear.* The material conditions of fatness do not themselves exist outside of the space of emotions.

Fatness and (mental and physical) unhealth on the one hand and thinness and health on the other have become solidified as cultural assumptions, reinforced by institutions, imagery, and individuals in myriad ways.[2] Fat people hear that their bodies are symbols of moral depravity and poor health (and, by association, mortality and death) and must navigate assumptions that they intentionally engage in unhealthy behaviors even if people are presented evidence to the contrary. Thin people, by virtue of their thinness, must then be healthy. Driven and reinforced by emotions, the consequences of these assumptions can be lethal, as thin people miss important signs of ill health and fat people all too often avoid doctors or have inadequate healthcare based on experiences of relentless stigma. Here we find the dialectical notion that thinness *produces* fatness, that ideas of thinness create ideas of fatness as a social relationship. More specifically, fatness can only be acceptable on the terms dictated by thinness: assumptions of health, industriousness, and the pursuit of normativity.

Fatness has not yet been adequately theorized in relation to thinness. There is a missing discourse of how notions of thinness have come to define, castigate, and set parameters around fatness. Specifically, one of the arguments of this book is that emotions themselves produce the material conditions of being fat and underlie the operation and circulation of fatness both in public and in private. The transmission of narratives of fear have become preoccupying for many thin and fat people. I am a practicing psychotherapist and, when doing psychotherapy with fat patients, nearly all of them have repeatedly expressed a pervasive fear of their bodies functioning as a "ticking time bomb," waiting at any moment to explode, implode, or malfunction. They have internalized the notion that their bodies are always/already failing, that their bodies cannot be trusted to function in a healthy or predictable manner.

Thin people, too, often engage in this rhetoric with fat people, through discourses of "concern" and "worry" for them, and by describing fat bodies in morbid terms. (The medical classification of "morbid obesity" absurdly reinforces these patterns even more intensely and dramatically, and will, I believe, be seen many years from now as embarrassingly hateful and malicious.) Fat people's subjective experience of feeling terrified of their own imploding bodies does not typically come from the *actual* experiences of their bodies failing them but from the ways that fat people absorb the near-constant messaging directed toward them about their bodies as dangerous and precarious. These sorts of projections also torpedo the kinds of self-awareness that fat people might otherwise have about their actual medical problems; fat people must simply endure their bodies. Emotions in this case are not felt but rather pushed into the cultural orbit around fat bodies such that fat people experience this paranoia as vivid and alarmingly real.

Missing or obscured in contemporary discourse about fatness is the fundamental problem that fatness is not merely an identity read from the outside by others, but one constituted by a complex series of emotional expressions both from without and from within. Fat bodies are *read* and *experienced* through affect. In this way, the fear of fatness—a framework that runs throughout this book—is not a byproduct of but a driver of fat oppression. Anti-fatness has at its roots an interface between fear, dread, terrorization, alarm, avoidance, anxiety, and hatred. Fear is not just a projection, but an experience of living in a fat body.

This production of fear results in the expansion of reality for some and the contracting and shrinking of reality for others. Many fat people are crushed by the physical and psychological sensation of absorbing fear, such that they withdraw, turn inward, and reduce their own possibilities. A claim I heard again and again when speaking to fat women either in therapy sessions or in research interviews was that they started to cut off certain life possibilities for themselves as they got fatter. They stopped dancing, or trying more inventive clothing, or flying on airplanes, and for some, they stopped dating or having sex. Some imagined that the entire concept of being loved, adored, protected, and cared for was permanently out of reach. This is perhaps one of the most painful aspects of fat oppression, at least to me. To hear women declare that they cannot imagine the futures they once did—having children, seeing themselves as desirable, traveling freely, applying for jobs they want, physically relating to the world with comfort and ease—is itself a great tragedy, one that we have not even begun to grapple with in cultural or interpersonal terms. The siphoning off of possibility is perhaps the most painful aspect of oppression, for it does not simply crush dreams and ambitions, but it frames these things as permanently extinguished.

In contrast, thin people absorb the experience of fearing the fat body with an expanded view of their own possibilities. I am reminded here of the now-famous line from ultrathin model Kate Moss: "Nothing tastes as good as skinny feels." The triumphant embrace of thinness here—the distance it establishes between very thin people and those who eat—can be seen as a cultural marker of difference that is generated and maintained by fear but also reinforced for thin people *as dominance*. The renunciation of food, the marking of their bodies as the opposite of fear, opens up possibilities and becomes expansive in its expression. Critically, these cultural articulations do not need to actually state that fat bodies are fearsome, as the prizing of thin bodies does the work of marking fat bodies as the other, as the containers of fear.

Still, the Moss mentality suggests that fat bodies do not generate fear in a static way; the generation of fear must be a continual process. People must constantly think about and manage their own relationship to fatness by situating it as a potentially injurious identity, *the self that one must not become* and *the body one must not succumb to*. Fatness is often constructed in this way, as letting oneself go, as surrendering, as not working hard enough to ward it off. Here fatness and injury become intertwined. For women, the potential injury of fatness looms even larger. As a researcher, I have felt astonished by how often thin women imagined fat women as wholly disabled, unable to walk or move or exercise, stuck in their house, rotting away. Even as I sat across from them, myself inhabiting a fat body that clearly did not experience these things, the fantasy of fatness—the injurious potential of it—overshadowed the relation between us. *I must not become you (fat) because I will then experience the shrinking of my reality; my reality is only so big as my thinness allows. Nothing tastes as good as skinny feels.*

Fear, then, informs the way that certain bodies are constructed through relations of opposition, disavowal, the "not me" and "never in the future will be me." Thin people engage in a continual assessment of fat bodies as fear-producing and different from themselves. This brings us to one of the core arguments of this book: Because individual bodies do not themselves generate fear—I do not have to intentionally generate fear in thin people—but my body is read as a category tied to other fearsome bodies, the experience of sitting in the room with thin people is often one of understanding myself as part of a terrifying collective. I am not merely myself, but a symbol of what they may become. I am not merely a single body but the imposition of lots of other fatter bodies into their psyches. I am not knowable as an individual because of my affinity with a collective mob of terror-inspiring "monstrous" bodies. I am the embodiment of threat, the self that they are not, and the borders of my body are constructed of their fear. These patterns are alarmingly common, felt both by thinner and fatter people, as their worlds expand and contract in accordance with the adhesive qualities of fear.

NARRATING FAT WOMEN'S LIVES

To make these arguments concrete, and to enrich the stories and ideas presented throughout, I draw from two primary groups. First, in 2021, I interviewed twenty fat women from all over the US about their experiences with fat embodiment. They ranged from small fat to infinifat. In some chapters, I include direct quotes from these conversations, while in other chapters, their narratives weave into the broader claims. Then, in the spring and summer of 2022, I interviewed ten fat activists from the US and the UK who mostly identified as radical fat activists and who have engaged in numerous forms of activism and advocacy. These ten voices of defiance, confrontation, and fury challenged anti-fatness and pushed for new narratives of fat embodiment. While the fat activists certainly had a broad range of targets for their fury, they seemed to share a worldview that demanded change not only within the minds of fat people but also within communities of thin and thinner people. In marked contrast to the first group I interviewed in 2021, who were often immersed in feelings of fat shame, the fat activists had more direct recognition of how fat people cope with social structures that perpetuate destructive frameworks for understanding diversity of body size and the lived experiences of fat people. All ten fat activists—Stacy Bias, Barbara Bruno, Kimberly Dark, Aubrey Gordon, Da'Shaun Harrison, Caleb Luna, Mikey Mercedes, Tigress Osborn, Esther Rothblum, and Virgie Tovar—agreed to be named directly in this book.

In both groups of interviews, because I spoke primarily with cis women and non-binary people, I chose to focus more on fat women's experiences rather than on fat cis men's experiences of fatness. Though at times I include and refer to the experiences of trans and non-binary people, especially when I spoke with fat activists about resistance to anti-fatness, the vast majority of this book focuses on understanding the specific experiences of fat women. This was a conscious decision, for fat women often carry more stigma than fat men related to their body size,[3] disproportionately do more care work than men (and thus have a heightened sense of their own vulnerability compared to men), and often suffer more dire consequences for being fat. These consequences, detailed in subsequent chapters, include more job discrimination, more negative representations in the media, increased likelihood of getting poor (or no) medical care, more negative consequences in romantic relationships, and far more exposure to violence and abuse related to body size compared to men, alongside many other examples.[4]

I have also spoken for many years with thin (and thinner) women about their bodies and their ideas about fatness. As a practicing clinical psychologist who has worked with clients for two decades, and as an academic feminist who works across humanities and social science fields, I have studied, and listened to, many women's narratives of their bodies across sizes and identities. I have been struck with the profound negativity thinner women have directed towards fatness, fat bodies, and the potentiality of gaining weight. In chapter 1, for example, I drew upon thin women's narratives about hypothetically gaining weight in order to capture how fantasies of fatness operate and how these fantasies often construct fat bodies as immensely fear-producing. I asked thin women to imagine their most dreaded body, which again pointed to the ways that fatness became tangled with other abject statuses, making them largely inseparable. A common thread in this book is that we cannot understand our cultural responses to fatness without also understanding intersectional cultural narratives about trans identity, Blackness, queerness, poverty, and disability. I consider the stakes for those already marked as marginalized by other statuses, and how the fear and dread associated with fatness reflects cultural values layered onto other bodies as well. The important work being done by Da'Shaun Harrison and Sabrina Strings on anti-fatness *as* anti-Blackness has been especially fruitful in this regard.[5] Collectively, these interviews help to enrich arguments both about the dire status of fat lives in this cultural moment, and about the urgent necessity of vehemently opposing the politics and practices of anti-fatness.

A CALL FOR FAT FURY

I have titled this book *Fat and Furious* as a gesture of resistance, as a marker of revolt, and perhaps mostly as a fantasy for what could happen if the workings of oppression did not sink their teeth so deeply into our skin. A fiction writer I knew once described her job as being an "archeologist of possible futures," digging into the past while simultaneously imagining and manifesting the various possibilities of the future. The story of widespread fat fury—still far off in the distance, though the tremors of it appear closer in proximity and more frequently than ever before—is a collision between fat histories and fat futures. Many who have come before have worked to build something different, something new. They have raged and wanted and desired and fought for fat bodies to live in a different sort of world. The voices featured in this book—fat women's voices struggling with what it means to make space for themselves alongside the voices of fat activists, kicking down doors and razing entire structures to the ground in a fiery blaze—illuminate the challenges of the present and the work that is yet to come. They invite new conversations and provoke new directions in this cultural moment.

This is a book for lots of different kinds of readers, regardless of your background, size, or previous knowledge about these subjects: those who feel their experiences have been sidelined and not allowed a real politic, those who are not sure if they should take fatness seriously as a feminist issue, and those interested in how oppression gets grounded and expressed through bodies. I welcome those who resonate with the fat activist work they've seen online and feel the impulse to resist anti-fat attitudes, those who currently read Roxane Gay and Lindy West but are also looking for a guidebook for what to do next or how to go further, fat women who are tired of empowerment-only memoirs, and fat kids questioning what feminism has to offer them beyond Taylor Swift and Beyoncé. Most importantly, this book is for those who feel anger and rage about gender politics but who may still be terrorizing themselves about body size and weight gain. There is so much more work to be done, and I consider this book an open invitation to join the struggle.

In many ways, I work in this book to deeply examine a whole host of complex emotional experiences of fatness—how thinness and fatness interact and become inseparably intertwined, how fatness becomes as much a fantasy and a projection as a lived experience, how anti-fatness operates both as a subtext and as an explicit narrative that can have devastating consequences. Several claims run throughout this book: anti-fatness infects us all, becomes adhesive to other experiences of marginalization, and carries deep emotional weight. To understand the mechanisms by which anti-fatness impacts our consciousness of our bodies and our worlds is an impossibly difficult task. To understand how to manage the damage done by it, how to resist or redefine or reemerge from it, is even harder.

It is an intensely vulnerable thing to speak about, write about, think aloud about, or draw attention to one's own fatness, let alone fight against cultural norms of shame, dread, neglect, disgust, and self-loathing. At times, this book has felt like it's made of my skin. It is a way to see my body from different vantage points, to map my own experiences onto those of others, to draw in the margins of the forgotten stories of fat people's lives, and to make room for the emotions too often suppressed in the stories we've already told about fatness. I want to feel freer—maybe freer to be angrier, sure, but also *just freer*. I wrote this book because I had to, because I am in this struggle too.

Writing about fatness can sometimes feel like a trap. If we talk openly about the more vulnerable parts of fatness—the siphoned-off possibilities, the lived experience of being in a body marked as an object of dread, the self-inflicted wounds of fearing mortality and rejection, the literal and meta-phorical feeling of being squeezed—we may unwittingly undermine or lose sight of the possibilities for resistance, joy, self-love, desire, and community. If we explore how bad things can really be for fat people—particularly in the form of discrimination and injustice—this can undermine the importance of also understanding fat people's lives as rich, multifaceted, provocative, and hyper-ordinary. I want this book to form a bridge between these realities, to make space for fat vulnerability *and* fat resistance, to rummage through the stark realities of anti-fatness while also opening up new understandings of complex and often rebellious fat subjectivities. This is a tall order.

I might argue that all forms of embodiment are a struggle, that we all live within the sticky webs that trap us within certain ideologies and emotions. Fat embodiment feels like a particularly complex experience to even begin to outline, let alone capture in more vivid detail. It carries much confusion, ambivalence, contradiction, and struggle. Because of this, it is full of pos-sibilities for consciousness-raising, reflection, and revolt.

Still, so much of what we know (or could know) about fatness is stifled and blocked through silences and gaps, filtered through the insidious prac-tices of capitalism, reflected back to us through grotesquely false media representations, and undermined by people and institutions eager to sideline fatness as dreadful and disgusting. As so many of the fat activists featured in this book have implied, we have to feel our way through the dark, sensing cracks and fissures in these suffocating stories, finding bits of freedom where we can. And we have to allow ourselves to feel things about fatness and make room to understand what others feel about it. It is through the intensity of emotions people have about fatness that we can make sense of what our bodies carry. This is how things change—sometimes slowly, and sometimes seemingly all at once, but almost always ushered in by big feelings.

I offer a text here that I hope will feel cathartic, perhaps clarifying or illuminating, and certainly infuriating. This fury is necessary. As fat women, we are counting on this fury—in ourselves and in others—to catalyze and transform the future. Perhaps you are already furious. Perhaps you're newly arriving to the discovery of your own anger. Perhaps you're so angry that you can't remember a time otherwise. Perhaps you're waiting for the spark to ignite something in you. I am fat and furious, and I hope you are—or will be—too.

PART ONE

THE TERROR OF FATNESS

CHAPTER 1

THE TERROR OF FAT FUTURES

Thin Women Imagine Weight Gain

"No offense," she said, her eyes darting away. "I just can't get fat. I just *cannot* get fat. My life would be over. I think about it all the time and I just *can't*." My conversations with women with a multitude of body types and shapes, spanning from young to old, have often included snippets such as this. I speak to women as a researcher, wondering aloud about how they view their bodies and how these attitudes interact with the social realities of fatness. In this exchange, fatness is held as an idea in their minds, a body divorced from a self. For many thin women, fatness appears viscerally as a gnawing sense of unease built into the core of their minds. *I just can't. I just can't. I just can't.*

For this person, and for many women, fatness operates as a specter, a haunting, a terrifying prospect of a body they devote considerable effort to avoid having. The anticipated condemnation of becoming fat—often imagined as a possible future that fills women with fear—can powerfully shape women's ideas about their bodies, relationships, and consumption. In this way, fat and thin do not operate as a dichotomy, as two separate realities of fat *or* thin, but as a continuum between the two. Along this continuum, fatness takes on characteristics of a projection, a fantasy, and a material experience of what *not* to become. Fatness exists as a lived reality for some and as a fantasy or imagined identity for others; for many, it is a combination of the two.

Fat and thin women are bound together, born into existence simultaneously, a subject and a projection, a person and a fantasy. The quest for thinness and the fleeing from fatness are tangled up with each other. One byproduct of this relationship is that thin fantasies about fat women take over and dominate fat women's self-understanding of their bodies. They operate instead as a spectral, haunting presence for thin women, the self they must not become. It is this binding, adhering quality of dread and terror that links fat and thin women together. Social reality exists through the binding of emotions. Thin people understand their fear of becoming fat quite intimately, and this continuously shapes their social world and burdens fat women with the weight of their fear.

In some ways, fatness operates as a kind of "bogeywoman" character for many thin women (and, as I'll explain later, for some fat women too). The intensity of emotion felt about fatness allows thin people to construct themselves outside of fatness, through a pervasive endless loop of *I'm not fat.* The fact of being *not fat* is perhaps as critical to the social development of normative femininity as other mundane aspects of adolescent life: separating from one's parents, falling in love, raging with hormonal expressions, and so on. This leaves fat adolescent girls in a dangerous dilemma, for if the disavowal of fatness reflects the experiences of normative teenage girlhood, what then of the bodies that cannot "fend off" or deny their fatness? What if you *are* the bogeywoman?

If fatness and thinness are endlessly bound up together, they come to represent a subject and a mirror. Much like French philosopher Luce Irigaray's conception of men and women in the sexual economy, where men operate as subjects and women operate as mirrors reflecting men's sexual power,[1] thin and fat women operate similarly. Thin women construct a subjectivity based on the disavowal of their own fatness, and fat women become hollowed out, existing instead as the physical embodiment of thin women's fear. Note, too, that this story has repeated itself again and again—between white people and people of color, cis people and trans people, rich people and poor people, straight people and gay people, and nondisabled people and disabled people.[2]

As scholar Sara Ahmed says of the emotional dimensions of bogeyman figures like the racialized Criminal or the Terrorist: "The bogeyman could be anywhere and anyone, as a ghostlike figure in the present, who gives us nightmares about the future, as an anticipated future of injury."[3] So much of what constitutes these hierarchical and uneven social relationships is the ability for those with less power to generate fear in the powerful or dominant groups. In the case of anti-fatness, the anticipation of future injury is not as explicit as in the figure of the Criminal or the Terrorist but instead operates through the pervasive infusion of fear into thin people's consciousness.

To exist as a projection, stripped of subjectivity, is itself a horrifying reality; fatness becomes permanently lodged as an abject status. Consequently, articulating the experiences of fat women, as I do in this book, is to wade through layers of fear and anxiety that have adhered to them. It is a process of showing how the social relationships between thinness and fatness have devastated fat women's ability to see and understand themselves, let alone to ask for or demand something different. It is hard to know ourselves when we have been constituted as an object instead of a subject, as a repository of fear, loathing, and pity rather than a complex, full human.

Enormous amounts of time, money, and energy are spent on generating and perpetuating these fears, and on treating fat people as abhorrent and fearsome. And yet, the palpable fear of becoming fat is made all the more absurd by the relatively mundane qualities of weight gain that occur over longer periods of time. People might become fat; many people in this country do, because of aging, genetics, gradual hormonal changes, lifestyle (starting a family, working a desk job, or living without access to the outdoors), or simply existence in a society with a dysfunctional relationship to eating, with "good" or "bad" foods, a diet culture, large restaurant portion sizes, and so on. Fatness comes to absorb dread and fear because it is a realistic possible future for many women. The reality is that fatness *is* often a part of our future, and our bodies will inevitably change as we get older. Portraying these changes as a dreaded desent into a stigmatized social status only further harms people as their bodies age and change.

The reality that many people will become fat exists in direct contrast to the portrayal of fatness as an outlier or an outer limit. Becoming fat or fatter could simply be a matter-of-fact reality for many people, yet it is often pitched as a fear-producing process driven by moral failure. Similar to conservative and religious moral panics about people becoming queer, the generating of fear around fatness provides an especially potent backdrop for hatred, discrimination, and stigma to thrive. It makes fatness "hateable" not only in terms of directing negative emotions toward currently fat people but also in imagining the eventuality that many people will become fat. In short, we could view becoming fatter as a simple development that *just is*, but instead we often attach a frenzy of fear around it, casting fatness as the dreaded outer limit.

According to the data, weight gain is far from an aberration. Roughly one-quarter of American women of reproductive age will gain a substantial amount of weight, with many gaining over one hundred pounds in their adult lifetimes.[4] While weight gain does not necessarily overlap with health status, it is still notable that the Centers for Disease Control and Prevention (CDC) estimates that over 35 percent of women have body mass indexes (BMIs) that place them in the "overweight," "obese," or "extremely obese" categories, with many women weighing well over two hundred pounds; the National Institutes of Health estimates that nearly 42 percent of American women would qualify as having "obesity."[5] The average American woman is 171 pounds.[6] Becoming fat, therefore, is a relatively normal and mundane experience for many people. Fatness *is* the norm.

The normative qualities of fatness have collided with the pervasive and relentless fear of fatness, leading to sharp increases since the 1990s in body hatred, anti-fat discourse, and body-shaming. Feminist scholar Susan Bordo famously identified that the fear of fatness was also no longer an aberration. Girls and women hating their bodies and being afraid of becoming fat (or fatter) is so normal that it is unremarkable, in part because so many of them—94 percent in a recent study—experienced body shame from others.[7] Many psychologists and sociologists now identify body hatred as part of normal adolescent development for girls, no longer seeing it as divergent from typical adolescent development.[8] The fear of fatness is seen as a typical feature of normative adolescence.[9]

Internalized anti-fat bias tends to follow women developmentally throughout their lives but disproportionately affects younger women. Adolescent girls, for example, held particularly negative views of fatness, often using fat-negative phrases and terminology behind their friends' backs at school and choosing friends who had similar body weights.[10] For college-aged women, having traditional beliefs about gender roles and consuming fashion-related media, particularly social media, correlated with more negativity toward fatness and more fear of becoming fat.[11] For some women in their twenties and thirties, dread of fatness and fat phobia impacted those whose bodies changed temporarily, such as in pregnancy. For many women, pregnancy elicited fears about becoming fatter and resulted in distortions about weight gain during pregnancy.[12] Pregnant women often described weight gain during pregnancy as disturbing, though these effects were felt more by white women than by African American women during pregnancy.[13] The meanings attached to fatness at different ages show how women grappled with tensions about body weight at many different life stages and that anti-fatness infused women's normal developmental stages throughout their lives.

To paint a starker and more realistic portrait of what normative body hatred and anti-fatness looks like for women, we should look at more disturbing cultural fantasies that emerge around fatness, particularly when people consider hypothetical scenarios about becoming fat. For example, a survey of *Esquire* magazine readers in the early 1990s found that over half of young women would prefer to be run over by a truck than be fat. A whopping two-thirds of these same women would choose stupidity over fatness.[14] Another study found that 24 percent of US college women admitted to always being fearful of gaining weight, while 42 percent of Canadian undergraduate women said that they were pervasively terrified of gaining weight.[15] These results send a clear message about the imagined fear of fatness and the severity of how much thin people would do to avoid fatness as a social status.

Appalling forms of anti-fat bias appeared frequently in other studies related to how the fear of fatness infects schooling, healthcare, and interpersonal relationships. The fear of fatness is also connected to other sorts of phobic or disgusted reactions to marginalized bodies and has substantial overlaps with symbolic racism and the fear of fat bodies of color.[16]

The fear of fatness also had strong connections to women's eating-disordered thinking and behavior, particularly as the fear of gaining weight formed the center of women's narratives about their bodies. The slippery slope between "normative" dieting and more extreme, potentially lethal, expressions of anti-fatness reveals the fear of fatness as infusing a wide range of women's experiences with eating. Young women in a bulimia treatment center described eating-disordered behavior as linked to a strong fear of fatness.[17] Another study found that underweight college students overestimated their body size while most other groups underestimated their body size, suggesting that distortions to understanding one's size are common.[18] Both dieters and non-dieters described strongly negative attitudes about fatness, but dieters had internalized stronger negative feelings about fatness than did non-dieters.[19] Those women who looked for external validation of their bodies struggled more with fear of fatness than those who found intrinsic value in their bodies.[20]

Attributions for why people become fat also affected attitudes about fatness, as most women blamed fatness on individuals' lack of self-control and restraint.[21] These ideologies highlighted individuals as responsible for weight gain while minimizing institutional practices and their impact on body weight related to workplaces, food culture, capitalism, and family and economic systems. The beliefs that personal willpower determined fatness led to far more endorsement of anti-fat attitudes than those who saw a broader picture of culture, evolutionary causes, and genetic predisposition, suggesting that attributions are ideological frameworks for understanding fatness.[22] A study of six countries found that those who attributed fatness to personal responsibility held more anti-fat prejudicial views.[23] Further, the increasing prevalence of "food addiction" discourse, which also attributes fatness to individual behavior and beliefs (in this case, addiction to food), portrayed fatness as a consequence of loss of control and personal responsibility. Belief in food addiction also increased fat people's self-stigma and moved them away from structural and cultural explanations for fatness, such as availability of junk food.[24] Overwhelmingly, weight gain is currently seen by both thinner and fatter women as a lack of self-control—and, by extension, a personal moral failing—which contributes to negative or hostile belief systems about fat bodies.

It is useful to remember that anti-fatness, and specifically attributions for becoming fat, also have a *history*, and have been informed by the social and cultural conditions of each historical period. Nicolas Rasmussen traced the historical development of medical literatures making attributions about fatness and discovered a significant shift after World War II. He found that psychiatrically oriented postwar medical thinking about fatness was far more stigmatizing than the endocrinologically oriented thinking of the interwar period, in part because fatness became linked to notions of addiction. This change then shifted attributions for fatness away from the physiological and toward ideas about moral failure, prompting a huge surge in anti-fat attitudes during the 1950s.[25]

These frameworks of moral failure, alongside pervasive hostility toward fatness, have had damaging consequences for fat women. Women who experienced fat stigma had far worse health outcomes than those not dealing with fat stigma, suggesting that stigma was itself a health hazard.[26] Mental health outcomes were typically worse for fat women than for thin women, as fat women who reported high levels of fat discrimination also reported greater levels of anxiety and clinical depression compared to thin women, in a study of twenty-two thousand people.[27] Some studies have identified

excessive fear of fatness as connected to eating disturbances, negative connotations about fatness, and women's desire for thinness, but critically, this
fear was not linked to weight loss or healthy body treatment.[28] Fat women
subjected to fat-shaming rhetoric ironically reported consuming more calories and feeling less capable of controlling their eating compared to those not
exposed to weight-stigmatizing content.[29] A study of middle-aged healthcare
professionals found that the fear of becoming fat seemed to have no relation
to eating healthy diets or doing cardiovascular exercise, again suggesting
that pushing fear narratives did not translate into people engaging in more
health-related behaviors.[30]

Studies show that fat discrimination has outsized negative social and relational impacts on fat women in particular. Fat women and girls sometimes
felt cut off from romantic and dating contexts, as 50 percent of fatter girls
in ninth through twelfth grade had never dated, compared to 20 percent of
their thinner classmates.[31] No such distinctions occurred for boys.[32] Further,
fat women with intense body shame felt less satisfied with their sex lives than
fat women who validated their bodies.[33] Fat women who felt more negatively
about their bodies also experienced more unwanted sexual activity than fat
women who considered fatness a good quality.[34] This may stem in part from
how fat women are portrayed, as either sexless or as having insatiable sexual
appetites, or as not being considered sexually attractive or having sexual
agency, leading to distorted views of fat women's sexual lives.[35]

The fear of fatness is reproduced and reinforced throughout the social
and political landscape, from everyday interactions to structural inequalities
that favor thinness. "Fat talk," or the way that women speak negatively with
each other about the size and shape of their bodies, also impacts how women
feel about their bodies.[36] Women often use fatness to demean their own body
in order to gain sympathy and affirmations from people who feel obliged
to say *You don't look fat!* Women who overheard fat talk not only used more
fat talk themselves but also described more body shame and dissatisfaction
compared to those who were not as exposed to fat talk.[37] For thinner women,
merely *hearing* other women denigrate their bodies seemed to infect their
psyches and led to behavioral shifts like restrained eating, a notable contrast
to fatter women eating more when hearing anti-fat rhetoric.[38] Studies have
repeatedly shown that thin women of all ages participate in fat talk, as do
women across the size spectrum.[39] The demographics of women most likely
to use fat talk included those of an average weight, younger women, and

more educated women (those with more than a high school education), again suggesting some notable dynamics for the role of education and fat talk.[40] As women became more educated, they denigrated themselves more, not less, often. African American women were perhaps more protected from these negative attitudes, as they reported far less emotional distress about weight gain than white women.[41] In general, though, women took their cues about fat talk from their immediate social environments, mimicking friends' and acquaintances' fat talk, and their mothers' fat talk, more than strangers or distant others.[42] Even more notably, women expressed more surprise when other women talked positively about their bodies than when they spoke in negative ways about their bodies.[43]

WHAT WOULD IT BE LIKE TO GAIN ONE HUNDRED POUNDS?

Feminist psychologist Leonore Tiefer wrote that social norms serve as a mechanism of social control and that "the problem is that the very existence of standards of normality breeds negative psychological consequences for those who deviate—that is known as the 'social control' function of norms."[44] That is, social norms are not merely passive suggestions for how people should look and behave but operate as standards that separate those who conform and those who deviate. These norms push people into conformity by denigrating those whose bodies stray outside of social norms, suggesting that anti-fat attitudes cast fat bodies as nonnormative, deviant, and less than fully human.

Several years ago, I designed a study that asked thinner women (all but one weighed under two hundred pounds) about their bodies, sexualities, and beliefs about fatness. This group of women came from diverse backgrounds in terms of race, ethnicity, sexual orientation, and age.[45] All of them lived in Phoenix, Arizona, and participated in a face-to-face semi-structured interview that lasted 90 to 120 minutes. Given that weight gain is fairly common and that drastic weight gain is also commonplace for women throughout their lifespans, I posed the hypothetical question: "What would it be like to gain one hundred pounds?" I chose a question about significant weight gain so they would then have to imagine a body different enough to enter them into the identity category of fat rather than merely "fatter than they are now."

Most commonly, thinner women reacted to my question by saying that gaining weight would make them feel incredibly angry and frustrated with themselves, and that they would feel like it represented their personal failure.

The highly moral language of fatness and thinness appeared vividly in these descriptions. For example, Rachel (thirty-nine, white, bisexual, 170 pounds) talked frankly about the self-hatred she would feel if she gained a hundred pounds, citing the importance of vanity: "I feel like I would hate myself. I would feel so disappointed in myself for allowing myself to forget the healthy part of vanity. Everyone should own a full-length mirror!" Similarly, Joyce (twenty-one, Filipino American, bisexual, 130 pounds) said she would compare herself negatively to her thinner self and would miss her "better" self: "I feel like I would just think about when I was lighter and younger and having that comparison would get to me. It would be scary!" This sense that the good self is thin and the bad self is fat appeared as a shared assumption about fat bodies, as thin women assumed individuals become fat because of individual choices and deficiencies. The fantasy of controlling weight gain and chastising themselves for gaining weight further reinforced this.

The connection between self-directed anger and feelings of disgust also surfaced. Four women shrieked in disgust when asked this question, or started laughing uncontrollably, imagining that the seemingly outlandish question was a joke. This sense of outrage directed at themselves for becoming fat, combined with women's remarkably strong emotional reactions to this question, revealed the strong affective underpinnings of the terror thin women feel about fatness.

In contrast with these reactions, three thinner women mentioned that they had gained weight before and had weathered fairly sizeable weight gains and losses over the years. In this sense, the hypothetical question about weight gain elicited reactions based more in reality than in fantasy. Emma (forty-two, white, heterosexual, 125 pounds) described her previous weight gain during a medical treatment and her experience with having fat family members, saying that these changed her perspectives about fatness: "There was a stretch of time in my lupus treatment when I was on heavy steroids and I gained about sixty-five pounds (the biggest I've ever been). It didn't bother me. I can accept my body. A lot of my family are overweight. They're bigger and they're beautiful." Contrasted with this view that weight gain could be managed and coped with, others described feelings of devastation, as it reminded them of a former fatter self they wanted to reject. Kathleen (forty-nine, white, heterosexual, 185 pounds) described her weight shifts and the severe personal and relational consequences she endured in the past: "Devastating. I've been there. Absolutely devastating. More than anybody can even know. I've done it a couple of times actually. I gained eighty-three pounds during my first pregnancy when I was seventeen, and it completely changed how I felt about myself. My husband had a lot of affairs on me. I remember vividly one time he said, 'Look at yourself. Just look at yourself in the mirror and you wonder why I screw around.'" Kathleen's fear of returning to her fat body seemed to locate the negative aspects of fatness in the physical body rather than in the traumatic and high-conflict relational aspects of her life. She also seemed to internalize the legitimacy of blaming betrayals on her fatness.

The most common response from women when they imagined gaining a hundred pounds focused on their perceptions of the physical limitations they would face by becoming fat. Here, the terror of fatness took the shape of fantasizing about fatness as fundamentally disabling. Sofia (forty-two, Mexican American, heterosexual, 167 pounds) felt fat being thirty pounds overweight and imagined getting fatter as terrifying: "I don't feel good for me. I'm slow, I get tired easily, and I breathe harder, you know? With more weight, all of these would get worse." Escalating these worries, Gretchen (fifty-two, white, heterosexual, 193 pounds) imagined she would lose her ability to stay active and would not move: "I would be so miserable. I couldn't move. It would be really hard to do things I like to do, like hiking, biking, traveling. It would be very physically difficult to do things, with a lot of stress on joints." Antonia (twenty-five, Mexican American, lesbian, 150 pounds) similarly imagined fatness as disabling and limiting to her sexual and physical life: "I feel like I would have a hard time breathing, and then sexually it would change things too." This sense that fat bodies are incapacitated or severely limited remained an unchallenged "fact" for these women.

The reactions were sometimes based on concerns about pregnancy weight gain or family members' health problems, but no woman mentioned knowing or even imagining a healthy fat person. Being fat and in shape or fat and *not* disabled appeared nowhere in the women's responses. For example, Bea (thirty-seven, Filipino American, heterosexual, 176 pounds) described her fear of diabetes and cancer, assuming that all fat people would have serious health complications: "If I gained one hundred pounds I'd be very unhealthy. I'd have full-blown diabetes." The inability to imagine fatness beyond illness and physical limitations also shows how thinner women constructed becoming fat in purely negative terms, through various imagined losses they would face.

Another perceived loss related to imagined weight gain was a lack of partner attention and not feeling sexy. Notably, women did not mention fearing negative responses from parents, siblings, children, or others, but did fixate on their partners losing interest in them. For example, Gail (forty-six, white, bisexual, 195 pounds) admitted that she would enjoy sex less: "I would feel less sexy. It would take me probably a lot of time again to make myself more comfortable in my skin again and feel like I could act sexual again." Similarly, Trish (nineteen, white, lesbian, 125 pounds) felt convinced, based on her previous slight weight gain, that she would lose her sexual appeal and become deeply depressed and agoraphobic: "I would probably live off the couch and play video games and just not have any confidence in the bedroom." This sense of losing confidence, feeling unattractive, withdrawing from the public eye, and experiencing a loss of sexual attention permeates thinner women's narratives.

Thin women also imagined that gaining weight would *require* eating-disordered behavior to get their bodies back into control, highlighting yet another problematic fantasy about body weight. Yvonne (forty-one, Mexican American, heterosexual, 130 pounds) imagined eating disturbances in response to feeling fat: "I would have to work really hard at it, want to exercise more, watch what I eat, diet, stuff like that. It would probably go too far." Lila (thirty-six, white, heterosexual, 145 pounds) felt certain she would develop an eating disorder due to a combination of self-hatred and the loss of male attention: "I would just hate myself. I would have an eating disorder and starve myself again. I'm sure of it. I would be so unable to be with somebody else because even if they said, 'Oh, you're so beautiful,' I wouldn't believe them. I wouldn't even want to go out of the house. I wouldn't show myself to anybody. Who would want to be with someone who was that much overweight?!" Not being able to imagine dating while fat points to how especially consequential fatness feels to many women. Dire consequences in their social relationships and feelings about eating also show how fatness is constructed with deep fear and dread, a self that must be pushed to the margins of the imagination.

While it should not have come as a surprise that many women expressed feelings of severe distress about fatness—imagining, for example, that their lives were over—it was startling nevertheless to hear it expressed so directly. Several women talked about extreme options if they gained a hundred pounds. Zari (forty-three, African American, heterosexual, 120 pounds) imagined wanting to kill herself: "Devastating. I would have a heart attack. I would be anorexic. I would be killing myself, starving myself." Veronica (forty-nine, African American, heterosexual, 260 pounds), already fatter than most of the other women I spoke to, said plainly: "I would want to die if I got that fat. I just don't see a point in still living like that." Her reaction was also notable because the weight gain would mean a launching into superfat status rather than medium fat status, a line that provoked reactions of extreme distress.

These narratives, this full-throttled internalization of fat-shaming, suggest that thin women did not contest or challenge dominant cultural scripts about fatness. The absence of any oppositional narratives is all the more alarming given that messaging about body positivity, fat acceptance, and fat activism is growing in visibility. Certainly, many members of oppressed groups find hidden or overt ways to challenge their own subjugation.[46] The difference here is that thin women were asked to *imagine* a different embodiment, which did not produce fat-affirmative ideologies. The reactions here are not only disturbing but also connect fatness to dread, disgust, terror, fear, abjection, and disability. That women's notions about fat bodies were largely alarmist, hyperbolic, and unrealistic—fat women do not routinely and frequently lose their full mobility, die of heart attacks, hide themselves in their houses, stop having sex altogether, flee from their families until they lose weight, or feel constant anger with themselves—reveals another disconnect between the realities of living in fat bodies and the imagined sense of living in fat bodies. Thin women detested fatness, indicating that terrible things would happen to them if they became fat. Central to this discourse is the reality that thin women often perpetuate anti-fatness, that their drive to avoid stigma actually *produces* anti-fat stigma for fatter women. The fear of fatness was far more extreme, exaggerated, and distorted than the realities of living in a fat body. Understanding thin women's emotions about fatness, coupled with the reality that this sort of weight gain is actually relatively commonplace among large subsections of American women, is critically important to understanding contemporary fat negativity.

It was striking that no one mentioned anything about how anti-fat the world is; they talked only about fatness as an inherently monstrous fate. Thin women did not frame fatness in defiant terms as a symbolic challenge to the pursuit of unattainable bodies and unrelenting thinness. They also did not question the conditions or context for their hypothetical weight gain or qualify their answers accordingly: Am I a new mother? Am I injured or ill? Am I an Olympian? Am I going through a breakup or perhaps in the honeymoon phase of a new relationship? Am I in prison? Am I living in opulence in the South of France? Thin women did not even make space for a "So what?" attitude about fatness. Rather, similar to earlier studies of women choosing stupidity or death instead of fatness, thinner women would do almost anything to avoid living in a fat body. There is no room for imagining fatness as good, normal, mundane, or fun, or as a nonissue. The void here, it seems, was a near-complete lack of imagination of how the world might operate differently, better, or in a less harmful way.

In a final thought on this group of women, I want to note that the thin women I interviewed gave these vivid, emotional, anti-fat responses while being interviewed in person by me, as a fat woman. Listening to the interviews as a researcher left me not with feelings of personal injury (though a few comments made me wince internally) but with a sense that thin women harbor a pervasive sense of dread and fear about fatness that spans demographic differences of age, race, sexual orientation, and relative degree of thinness. That women were so willing to disclose hateful feelings about fatness to me raised questions about what sort of anti-fat attitudes would have emerged if these thin women had spoken with a thin interviewer. Research shows, for example, that self-censorship is often present in mixed-race dynamics given that social desirability makes students not want to appear racist to their classmates.[47] This leaves me wondering, chillingly: Are women's responses to this question the *censored* version of their feelings about hypothetical weight gain, or is anti-fatness such an accepted reality that articulating these views is not seen as a problem at all?

OTHER DREADED BODIES

To understand the deeper stories of how people relate to fatness through fear and dread, I also want to consider how thin embodiment and desire for thinness are often constructed against a backdrop of anti-fatness, especially for women. The disavowal of fatness, and the perception that fatness is somehow ugly, forms a key part of thin women's understanding of themselves and their bodies. Sociologist Heather Laine Talley has theorized, using people with facial variance and facial disabilities, that women are more driven to avoid being ugly than to be beautiful; in her model, fear of ugliness serves as a central driving force of women's relationship to their bodies and to social norms. People are driven to avoid the social punishments of being perceived as different or abject. In essence, women want to be perceived as normative, and therefore avoid the punishments associated with ugliness, more than they want to be beautiful per se. She writes, "Girls dream of being beautiful—but perhaps equally important, girls fear being ugly. While the intense desire to be beautiful certainly generates insidious consequences, anxieties around ugliness can be taxing too . . . fearing ugliness is, at core, a fear about the future—as if a good life is exclusively determined by what we look like."[48] How this translates into thin women's understanding of fatness is an open question, but Talley's work serves as a reminder that avoidance of stigma and disavowal of "ugly" identities may drive thin women to associate fatness with anxiety and a lack of safety in a patriarchal world that relentlessly denigrates women's bodies. In this sense, anti-fatness is perpetuated and expanded through the systems of oppression and power that require bodily compliance, efficiency, productivity, and narrow beauty standards. White supremacy, patriarchy, and capitalism *create* anti-fatness and infuse people's realities with the sense that fatness represents loss, precarity, and frank danger.

Connected to discourses of ugliness and abjection, research on disgust is a better predictor of punitive moral judgments than other emotions, like sadness or despair. Disgust works to distance the self from those perceived as morally inferior, thereby allowing people to create moral judgments rather than rational cognitions.[49] These disgust framings are often combined with feelings of contempt and resentment, such as the cultural framing of the racialized enemy during wartime, or the racialized and classed "morally degenerate" welfare mom. These contemporary examples reveal how conservatives deploy disgust in service of denigrating entire groups of people.[50] Like fear, disgust has a sticky, adhesive quality to it; we become more disgusted as we get closer to someone deemed as disgusting, and yet disgust can also stick in our imaginations and fantasies about certain bodies or objects. Disgust is often tied to notions of cleanliness, goodness, and social ideals, suggesting that disgust can effectively *produce* negative attitudes and anxieties.[51]

The emotion of disgust can also work to stigmatize less powerful groups of people and frame them as immoral, degenerate, and unworthy of respect and dignity. People who felt disgust for fat people—not pity, sadness, or a different negative emotion—judged them as morally deficient.[52] Further, people rated crimes against the wealthy as more problematic and disgusting than crimes committed against poor people,[53] and they assessed welfare recipients as more disgusting than others.[54] Homeless people have often been judged as the most disgusting population of all.[55] Doctors tended to feel more disgust toward patients who were fat, intersex, and trans.[56] These findings collectively suggest that disgust regulates bodies and reproduces social biases, ideas about beauty and ugliness, and hierarchies that disproportionately value those with higher status.

Building on the results of the study where I asked thin women to hypothetically imagine gaining a hundred pounds, I asked these same women to imagine other kinds of abject or debased statuses related to their bodies and embodiment. I posed the question: "What is the most dreaded body you can imagine? In other words, whose body would you least want to occupy?" The question was designed to access a wider range of social statuses women found abhorrent, and it implicitly asked women to imagine an embodied form for the emotion of dread. I was interested here in how fatness might connect to other kinds of embodiment and how the imagined dreaded bodies operated differently than responses to more straightforward questions about body image, weight, and feelings about their own identities.

The most common response to the question about dreaded bodies centered on women's fear of fatness. Fourteen out of the twenty thinner women I interviewed mentioned fatness in their answers, again suggesting that anti-fatness dominated women's ideas about dreaded bodies. The intense fear of fatness also morphed into fears about smelling bad and other kinds of abject, visceral body markers. For example, Naomi (eighteen, white, bisexual, 142 pounds) said, "I already have problems being the way I am now—being a little obese—so I just would not want to be any fatter. That would be terrible. I don't want to have a bunch of acne on my face, or a dirty body. I wouldn't want sicknesses or STDs or cancer. I don't want a body that has cancer in it." In these kinds of responses, thin women's fear of fatness morphs into broader fears about poverty, disease, and other markers of abjection, showcasing fatness as a launching pad for other kinds of dreaded body statuses.

Thin women imagining dreaded bodies also portrayed fat women as grossly negligent of their bodies, coding their fear of fatness as both about body size and about moral judgment of poverty, eating choices, and aging. Yvonne couched fatness in ideas about negligence and disgust: "Somebody that's not healthy and not taking care of themselves." In another example, Lila described fatness and sagginess as interconnected, and spoke about the loss of sexual desirability: "I would just not want to be saggy, just like a huge stomach that had to be lifted to get to my vagina, to be really, really fat and loose and just have like no shape." Martha (fifty-two, white, heterosexual, 130) also described a fear of sagginess and aging connected to the fear of fatness: "Somebody who's worn out, drug-addicted, saggy, and with missing teeth. I would hate to be fat and saggy." This Frankensteinian figure of a fat woman with missing teeth, a huge stomach, a shapeless body, and sagging body parts reveals again how thin women's terror about fatness serves as a baseline for other kinds of bodies they loathe or find disgusting, as if fatness itself absorbs these other markers of bodily dread. This frank sense of monstrosity embedded in these narratives—the way that fatness seems to conjure other kinds of "horrors"—shows the way that affect links with absurdity and fantasy to produce vivid portraits of embodied fear.

In tandem with the explicit fear of fatness was anxiety about illness and disability. Some women directly stated that they had a fear of being disabled, such as Bea, who imagined being in a wheelchair: "I think it would be hard for me to be in a wheelchair and stuck like that. I don't want to be stuck with people pushing me around and I'm too lazy to push myself around. I just want to be able to control my body and not rely on others to help me." These associations between dread, loss of autonomy, fatness, and disability painted a portrait of how dread seemed to fuse together different abject body statuses.

Thin women feared having bodies outside of white, cisgender, hairless, and traditional beauty norms, again revealing how dominant ideas of embodiment guided their emotional reactions to bodies. In an especially problematic and alarming response, Antonia (twenty-five, Latina, lesbian, 150 pounds) noted that she found Black women's bodies ugly, giving a disturbingly racist description of Black women's genitals in her answer: "It's really fucked up, but Black people gross me out. I've always joked about it but there's probably some truth of my feelings for this. I've never been with a Black girl and I just imagine their vaginas and like labia and stuff being like roast beef sandwiches. I don't know. I don't like roast beef and that association kind of grosses me out." The relative lack of questioning about why these feelings existed and where they came from also allowed narratives of hierarchy and dominance, coded as being "grossed out," to exist in an unquestioned form. Disgust and dread often take on these forms: *I just don't like it/them. I just don't!*

Finally, the answers to this question show how abject bodily statuses are often woven together in intricate ways. Trish feared hairiness and fatness at the same time: "I wouldn't like to be bigger or obese. It would be this total loss of self. I guess being really hairy would be different for me too. I know a lot of women with hair on their arms. That's gross." In another example of nonnormative body anxiety, Bea described trans and intersex bodies as abject: "I wouldn't want those bodies that have both male and female parts, or bodies that move between them. It would be so hard on me emotionally." This sense that certain bodies—especially fat and trans bodies in these examples—produce troubling associations shows how the avoidance of ugliness creates an all-encompassing fantasy of the *dreaded other*, one that contains multitudes of fear, a bodily repository of all our moral and political panics.

This group of thin women easily and readily formulated ideas about abject and dreaded bodies by conjuring up ideas about fatness, excessiveness, and bigger bodies though fatness often fused together with Blackness/Brownness, trans identity, and disability. This also suggests that ideas about fatness are not related to women's own bodies ("My arms are too big" or "I need to lose weight") but link to a specter of fatness in the culture at large ("I do not want to eventually be fat" or "I must do everything I can to avoid becoming fat"). Thin women's fear of fatness is located both in their immediate sense of embodiment ("I am/am not fat") and in their imagined embodiment ("What will I or could I become?").

For thin women, fat bodies are not drawing on realistic examples but on the emotional production of the dreaded, monstrous other, embodied vividly in the kinds of narratives that saturate our media landscape, such as *The Whale*, *What's Eating Gilbert Grape*, *1000-Lb. Sisters*, and *My 600-Lb. Life*. Women here had an emphatic sense of what to *avoid* becoming.

All of this points to the premise that emotions—specifically, dread, fear, and terror—are deeply political and cultural entities, situated not only within the individual person, but adhering to bodies—both material and imagined—that surround those individuals. As critical theorists Sara Rodrigues and Ela Przybylo have argued: "The process of thinking about abjection, disgust, and revolt is less about thinking ugliness than it is about visceral reactions to ugliness . . . Thus our visceral responses to dirt, the grotesque, plainness, and/or monstrosity are about maintaining social relations and social margins."[57] Visceral reactions to dreaded bodies reveal thin women's ideas about the social order and the hierarchies that uphold that social order. The body, in its idolized or dreaded forms, exists as a fantasy or a flight of imagination; as such, it has the power to wound, to maintain inequality, and to reinforce the worst kinds of social and cultural narratives about good and bad, ideal and dreaded.

A FATE WORSE THAN COVID

The bigger question of how thin women react to *actually* gaining weight brings together a collision of these fantasies of fatness (what it might be like) with the realities of weight gain (what getting fatter feels like in practice). The early days of the COVID-19 pandemic, when people were adjusting to the world shutting down, provided a unique window into how people reacted to dramatic shifts in their bodies, as lack of movement and exercise combined with intense anxiety and fears produced the perfect storm for anti-fat attitudes.

In June 2020, after the George Floyd protests had begun, I was conducting a study of women's attitudes about body hair for a separate project. As the participants were recruited to the study because they intentionally grew out their body hair, the interviews primarily focused on their feelings about rejecting the social norm of hairlessness for women. The interviews included a range of questions about contemporary political issues, including reactions to Black Lives Matter protests, feelings about feminism, and ideas about how the pandemic had affected their lives. At that point, racial tensions were erupting across the US, vaccines were still far from becoming a reality, the first Trump presidency dominated the news cycle, and COVID cases were spiking, particularly in red states. In this context, I spoke to a group of twenty-two individuals[58] (nineteen cis women, two non-binary women, and one trans woman[59]) and asked them several questions about COVID-19 and the lockdowns. One of these questions was: "How has COVID-19/the coronavirus impacted you in general?"

Notably, this particular study did not target discussions of fatness, nor did I imagine that fatness would be a theme that emerged in their responses about the pandemic's impacts on them. I had originally imagined that women would want to talk more about sociopolitical issues and current events. It came as a profound surprise to me that women's COVID narratives were not filled with discussions of isolation, solitude, missing friends and family, fear of sickness or death, concerns about health, anger about racial injustice, under- or unemployment, worries about domestic violence, exasperation about juggling multiple social roles, and other themes all-too-familiar during the early months of the pandemic. Thin women's fear of fatness has become so engrained that women identified becoming fat as their primary concern about the COVID pandemic. Thin women described their fear of gaining weight as debilitating, preoccupying, and terrifying. *Would I become fat? What would happen if I gained too much weight? I feel like my body is getting soft. I'm eating too much and I'm gonna get fat.*

Thin women's responses centered on the idea of weight gain as threatening, sometimes more threatening than illness itself. In fact, over three-quarters of the women I interviewed mentioned weight gain when discussing how the pandemic had impacted them. This was especially true for thin women who feared becoming fat. Ainsley (twenty-three, white, heterosexual, 125 pounds) expressed fear of gaining weight and how she had to fend it off to cope with the pandemic: "I've been trying to work out more and get in shape. I know that there's the whole 'Corona 15' like the 'Freshman 15' so I was trying to get ahead of the ball game."

At times, thin women imagined fatness as an identity to avoid, linking it to ill health and the idleness of staying home during the pandemic. Jasmine (twenty-eight, Taiwanese American, heterosexual, 120 pounds) described exercising to avoid increasing her risk factors for COVID: "I'm thankful that I'm in good shape because I exercise a lot and I know that people who are not in good shape like physically or nutritionally are at greater risk for contracting COVID."

Several thin women chastised themselves for perceived laziness, lack of exercise, and weight gain, seeing their behaviors as character flaws. The didactic links between thinness and morality, fatness and immorality, were striking. Thin women also engaged in relentless criticisms of their food choices and expressed anger at themselves about their weight during the COVID-19 lockdowns. Heather (forty, white, bisexual, 145 pounds) said she felt angry at herself for her lack of exercise and her food choices: "I'm not making the best food choices because I'm getting junk food and eating more when I'm home." Frances (forty-seven, Mexican American, lesbian, 138 pounds) verbalized and partially critiqued her acute fears of weight gain: "I know I should be more scared of the coronavirus but honestly I'm just scared of getting heavier. I can see that my body is different. I'm so mad at myself about it. How could I let this happen? I've never seen myself as a big person and I never want to be one!" These emotional descriptions laced with self-criticism and fears of fatness point to the ways that fatness operates as a dreaded possible self that can become real if they lose tight control over their bodies.

Reflecting on these narratives, I found it remarkable that these stories about weight gain (or feared weight gain) arrived unsolicited in the middle of a study about other aspects of bodies, politics, and social life. This group of women—all of whom openly rebelled against other body norms by growing out their body hair—expressed a pervasive fear of weight gain, one that guided their experience of the early COVID-19 lockdowns. Perhaps some of these feelings situated weight fixations as a distraction from the menacing world of the pandemic. Still, body size figured centrally in their feeling of stress, as their experience of the pandemic elicited fears of losing control, doing an insufficient amount of dieting or exercising, getting soft or flabby, gaining weight, and being lazy. Most notably, strong links between negative moral characterizations like laziness connected to feelings about weight gain or fatness.

There is a painful irony in these narratives: when bodily harm was literal and imminent during the early months of the pandemic, with many fearing they could die of the virus, countless people could only focus on the fact that they might gain fifteen pounds before the pandemic was over.

WHAT WE MUST NOT BECOME

What people least want to be—or most want to avoid—is a driving force of embodiment. For thin women, fatness is all-too-often framed as something they must not become. This assessment of dreaded bodies, laid out both psychologically and materially, is mediated through emotions and absorbed and transmitted through relations of power. As media scholar Lisa Blackman argues, "Affect refers to those registers of experience which cannot be easily seen and which might variously be described as non-cognitive, trans-subjective, non-conscious, non-representational, incorporeal and immaterial."[60] She goes on, "Affect is not a thing but rather refers to processes of life and vitality which circulate and pass between bodies and which are difficult to capture or study in any conventional methodological sense."[61] Emotions are fundamentally unruly, working to resist easy categorization. They bleed into each other, disrupt and reinforce hierarchies, and work as mechanisms of social control or markers of resistance and liberty (sometimes simultaneously). When we think about *what is possible to become*, whether in our bodies, our social statuses, or our careers, this is both a cognitive exercise and an emotional one. Thin women relate to the question of becoming abject—gaining a hundred pounds, becoming a "gross" or "dreaded" body—through narrative, emotions, and literal fantasy.

The specter of fatness (something many women will become over their lifetimes) carries a certain terror that is more vivid and easily accessible than the imagination about identities people can never change (like racial identifiers). For thin women, fatness is always a lurking possibility, a shame-filled double of the self that can push thin women outside of the bounds of the hegemonic—dominant, patriarchal, white, cis—gaze. In this sense, what is *imagined* haunts the edges of how women understand themselves now. Possibilities of the future, and the emotions invested into those possibilities, change how people see themselves in the present tense. *I'm not fat, I don't want to be fat, fat is bad*—these thoughts constitute so much of thin women's subjective takes on the world. Thin women do not merely understand fatness as a distant possibility; fatness shapes their *current* self-understanding, molds their embodied preoccupations, serves as a constant centerpiece of their imaginations.

For those of us living in fat bodies, it can be hard to face how distressing our bodies are to many thinner women. The narratives in this chapter are painful: *I find pieces of myself everywhere, and I cut myself handling them.*[62] Thin women may perceive fatness as a loss of desirability, a loss of mobility, a marker of shame and disgust, an excuse for self-chastisement, a shift away from normativity, and much more. Some of these reactions are inevitable outcomes of living in a culture that attaches women's value to their bodies, sees fatness as a personal and moral failure, and eagerly punishes any lack of conformity to white, heteropatriarchal standards of beauty. Becoming less desirable is a nearly universal fate for women; consequently, women do a great deal of emotional and psychological jockeying in order to understand themselves in relation to that dreaded future self. Their bodies will become more marginalized. This is painful for everyone, even if differently experienced.

Emotions guide and shape how we experience our bodies: joy, whimsy, acceptance, disgust, fear, dread, loathing, anger, embarrassment, shame, marvel, confusion, annoyance, sarcasm, humor, hesitation, ambivalence, sadness. I argue that emotions are a key factor in the construction and maintenance of bodies in social space. We become preoccupied with our bodies as we are, but we also become preoccupied with what we might become. This sense of possibility—things that could happen—is the space of expansive thinking and social change (revolution as well as making new systems and new lives for ourselves) but also one clouded by emotional frameworks for what we dread and who we fear. The imagined embodied self is thus a dangerous one, drenched in power and hierarchy, prone to jagged edges.

Fatness haunts thin women. It scares them. If this chapter has one clear message, it is this: thin women's fear and dread about fatness set the stage for enabling the harms done to fat women. And for that, there must be a reckoning.

CHAPTER 2

"LAZY, UNMOTIVATED, DEPRESSED, SEXLESS, OVEREATING, AND EMOTIONAL"

Fat Women Confront and Grapple with Fat Stereotypes

I cringe every time I think about the character that Chrissy Metz plays on the fictional television series *This Is Us*. Constantly tearful, overly generous, one-dimensional, vocally self-loathing, endlessly apologetic for herself, eating disordered, surprised that her husband loves her *in spite of* her body—these traits often circulate as facts of fat life. On the rare occasions that we get to see something else—Cardi B and Megan Thee Stallion's shamelessly lusty selves in "WAP," or Bridget Everett's fully-human-and-also-fat character in *Somebody Somewhere*—it feels like a revelation. Fat stereotypes have become ubiquitous even as fat characters are flattened out, cast as thinking about and fixating on their fatness, caricatured as either funny or pathetic but rarely anything more.

The range of spaces and relationships where fatness is treated as abnormal, abject, or inferior to thinness is staggering. Problematic stereotypes about fatness have staying power and have persisted for at least seventy years without significantly lessening. A 2016 study of over *four million* implicit bias tests taken between 2007 and 2016 found that bias decreased for sexual orientation and race but increased sharply for weight bias, marking anti-fatness as the only major form of bias on the rise.[1] Whether in film, television, literature, social media, magazines, political coverage, or advertisements, the portrayal of fat women overwhelmingly presents fatness as disastrous, negative, stigmatizing, and something to avoid. Weight bias persists across nearly all types of media and has worsened over the last several decades.[2] Even more alarmingly, a CDC survey found that over half of US residents who watched television at least twice weekly believe that health information presented on television is accurate. Another study found that mothers label the evening news, internet searches, websites, parenting books, and morning talk shows as the most reliable sources of health information after their pediatricians.[3] No wonder, then, that accurate information about fatness, health, wellness, the success (or lack thereof) of dieting, and the complexities of gaining weight continue to attract much misinformation and misdirection.

Consuming any kind of media typically skews feelings about fatness and encourages anti-fat bias and negative emotional frameworks for understanding body size. For example, the amount of women's media consumption predicted increases in disordered-eating behaviors, drive for thinness, body dissatisfaction, and feelings of ineffectiveness. Magazine reading was particularly effective in generating weight bias in women consumers, as were weight-loss reality television shows.[4] Those who watched even a single episode of weight-loss reality TV like *The Biggest Loser* more often expressed negative attitudes toward fatness, dislike of fat people, and a belief that weight could be personally controlled through willpower.[5] And watching weight-loss reality television contributed to the belief that individuals control their own weight, which then led to more anti-fat attitudes and biases compared to those who did not watch these shows.[6] Shows like *My 600-Lb. Life* and *1000-Lb. Sisters* feature fatness as grotesque, monstrous, and abject. Weight-loss reality TV focuses on the moral economy of good and bad fat people, and obscures any of the social and structural elements that shape weight and body size.[7]

In different types of media, television representations of fatness have reduced fat women to one-dimensional characters often devoid of an interior life. Fully half of television episodes on prime time in the 2010s contained at least one weight-stigmatizing incident, including programs targeting both children and adults.[8] In an analysis of the ten top-rated prime-time fictional television shows, only 14 percent of characters were fat. Fat women characters did not interact with romantic partners, did not display physical affection, and were treated as largely unattractive. Fat male characters, by contrast, were seen interacting with romantic partners and friends, talking about dating, and openly eating.[9]

Television viewers also found weight-related humor more funny when they endorsed more negative stereotypes toward fat people, suggesting that how people related to humor about fat people may also reflect deeper attitudes of anti-fat bias and hatred.[10] Fat stigma and fat humor, directed toward fat characters, originated from male characters three times as often as female characters on television.[11] In an analysis of twenty-seven different prime-time sitcoms, fat male characters frequently made self-deprecating and derogatory comments about their own body, which often provoked strong reactions from the audience.[12] In notable contrast, women characters in situation comedies *received* negative messages from male characters, as men making fun of women's fat bodies appeared as a common trope of comedy on television.[13] Fat women on television were also derided more than thin women, and dieting women were depicted as giving themselves more verbal punishments than non-dieting women. Additionally, fat bodies were depicted on television as the antithesis to what is "normal" or desirable, suggesting that fatness is a condition to overcome, a site of fear, and inherently humorous and degrading.[14]

That said, some television representations have tried to complicate the narratives of fatness as morally inferior and wholly negative. Several shows (*American Housewife, The No 1. Ladies' Detective Agency, Big Sexy, My Mad Fat Diary,* and *Super Fun Night*) have embraced body-positivity messages and have begun to critically examine the moral panics of the "obesity epidemic."[15] As blogger Gillian Brown has noted, depictions like Dan Conner in *Roseanne* and Sookie St. James in *Gilmore Girls* attempted to counteract more negative depictions, like Fat Amy in *Pitch Perfect,* Tracy Turnblad in *Hairspray,* and Po in the Kung Fu Panda movies.[16] Shows like *My Big Fat Fabulous Life* introduced fat women escaping the parameters of fat shame (but only if they fit into the "good fatty" archetype).[17] Series like *Dietland* and *Shrill* work to complicate the narrative of fat women, particularly by depicting women overtly struggling with internalized fat shame and externalized fat bias.[18] Still, no research has examined the possible impacts of watching these depictions of fatness, and critical reception of those shows have been mixed, with some celebrating the unabashed embrace of fatness as refreshing, honest, and game-changing while others argued that the shows reduced fat phobia to an oversimplified "fat is beautiful" message.[19]

In her astute analysis of films depicting fatness, media scholar Barbara Plotz points out that body size on television operates as a continuum, writing that the questions that emerge about sorting people into fat or thin "highlights how the social constructedness of this category is more obvious than those of other categories such as gender or race. Who counts as fat and who doesn't can vary over time, can vary from one nation/culture/region to the other and can depend on class, race and gender identity."[20] She analyzes fatness not as a particular body size but as a cultural construct around which representations operate. In this sense, films depicting fat women often rely on familiar tropes about fatness, even when characters sometimes move in and out of their status as a fat character. She ultimately argues that films themselves often point out, or make a big deal of, women's fatness and that they are worthy of particular scrutiny for their treatment of fat women's bodies. Films focusing on fatness often portray fat women (see Melissa McCarthy in *The Boss* or *The Little Mermaid*) as less feminine, sexually and physically aggressive, and dominant and overbearing in personality. Fat women are expected to engage in physical or gross-out comedy and are often depicted as engaging in negative or gross eating practices. For fat women of color, films often feature long-standing stereotypes of sexual availability, slapstick, and old tropes of supporting the "beauty" and "femininity" of white women characters.[21]

Conflicts about representations of fatness in film have often centered on the use of fat suits—prostheses often made of foam and latex—to allow otherwise thin or thinner characters to appear fat. There is a long history of film directors employing fat suits instead of casting fat actors, depicting fat people as humiliated, foolish, unsexual and unattractive, and overtly disgusting. From Gwyneth Paltrow in *Shallow Hal*, socially and romantically repulsive in a fatter body, to the more recent depiction of Brendan Fraser's extreme fatness in *The Whale*, fat suits often amplify the negative emotions and abject reactions viewers are meant to have about fat characters.[22] As fat studies scholar Kathleen LeBesco has argued, "The suits seem to allow for a moment of recognition that fat-phobia exists, followed by a mandate that fat people must lose weight to avoid this stigma . . . although on the face of things the fat suit is about transforming our values, it can in fact be understood as a conservative tool aimed at normalization and the degradation of difference."[23] According to *Atlantic* writer Megan Garber, films with fat suits like *Shallow Hal* "speak to a culture that still interprets fatness as a condition that deserves whatever mockery it might get."[24]

Anti-fatness also appears in children's media, which has become more fixated on weight, thinness, and body image. Two studies of children's videos and books found that body image content appeared frequently, especially in stories about Cinderella, Rapunzel, and the Little Mermaid.[25] In an analysis of children's movies over the past two decades, more appearance-related themes for women characters have appeared, as has more messaging about personal control of weight, compared to earlier time periods.[26] More than 70 percent of children's movies included weight-related stigmatizing content ("That fat butt! Flabby arms! And this ridiculous belly!" in *Kung Fu Panda*), suggesting that weight stigma is a normative aspect of children's films.[27]

Media targeting tweens (ages eight to fourteen) has pivoted toward even more aggressive anti-fat bias. For television consumption, an analysis of the five most popular Disney Channel shows in the mid-2010s found that *every episode* of these programs included appearance-related incidents and communicated content about food. Roughly half had content about exercise, and 40 percent discussed body weight directly, particularly around masculinity and muscularity but also around femininity and thinness.[28] The impact of these forms of media on tweens' body image was pronounced, as watching more television programs aimed at tweens produced more internalization of appearance ideals and anti-fat bias.[29]

Media content targeting older teens also has an abundance of anti-fat messaging and weight-related material. An analysis of 631 online advertisements found that weight-loss products were aggressively marketed to teenagers and directly emphasized the thin ideal.[30] When teens saw weight-loss advertisements, they interpreted the advertisements by responding emotionally rather than by critiquing their financial motives or credibility.[31] Teens who consumed more online content reported more appearance comparison, weight dissatisfaction, and drive for thinness compared to teens who consumed less internet content.[32] Further, teens who consumed and reacted more to media were far more likely to engage in extreme dieting than teens who consumed less media.[33] In particular, watching music videos predicted self-consciousness about weight and appearance more than television and video game usage.[34]

Social media has had a particularly deleterious impact on adolescent girls' feelings about weight and appearance, with a plethora of studies showing that more consumption of social media has resulted in more negative body image and anti-fat attitudes, particularly for teenage girls who compare their bodies to other girls' bodies.[35] The negative impact of social media usage on girls' feelings about their bodies was significant, even when controlling for demographics, active versus passive daily social media use, and other risk factors for body image problems, suggesting that social media engagement was itself problematic for teens across the board.[36] Different platforms had similar results, with TikTok overwhelmingly glorifying weight loss and ignoring weight-inclusive content (only 3 percent of one thousand videos analyzed included weight-inclusive content; the rest championed thinness and weight loss).[37] Across social media platforms, the pandemic era further intensified adolescent girls' exposure to anti-fat rhetoric, as 55 percent saw social media content about stress eating, and 41 percent saw weight-gain memes. These numbers were even higher for adolescent girls with higher body weights (66 percent and 48 percent respectively).[38] Teen girls' use of Instagram increased over time if they reported poorer body image scores initially.[39] This suggests that anti-fat attitudes and poor body image may fuel an increased hunger for social media content, making it all the more insidious as a promoter of anti-fat content.

Women's magazines have also contributed to spikes in fat stigma and anti-fat bias. Pictures in magazines strongly impacted girls' (fifth through twelfth grade) perceptions of their weight and shape, with 69 percent reporting that magazine pictures influenced their idea of the perfect body shape, and 47 percent saying they wanted to lose weight because of magazine pictures. The more women read women's magazines, the more they dieted or exercised to lose weight[40] and the more they disliked their bodies.[41] Fitness magazines overwhelmingly emphasized women's physical beauty over their health, again reinforcing how social conformity to beauty norms dominates health discourse in women's magazines.[42] Parenting magazines targeting mothers also included gendered and racialized content about food practices as moral and emotional decisions made by mothers, women having an obligation to seek a thin body and to model thinness for their children, and fat children as inherently unhealthy and at risk of becoming fat adults.[43] These incessant associations between wellness, class status, thinness, and policing of food lay the groundwork for women's relationships to themselves and their children to fixate on anti-fatness.

How fat women see themselves reflected back to them in popular culture can impact not only how they feel about themselves but also how others interact with them. Representation matters, not just because it creates contexts for people to feel validated and seen, but because it shapes consciousness, maps out the terrain of what is possible, and depicts "typical" stories associated with certain kinds of bodies—who gets to fall in love, have a satisfying career, or travel the world.

POLITICIZING FATNESS IN THE NEWS MEDIA

As one of the most consistently aggressive anti-fat media spaces, political news coverage of fat people has communicated direct messages about the "problem" of fatness, using news stories to further degrade and humiliate fatness as a moral failure. The treatment of fatness has gradually moved more toward attributions that blame individuals for their own moral failings. Analysis of news media content from 1990 to 2001 found that fatness became a "postmodern epidemic," where moral panics around fatness emerged after no medically pathological basis could be found for it.[44] In essence, as the etiology of fatness became more diffuse and the cures less attainable, fatness acquired the status of a moral "defect." This phenomenon circulates abundantly in contemporary political news media about fatness, particularly in stories featuring fat women—including the ubiquitous headless fat bodies commonly repeated in news stories about "obesity." (As a satirical headline on Reddit touted, "Study: Obesity Linked to Headlessness.")[45]

News stories about fat women discussed fatness as a scourge and a pathology, using terms like "fat bombs," "killer disease," and "tax burden" to couch fatness as both an undue burden on taxpayers and a synonym for being undeserving of care; fat people were treated in news media as pathologized, gazed upon, marginalized, controlled, and gendered.[46] The impact of this on both thin and fat people has far-reaching negative consequences on perceptions of fatness. One study of exposure to news segments with anti-fat bias found that adults who viewed negative, stereotypical images of fat people increased social distance from fat people, particularly African American women, had more anti-fat attitudes, and rated fat people as lazier and more unlikable than those not exposed to stereotyped news media content.[47]

The vast majority of news coverage about fatness couch it within a discourse of concern, blame, and advice for fat people about the physical harms of fatness.[48] Kathleen LeBesco has traced numerous efforts by the state, covered extensively in news media stories, to engage in the "war on obesity," including bills targeting body mass index, obesity report cards, curtailment of custody, and state-sponsored health insurance discrimination. Each of these, she argues, undermines human wellness and reinforces the ideology of a neoliberal government that targets individuals for their own fatness.[49] The overuse of the labels "overweight" and "obesity" also suggest that political news coverage of fatness continues to place fat bodies as outliers rather than as normative.[50] Rampant size discrimination has led news media outlets to speak about fatness with "authoritative" anti-fat rhetoric while also implicitly and explicitly encouraging fat people to have a disordered relationship to food, with crash diets, extreme restriction, and so on.[51]

Fat people are framed in the news media as contributing to the demise of culture and society. Obsessive coverage of the "obesity epidemic" has attributed a number of social and psychological diseases and ailments to fatness: cancer, climate change, spikes in young people's death rates, childhood disorders, and more.[52] Talking about it as an "epidemic," despite inconclusive scientific evidence, particularly in light of the relative absence of safe and effective weight-loss techniques, likely does more harm than good. Americans have actually gained a relatively small amount of weight—about eight to twelve pounds—between 1986 and 2006,[53] suggesting that moral panics about the "ever-expanding waistline" of Americans more often feed the need for news stories rather than represent anything actually new. Media discussions of the "obesity epidemic" serve the financial interests of the diet and wellness industry and the for-profit healthcare system and rarely present scientific studies about harm or the relative long-term lack of effectiveness of dieting.[54] The language of moral panics is even more severe for coverage about fat children, as hand-wringing and assignment of blame to parents, particularly mothers, for children's fatness has become a staple of mainstream news media coverage about the "obesity epidemic."[55] (The *Washington Post* once even suggested schools have standing desks to combat fatness in children.)[56]

Blame for fatness has been assigned to a wide range of causes: food culture, the growth of Walmart, the normalization of fatness, a contagious "obesogenic environment," an extra cookie, restaurant eating, and parental neglect.[57] While some articles apply a more nuanced and scientific reading to fatness, the majority still portray fatness as a problem that urgently needs solving.[58] The "redemptive" and "health-promoting" stories of diet culture in the mainstream news media often support anti-fat rhetoric couched in stories about health and wellness. Conversations about good and bad foods are ubiquitous in dieting culture conversations in the news media, with foods like alcohol, chocolate, butter, and take-out foods having particularly negative (moral) status compared to healthier foods, with the benefits of extreme dieting appearing as the optimal goal.[59] Anti-fat rhetoric also appears prominently in news stories about pregnancy and women losing their baby weight, with clear implications that residual weight after childbirth is undesirable and unattractive.[60] The news media shamelessly promotes diet culture to women, suggesting that dieting will increase their worth and value as people.[61]

For right-wing news outlets like Fox News, coverage about fatness takes an even more aggressive and belittling turn. Notably, surveys of individuals found that conservatives felt more negatively toward fat people regardless of their own weight status, a finding repeatedly echoed in the coverage that comes from conservative news outlets.[62] Fox News reporters have (absurdly) blamed the "obesity epidemic" on Latinx children, increased occurrences of C-sections during childbirth, vending machines in break rooms, and yogurt.[63] Their solutions to these problems include an equally absurd list of answers: anti-hunger aromas to stop people from eating, aggressive fitness trainers, traditional gender roles, a neuromodulator device called vBloc implanted under the skin to suppress appetite, and avoiding fat friends because fatness is contagious.[64] A writer at the conservative *Washington Examiner* claimed that fatness was a threat to national security because it reduced the number of eligible soldiers.[65] Going even more extreme, right-wing ideologue Milo Yiannopoulos summed up his anti-fat sentiments by saying his desired goal is to "make America thin again"[66] and that "100% of fat people are fucking gross."[67]

THE IMPACT OF FAT STEREOTYPING

People's relationship to stereotypes about their own lived experiences has played a central role in psychological and sociological research about oppression and social status for decades. Stereotypes function not only as a framework that people negotiate about how others view and see them, but also as deeply internalized ideas about themselves. While stereotypes are generated outside of individual people, they often become folded into the core of how people see themselves. Psychologists offer the term "stereotype threat" to refer to the phenomenon that happens when people worry about confirming a negative stereotype of a group they belong to.

One way that stereotypes can be harmful is encouraging people to internalize negative feelings about their own groups, which can be hazardous to their well-being. There is a profound global dissemination of negative ideas about fatness[68] where fatness is often framed as *deserving* of stigma, with thinness as the only available escape from the harms directed toward fat people. Thinness becomes engulfed in a perspective of healthism, where having a thinner body reflects a supposed moral superiority in comparison to having a fatter body. Stereotypes about fatness persist even when negative health outcomes of fatness are scarce (such as in Iceland, where fear of fatness is abundant but negative health outcomes of fatness were relatively small).[69]

Fat people are read as perpetually self-loathing and loathsome, with fat bodies carrying scripts and narratives that label fatness as negative even if people do not themselves feel negatively about their bodies.[70] Self-labeling as fat often sounds pejorative to thinner people, as the word itself has come to carry negative connotations. Fat people are not even allowed to call themselves fat as a matter-of-fact label. In one study, labeling people as "fat" versus "overweight" led to more negative connotations associated with fat people's bodies,[71] and another study found that thin people perceived the phrase "unhealthy weight" to have better connotations than "fat" in medical settings.[72] In other words, it's often assumed that the word "fat" carries excess stigma, while other descriptors that actually mark fat bodies as comparatively worse than thin bodies—"unhealthy" or "overweight"—are deemed preferable. Even though fat is a label that most fat activists and advocates choose, thinner people still approach the term with squeamishness and unease.

With regard to size, stereotype threat appears in how people relate both to groups of fat people and to themselves as individuals. One study found when faced with anti-fat rhetoric (fat people caricatured as lazy, unmotivated, lacking self-discipline, and so on), fatter women anticipated rejection, showed greater heart rate reactivity, and had lower cognitive performance, lower self-esteem measures, and increased negative emotions like anxiety and rumination than women who were less fat.[73] Fat people exposed to stereotype threat conditions also showed reduced skills in performance, learning, and memory, as well as perceived competence, compared to fat people not exposed to stereotype threat.[74] Another study similarly found that the level of stereotype threat increased as people's size increased, and that women were more susceptible to stereotype threat than men, as sexism and the need for women to embrace conventional femininity and attractiveness added to the burdens of fat embodiment.[75] Further, when fat women's bodies were visible to onlookers during an experiment, fat women had higher blood pressure and poorer performance on measures of executive control compared to when they were merely audiotaped, again suggesting that weight stigma and stereotype threat can reduce women's cognitive performance.[76] Fat children also respond intensely to stereotype threat. When playing video games, fat children assigned an avatar of a large body size performed far less well than those assigned a thinner avatar or those in a "weight neutral" condition.[77] These studies collectively suggest that when fat people anticipate negative attitudes toward themselves as fat, they have severe negative reactions both cognitively and emotionally.

Stereotype threat can also impede the diversity of images fat women have about themselves, leading to negative health impacts. Because positive representations of fat people exercising are largely absent within pop culture, fat women often react to stereotype threat by rejecting notions of themselves as active and athletic.[78] Priming fat women to think about weight-related stereotypes led them to exercise far less often, reject healthier eating, and consume more calorie-heavy foods.[79] Even if harsh comments about fatness were done with "good intentions," fat women exposed to weight stigma ate *more* calories than those not exposed to weight stigma.[80]

Weight stigma has a variety of negative health outcomes for fat women: increased physiological stress, poorer psychological health, more binge eating, and increased motivation to avoid stigmatizing places like the gym.[81] Ironically, many of the behaviors thought to "help" fat women, such as friends expressing concern about their weight or gyms advertising weight loss and fitness, are often detrimental and can themselves worsen fat women's relationship to health and exercise, a claim long espoused by fat activists.[82]

Stereotypes about fatness flourish at all stages of life—from within one's own family and social circles—and in entertainment, work, and school environments. The resulting social comparison about body weight leads to problematic outcomes for both thin and fat women. Disturbingly, in one study, thin women felt socially powerful when they endorsed anti-fat attitudes, as thin women who endorsed fat stereotypes and engaged in comparison to fat women had better body image compared to those who rejected fat stereotypes.[83] Similarly, when average weight or heavier women explicitly compared their bodies to thin women, they reported more dissatisfaction with their bodies and less optimism about future life outcomes; this suggests that social comparison based on weight reinforces the thin ideal and denigrates fat bodies.[84] The more that women had internalized societal views of fatness as bad and thinness as good and the more they reported restricting their eating, the more extreme their self-loathing responses became when exposed to media images of thin women.[85] For fat women and girls, the more they interacted with other fat women trying to lose weight, the more likely they were to try to lose weight using unhealthy behaviors, even if it produced negative feelings when doing so.[86] The desire to avoid social disapproval joined with media and fashion influences to be the strongest predictors of women's problematic weight-loss behaviors.[87]

Notions of respectability, or attempts to portray a group as "normal" and conforming to social rules, also play a role in how fat women react to stereotypes. Not wanting to confirm negative stereotypes led to clear ideas about good and bad versions of fatness, which are themselves tied to notions of healthism, morality, and ideas that link thinness to morality and good health, and fatness to immorality and bad health. "Good" fatness involves actively working to *not be fat* or, in lesser ways, to paint fatness as more normal and normative. Fat activist Stacy Bias has called out the narratives of being a "good fatty" or "bad fatty" as particularly insidious and deeply internalized both within and outside of the fat community.[88] Scholar Zoë Meleo-Erwin has cautioned fat activists against linking fatness to health, saying that such a strategy may lead to an ethic of assimilation that excludes many people (the "bad fatties"). She instead argues that fat activists should work to upend notions of bodily normativity and to fight against healthism and norms that people are only valuable if they engage in healthy behaviors.[89]

Stereotypes about fat women can also veer toward more positive representations, though these continue to be limited to certain moral frameworks about good and bad fat people. Many stereotypes of fatness, particularly happiness, sweetness, kindness, humor, and generosity, have been noted in research on attitudes about fat people.[90] But, these positive characterizations are notable for what they *don't* include: sexuality, desirability, complicated inner lives, sociability, and so on. Notions of being a "good" fat person dominate portrayals of fat women, situating a good fat woman as someone who apologizes for herself, is well-groomed, fashionable, and active, and repeatedly acknowledges that she should be pursuing healthier choices.[91] If the primary positive stereotypes of fat women emphasize maternal roles of nurturing and care, or the energetic "good fatty" attempting to demonstrate healthy behaviors and lack of personal responsibility for fatness, this situates fat women as only portrayed positively if they are working to end their own fatness, or use their fatness for the good of others. It enters them in an endless loop of self-loathing, anti-fatness, and other-directedness and does little to change actual attitudes about fatness as morally bad.

FAT WOMEN RESPOND TO MEDIA PORTRAYALS

Building on the concept of stereotype threat, caricatured portrayals of fat women, moralistic and overtly hostile news representations, and more, I wanted to better understand how fat women made stories about their relationships to media stereotypes about fatness. As part of my individual interviews for this book, I asked a group of twenty self-identified fat women: "What are the stereotypes of fat people?" "What portrayals of fat people do you see repeatedly in the media or in popular culture?" and "How do you feel about these characterizations?"[92]

The fat women I interviewed could readily access numerous negative stereotypes of fat women in the media, often describing these with an overt sense of anger. Many expressed anger at the overwhelming amount of negative stereotypes similar to what Isabella (thirty-six, Mexican American, heterosexual, 236 pounds) saw in the media: "That you're big and you're lazy and that you're gonna blow up the bathroom . . . They think they're gonna break every chair that they sit on, or that they're gonna go to a buffet and outeat everyone there, and there's gonna be no food left. It's ridiculous!" Jayden (fifty-seven, white, lesbian, 220 pounds) was upset at the reductive stereotypes directed at fat women and other people with lower social status: "Fat and lazy, sloppy, let yourself go. That kind of stuff. I hate those stereotypes! I hate them! Let themselves go? Are you kidding me? It's like Black people are lazy, fat people are lazy, women are lazy, it comes down so obviously anti-everything you don't like as a group. Everyone's lazy unless it's a white straight male who's also not fat!" These overlapping descriptions also point to the kind of easily accessible stereotypes that fat women have in their minds. Their anger and disgust about them suggested a refusal to fully internalize them as true or valid, though they did not mention any particular actions they would take about these stereotypical representations.

In contrast, a few fat women described fat stereotypes along with their efforts to combat them. Tahi (twenty-nine, Pacific Islander/Tongan, heterosexual, 265 pounds) described how she wanted to fight back against stereotypes of fatness: "Anytime I see comments online about people saying, 'Oh, they're too lazy to cook' or something, I just feel that's the time to start creating content that's not like that." Georgia (fifty-three, African American, heterosexual, 275 pounds) identified her competitive nature as a way to combat negative stereotypes of fatness. When I asked her how she reacted to these stereotypes, she added: "I'm very competitive. If I was at a tennis match or volleyball game, I would feel I have something to prove, and it is just because that's my nature. Not because I'm overweight, but I'm here to have fun, and if you get surprised by seeing my performance, then that just goes to show you what you really thought of me." These reactions, however defiant, suggest that fat women have to formulate parts of their identity around reacting to stereotypes and combatting them actively. This exertion of energy maintains these stereotypes as a powerful framework for women's choices and behaviors.

Some women reacted to negative stereotypes of fatness by believing that stereotypes were inevitable and that nothing could change them, suggesting a more resigned and passive stance. Esther (fifty-nine, white, heterosexual, 318 pounds) described the stereotypes and her efforts to simply ignore them: "They're dirty, they're slow, their feet are probably dirty. Their hair's greasy. Their clothes don't fit and they shop at Walmart or Kmart. I just ignore everybody." Yvette (thirty-one, African American, heterosexual, 325 pounds) acknowledged painful negative stereotypes of fat women but begrudgingly felt she could not do anything about them: "I've gotten accustomed to it and I try not to listen to it. There's not much you can do about it." These reactions—ignoring people, feeling it's inevitable, or questioning one's competence—suggest the beginnings of internalizing, accommodating, or avoiding stereotypes rather than combatting them.

Many fat women also directly internalized stereotypes as true and lacked any impulse to fight back against them. Octavia (thirty-two, white, bisexual, 200 pounds) talked about accepting negative stereotypes and believing these things about herself and other fat women: "Lazy, insecure, funny at the expense of others. No one fat in pop culture has protagonist energy. You don't get the sense that they have a deep inner life." Sharon (forty, white, heterosexual, 323 pounds) felt plagued with a constant feeling of smelling bad that came from negative stereotypes presented in the media: "I am kind of lazy and I do have an awful smell. Maybe I'm just self-conscious but it seems bad." This awareness that stereotypes can sink their teeth into women's consciousness suggested that merely recognizing negative stereotypes did not sufficiently allow for resistance to them.

Even as many fat women slowly internalized negative stereotypes of themselves, they also reacted intensely to celebrities who embodied or rejected fat stereotypes: Oprah, Lizzo, Rebel Wilson, Adele, Ashley Graham, and more. Laila (thirty, African American, heterosexual, 200 pounds) talked about several celebrity women but expressed dismay at their constant weight-loss stories: "I love Meghan Trainor. Monique before she lost weight. Jennifer Hudson before she lost weight. Aretha Franklin, but she had cancer I think. Everyone I can think of like that, they're just losing weight. I love Lizzo. That's my girl! She doesn't give two fucks. I love her. I love the confidence." Similarly, Hannah (twenty-seven, white, bisexual, 220 pounds) reacted strongly to Adele's weight loss, saying: "I feel bad saying this but I almost feel a little bit like she jumped ship, that she pandered to everyone talking about her as a stereotypical fat girl. She lost *so much weight* over the last couple of years. She's a completely different person." These reactions to fat women in the media point to the struggle fat women have with identifying or seeing themselves reflected in celebrity culture.

While women disliked the barrage of fat-women-must-change narratives, they also longed for more normal and realistic representations of fatness in the media and felt fed up with the one-dimensional fat woman characters they saw repeatedly portrayed. Vaiana (twenty-eight, Filipino American, bisexual, 217 pounds) longed for a wider range of romantic and professional roles for fat women actors: "They're usually someone that plays a comic relief character, or the villain's minion, or a side character. They're someone to be made fun of, someone completely stripped of humanity. Sometimes fat men get to have real roles, but fat women are always a characterization or stereotype. Either we're cast aside or we're sexualized." This clear sense that fat women are reduced and restricted to a small range of unflattering and inconsequential roles was something that fat women emphatically argued needed to change.

Collectively, fat women reacted strongly to stereotypes of fat women and their bodies. They rarely mentioned positive connotations of how the media portrayed fat women, and they lamented the constant mocking and trivialization that fat women endured. These portrayals shaped how they felt about themselves and revealed that even when they had an impulse to resist or fight back, fat stereotypes often felt overwhelming. These narratives also give nuance to the ways that seeing stereotypes portrayed in the media translated into fat women internalizing and shaping their reality around them, either by fearing that they confirmed the stereotypes or by proving themselves to *not* behave in stereotypical ways. This can be dangerous for fat women's well-being, in that reacting to stereotypes can produce a cascade of hazards: women not seeking help when needed, buying into weight-loss-as-redemption stories, fearing how others react to them, or generally viewing their bodies as something to manage and overcome rather than something to feel joy or acceptance about. Within these narratives are also stories of fat women rejecting these stereotypes, feeling anger about them, and wishing for something better.

The variability of women's responses to fat stereotypes in the media demonstrated the gaps between the subject and the object. The lessons of the object (that is, the fat female body as represented in the media) are more straightforward: fatness as shameful, the "good fatty" as possibly redemptive, fat women as caretakers and mothers and nurturers (at best) or morally bankrupt, self-deprecating, or gross or disgusting (at worst). The lessons of the *subject*, however, are more muddied, complicated, and uncertain. Women at times felt overwhelmed and defeated by stereotypes of their bodies, seeing these images as an exhausting trigger for self-loathing. Others described ideas about wanting more diverse images and representations or felt anger at being derided and reduced. Some celebrated fat celebrities who embraced their fat bodies publicly, and still others expressed resignation about fat stereotypes as "just simply true." One unifying thread in these stories is that fat women were paying close attention, even if their interpretations diverged sharply from each other.

One of the stranger aspects of studying fatness is the overwhelming sense that fat bodies exist only as objects of the (disapproving) gaze. Looking *at* fat bodies, as seen in media representations, for example, is more familiar than imagining fat people as having a rich interior lives and subjectivities. Fat women's bodies have become objects or things, and fat women understand their own bodies in relation to this. This latter aspect of fat subjectivity has been far too neglected, in part because of the relative lack of serious reflection around fat bodies and fat lived experiences.

Feminist philosopher Elizabeth Grosz writes of the relationship between the body and the social world: "The body is a most peculiar 'thing,' for it is never quite reducible to being merely a thing; nor does it ever quite manage to rise above the status of thing. Thus it is both a thing and a non-thing, an object, but an object which somehow contains or coexists with an interiority, an object able to take itself and others as subjects, a unique kind of object not reducible to other objects." She adds, "Bodies are not inert; they function interactively and productively. They act and react. They generate what is new, surprising, unpredictable."[93] In this way, fat bodies, too, are saddled with the impossible task of being a thing—looked at, imagined outside of humanness, objectified, judged, evaluated, reduced, and so on—and also a non-thing, something with the status of a subject, co-constructed by self and other. This work on fat stereotypes shows this malleability, as fat women appeared on screen as comedic reductions, slapstick caricatures, or bodies prone to shame-eating; these representations served as emotional frameworks that shaped fat women's own interiority about themselves in tandem with feeding thinner people stories of their own "success" and moral superiority. And yet, fat women's bodies are not only reduced to the status of objects—fat women at times invest their bodies with potent power to shape their social world, to act and react to the images and stories around them.

Building on Grosz's claims that bodies are not inert, I would add that it is through the process of recognizing fat interiority as attached to the fat body that we can understand some of the sites of injury that fat women carry and hold. Fat oppression is built and maintained; it is not merely inevitable. It is upheld and supported by institutional practices that then inform social and political realities. We do not "accidentally" have terrible representations of fat bodies in the media, and of course, it comes as no surprise that fat women often carry these stereotypes within them, furthering the potential of these stereotypes to damage and injure. Fatness is cast as a terrifying and terrorizing identity, with fat suffering, foolishness, and belittlement on a perpetual loop. The question of who wields the power to maintain, uphold, and perpetuate these stereotypes is complex, but it is necessary to face the discomfort of why people need to deride fat women's bodies in these ways, and what purpose it serves in maintaining hierarchy, oppression, and powerful, systemic anti-fat ideologies.

PART TWO

BEING FAT IN PUBLIC

CHAPTER 3

FINDING A "BETTER YOU"

*How the Wellness Industry Frames
Fatness as the Ultimate Failure*

I recently saw an advertisement for a burger, fries, and soda from the fast-food restaurant Blake's Lotaburger with the caption "Practice Self Care" underneath it. The ubiquity of these types of advertisements, and the way that corporations have appropriated the rhetoric of self-care to pressure consumers into buying their products, reveal what has always been true of the self-care industry: it was never about health and always about selling products. The particularity of this fast-food advertisement, though, struck me as especially disturbing, as the wellness industry has taken as its central premise the framework of anti-fatness as a selling point for making billions of dollars. Being "healthy" has become synonymous with capitalistic greed; in this fast-food advertisement, the premise of health was even more flimsy, even more absurdist. Take care of yourself by consuming a burger, fries, and soda, and then feel proud that you're taking "me time" to do so. The circular logic here—anti-fatness as the basis for the wellness industry, the wellness industry appropriating the language of self-care and mental health, self-care entering capitalistic discourses of buying-more-things, and advertisements selling this back to us in the form of a burger and fries—at least shows an honesty often sorely lacking in other aspects of the wellness industry.

Under the guise of helping people pursue activities and lifestyles that contribute to holistic health, the vast wellness industry, which now encapsulates everything from food services to health-food stores, gyms, spas, retreat centers, exercise programs, and more, has emerged as an economic powerhouse. The wellness industry is a behemoth force in contemporary US society, raking in a staggering $4.9 trillion dollars in 2019 and an estimated $7.0 trillion by 2025.[1] The wellness economy, as some experts have labeled it, now represents an astonishing 5.1 percent of global economic output.[2] The majority of this industry is built around the idea that weight loss and anti-fatness define the core of wellness and health. Clearly, the practice of selling people on weight-loss-as-wellness is big business, with a whole host of industries exploding around this concept. A 2020 estimate illuminated the immense profits made from wellness and weight-loss products: personal care sales reached $955 billion; healthy eating, nutrition, and weight-loss sales pulled in $946 billion; wellness tourism amassed $436 billion; wellness real estate made $131 billion; and workplace wellness programs earned $49 billion.[3] Entire segments of the economy are designed and marketed around the moneymaking potential of selling people on the business of so-called wellness, with fatness as the ultimate marker of not caring for the self.

The ubiquity of tying together weight loss and self-care, as if weight loss is inherently a form of caring for the self, underlies nearly all corners of the wellness industry. Assumptions about weight loss as morally and personally good, and weight gain as a symbol of failure and a lack of caring for the self, permeate a huge range of wellness products, programs, advertisements, and centers. In this world, fatness stems from "emotional eating," a lack of being in tune with the body's hunger cues, excess stress and anxiety, and a whole host of other "imbalances." Weight-related social control, where women bear the brunt of messages that they must not gain weight and should craft their bodies to meet the thin ideal, has fixated on body size as a marker of social status. Incessantly telling women to lose weight and/or maintain a thin body reveals the exertion of patriarchal—and ableist, ageist, white supremacist, classist, and heterosexist—power over women and their bodies. Fatness is, in essence, seen as the ultimate marker of shame and the decisive symbol of a person's lack of concern and care for the self.

Bound up in ideologies of weight loss as self-care are clear ideas about gender, race, class, and sexuality, told repeatedly through the embodied story of "ideal" womanhood and femininity. By telling women they will be happier when they are smaller and fitter, the wellness industry is also crafting clear ideas about womanhood as a tightly controlled form of embodiment. Fatness, then, may serve as a form of resistance to these representations of idealized womanhood and may shed light on the social construction of weight as tied to femininity.[4] Fatness is also portrayed as the antithesis of sexual desirability, as traced in the work of critical race scholars Sabrina Strings and Da'Shaun Harrison.[5] Strings's historical work has traced the origins of anti-fatness to the sexualized rejection of the fat Black body and to the ways that white colonial power has consolidated itself around the prizing and disciplining of thin white traditional femininity and disdain for Black femininity.[6] She argues, "The fear of the imagined 'fat black woman' was created by racial and religious ideologies that have been used to both degrade black women *and* discipline white women. . . . It entails the synchronized repression of 'savage' blackness and the generation of disciplined whiteness."[7] In this way, patriarchal and racialized control of women was *enacted through* anti-fatness.

Fatness and social class status are also deeply intertwined, as lower class status is associated with higher body weight and wealthier class status is associated with greater concern about weight along with social support for healthy eating and exercise.[8] These findings suggest that fatness may also symbolize loss of class status and the inaccessibility of the wellness industry, particularly as many of its products often require money, time, and education to access. Women in particular are expected to curate a particular kind of body mostly reserved for thinner and wealthier white women: sexually desirable, fit, conventionally attractive, and connected to wellness activities and "self-care." Ultimately, fatness operates as a form of racialized, gendered, and classed social hierarchy.

FROM DIET CULTURE TO WELLNESS CULTURE

Weight-loss industries, particularly those pitched to consumers through savvy marketing departments, have begun framing weight loss as a daily necessity in order to care for one's self. For example, the ubiquity of advertising for the dieting app Noom links wellness, behaviorism, and weight loss together by using an array of shrewd marketing tactics. With ads that read "No Food Is Forbidden" and "Eat More Water," Noom uses a calorie restriction model by telling people which foods are acceptable or not through a red-yellow-green "traffic-light system" that signals whether to eat or not eat certain foods. Still, Noom markets itself as a non-diet approach to health, drawing on the language of wellness to convince people they are not dieting but participating in a wellness program.

The model of selling women on self-care while actually promoting harm-ful dieting culture is far from a new approach for weight-loss companies. The tactics Noom uses present a bizarre series of contrasts. One ad explicitly reads: "Stop going on a diet. Start going on Noom."[9] Another Facebook advertisement lists a variety of things Noom users can now do, including "Buy those skinny jeans" and "Show yourself off, not hide yourself away." The emotional assumptions here about fatness-as-shame and fatness-as-deprivation-from-fashion are evident. In contrast to these marketing claims, women who have actually tried Noom called it "damaging to your psyche" and reported that its tactics promote eating-disordered behavior and "feel-ings of futility, self-loathing, and even death."[10]

Weight Watchers, now rebranded as WW, bases its program on food point systems and tracking of food intake alongside coaching, workshops, and weigh-ins. The newer emphasis on "wellness" at WW serves as a disguise for diet culture, critics say.[11] WW itself has admitted that people do not want to use the word "diet" because, according to former WW president Mindy Grossman, "they think it's a more short-term, punitive kind of issue, and that's not what we are."[12] WW and other dieting companies have repeatedly been criticized for their relative lack of screening for eating disorders, encouragement of body surveillance and rigid rules, overemphasis on processed foods, and assumptions that severe calorie restriction is a successful long-term solution for weight man-agement.[13] Leading dieticians have rejected formalized weight-loss programs and have instead argued for more sensible solutions to overall improvement of health. Nutritionist Samantha Cassetty explains: "Rather than focus on a goal weight, I think a better way to go is to focus on small steps you can take to create healthier habits. Examples include limiting soda, upping your veg-gie intake at lunch and dinner, cooking an extra meal or two, drinking more water, and aiming for seven to nine hours of sleep each night."[14] Weight-loss programs and apps, by contrast, funnel people toward their products at the expense of looking at longer-term, sustainable health choices.

Weight-loss programs also fail to acknowledge the most fundamental problem built into their business model: they are not successful. Several studies that have looked at dozens of weight-loss programs and diets found, point-blank, that they did not lead to weight loss or even any health ben-efits to the majority of people trying them. Long-term weight loss occurred infrequently, and weight stayed mostly the same regardless of the dieting interventions people attempted.[15] Experts warn that yo-yo dieting—the rapid gaining and losing of weight—is harder on the body than staying the same weight over time. In fact, in a study of African American women, those who repeatedly cycled between different weights had higher current and peak weights, a higher drive for thinness, less body satisfaction, and less self-esteem about their appearance than those who maintained a stable weight.[16] A study of the psychological impacts of yo-yo dieting found that such dieting led to negative moods, more eating-disordered thinking and behavior, problematic relationships to family members and partners who encouraged excessive dieting, and feelings of losing control and identity while dieting.[17] With the rise of expensive and effective new weight-loss semaglutide medications like Ozempic and Wegovy, where people can lose significant weight but only if they remain on the drugs indefinitely, the problems of weight fluctuation may only worsen over time, particularly for those who cannot afford to continue accessing these prescriptions.[18]

The apparent transition from diet culture to wellness culture has been carefully curated by weight-loss and dieting companies, a move that has situated weight loss *as* wellness. *Washington Post* reporter Allyson Chiu has rightly pointed out that even mentioning the word "diet" or "weight loss" has fallen out of fashion. She notes, "It is not a surprise that diet brands, like WW, would be inclined to shift to promoting holistic, and perhaps vague, wellness approaches in a climate where dieting has largely fallen out of favor with the masses."[19]

Even more benign versions of fitness and weight-loss products often (ironically) fail to achieve their goals. Step trackers embedded in Apple watches and phone apps like Pacer, Fitbit, and Sweat, which purport to track steps to encourage more movement, have led people to exercise and walk *less* than those who do not track their steps. The reason? People enjoy walking and exercising less when they consider it a chore. When walking moves from an enjoyable activity to a form of required labor, they have less motivation to move.[20] Step counting narrows our ability to imagine joy in movement while encouraging the over-monitoring of our bodies.[21]

The interest in monitoring and tracking people's bodies and the subsequent data raises significant questions about how that could impact fat people's health and their interface with medical systems. As people become more self-conscious about their dieting, movement, and biological health, it remains an open question whether this actually translates into wellness—that is, better health outcomes—at all. For example, studies suggest that weigh-ins at doctors' offices can result in fat people feeling more shame about their bodies, resulting in avoidance of medical care altogether. Asking to be weighed in kilograms instead of pounds (so it's more difficult to calculate precise pounds), closing eyes during weigh-ins, and consenting to weigh-ins only for treatment-related issues like unexplained weight fluctuations or pregnancy are possible options for reducing the stigmatizing impacts of weigh-ins.[22]

Even some of the apparent victories in wellness culture can operate as a double-edged sword. Exercise clothing company Athleta recently added 1X to 3X to its sizing for some products (priced and designed the same as thin-sized clothing, a rarity in the clothing industry). The company even introduced bodySTRONG inclusive sizing training for all employees. These developments seem positive and affirming, but when questioned about the motivations behind such changes, then CEO Mary Beth Laughton touted the fact that plus-size customers shop twice as frequently and spend almost 90 percent more money in their stores than thinner-sized customers.[23] (Fat women do spend more on clothing than their thinner counterparts, if given options to do so,[24] and often approach clothing through the lens of scarcity and "managing" the body rather than pleasure and aesthetics.[25]) One wonders, then, if the move is motivated by efforts to expand their brand to new audiences or simply to squeeze more profits out of their monied plus-size customers. Still, Athleta's decisions are progressive compared to most of the fashion industry. Designing athletic clothes in plus sizes at all is relatively new, another testament to how wellness culture has long considered only thin people as being "well."

THE RHETORIC OF THE "GOOD FATTY"

The sheer number of approaches to weight loss attempted among the group of twenty self-identified fat women I interviewed was astonishing: Weight Watchers, Nutrisystem, Jenny Craig, SlimFast, the Hollywood Diet, Lipozene, Atkins, the Paleo Diet, keto eating, CoolSculpting, apple cider vinegar consumption, veganism, vegetarianism, covering in Saran Wrap, the cabbage diet, lemon juice cleanses, low-sugar, gluten-free, or high-carb diets, eating only beets, drinking only smoothies, intermittent fasting, diet pills, intuitive eating, fat camps, laying on vibrating tables, consuming only lemonade with cayenne pepper, and flat-out starvation.

In story after story, fat women described diets that they initially hoped or believed would work, only to be disappointed that they once again "failed" to lose weight. The overwhelming feeling about dieting, repeated over and over in the interviews, was that they either did not work at all, worked for a time and then stopped, or set them up for cycles of weight loss and weight gain that never stabilized over time.

Their stories revealed the tensions between a culture that equates weight loss with wellness, and women's own sense of self-care that often moved beyond food restriction. The list of what women did to care for their bodies revealed an expansive sense of what self-care meant to them. Women talked about some of the more typical aspects of wellness, such as running, fitness classes, weight lifting, yoga, and stretching, along with eating a healthier diet, drinking juices or more water, taking vitamins and supplements, avoiding desserts, and consuming more fruits and vegetables. They also described versions of wellness based on the use of beauty products and treatments, including face creams, Botox, skin hydration, massages, facials, pedicures, and hair coloring. Some women stripped wellness down to basic forms of regular hygiene, like showering and brushing their teeth, while others imagined wellness more expansively as a mind-body endeavor like a spa vacation. Many women described wellness as medical care, such as preventative appointments for Pap smears, immunizations, and colonoscopies, and also treatment for their skin, joints, and heart and taking medications as prescribed; this was notably folded into their idea of wellness, even with routine mistreatment from doctors. Finally, women conceptualized wellness as attending to their emotional needs, such as slowing down, getting more sleep, connecting with religious or friend communities, seeing a psychotherapist, and logging off social media. They sometimes framed this as working on their emotional outlook—consciously feeling more gratitude or appreciation, trying to be more positive in their state of mind, improving their self-esteem, or engaging in meditation. Women also described wellness as removing themselves from stressful situations—giving up commuting by car, quitting their jobs, or leaving a bad relationship. Asked in an open-ended way, fat women identified numerous areas of their lives that constituted caring for their minds and bodies that expanded well beyond weight loss, fitness, and thinness. They were overwhelmingly upset with how wellness too often was coded as the pursuit of thinness.

Hannah (twenty-seven, white, bisexual, 220 pounds) noted that wellness was more all-encompassing than weight: "For me it's a much broader word. I think it's sort of an umbrella term that encompasses your physical health and wellness, but it can and should also include your mental, emotional, maybe even spiritual aspects of your being." Similarly, Vaiana described feeling that she had to educate her family and friends about more comprehensive meanings of wellness: "Wellness and thinness go together a lot. That's not how it works. It's not how it's supposed to be." The quest to expand notions of wellness represented one way that women resisted the overly narrow and anti-fat definitions of wellness they encountered in their lives.

Still, these critiques of wellness culture and dieting appeared far less frequently than buy-ins from women about these constructs, particularly around the idea that their size rightfully dictated their feelings about their moral selves. The notion of good and bad bodies—and ideas about how to "market" one's own fatness to others—dictated many of the behaviors that fat women engaged in.

Because fatness is so often cast in a negative light, particularly as fat women are portrayed as morally inferior to thin women, fat women are often in the position to prove their value and "worthiness" to others. The construct of the "good fatty," defined by Stacy Bias as "a fat person who at least believes in the socially constructed viewpoint that their number one goal in life should be losing weight," reveals how moral framings of fatness operate in certain archetypal representations of fat bodies.[26] In a comic zine that Bias developed for her blog, the "good fatty" is both an ideology that is internalized by fat people themselves, and a framework imposed upon them by others, including the media. The "good fatty" gets its definition through its juxtaposition to the "bad fatty," who is nonproductive, lazy, unable to do things, not sexually desirable, and highly stigmatized. Bias explains that the "good fatty" and "bad fatty" archetypes arise from capitalistic notions of productive bodies as valuable: "There is a mandate for self-sacrifice and for caring for our bodies in a way that maintains their productive and reproductive potential. So basically we are meant to be strong, able-bodied, heterosexual, and sexually desirable. Folks who don't conform to any or all of the above have stigmatized identities & are even denied rights."[27] Because fat bodies are often constructed in negative terms, these beliefs are used as a means to justify excluding fat people from spaces of privilege.

Bias identifies several different types of "good fatty" archetypes that make allowances for certain kinds of fat bodies to be seen as worthy or acceptable, including the Fat Unicorn, who does none of the typical behaviors assigned to fat people: "They mostly only eat healthy foods, they are fitness fanatics, their blood tests are perfect, their bodies are strong and able . . . These are the folks we talk about when we say fitness and fatness aren't mutually exclusive . . . And if they exist then logically fatness can't be universally declared a 'bad thing.'"[28] She also describes the Exceptional Fatty, who can "deadlift a bison, power through a triathlon, rock some mind-blowing choreography or even just tear up several flights of stairs without getting winded." In this framework, being fat does not stop them from excelling and is related to a sense of discipline and strong moral values along with brute strength. Bias also identifies the Work in Progress, defined as "a fatty in the process of becoming not-a-fatty." This can include the "fad dieter, the 'lifestyle changer,' the gym-goer, the post-operative" that celebrates moderation and labor through "aspirational thinness."[29]

Building on these more "desirable" fatties, Bias describes several other fat archetypes that circulate, often uncritically, throughout US culture. She lists the Real Woman, defined as the "heroine of the Dove Beauty campaigns," with a voluptuous body and an occasionally visible fat roll. This version of fatness is described as "normal" and indicative of the "everyday woman." Then, there's the Fat-Lebrity, the "[ambassador] of fatness . . . whose extraordinary artistry or performance skills create them as an exception to the general rules of social exclusion."[30] They are allowable, Bias writes, only if their individual bodies do not distract from their ability to entertain viewers and not offend thin people. Next on the list is the Mama Hen, or the maternal fat body, who, through adopting a comforting and compassionate presence, is "outside of the male gaze, non-sexualized and non-threatening" (even if she is still quite young); as a result of this archetype, many fat women are stripped of their sexuality and cast as comedic or shocking when even imagined as sexual.[31] Fat women are also sometimes cast as the No Fault Fatty, or those who are fat for reasons beyond their control, with conditions such as polycystic ovarian syndrome, those taking medications that increase their body weight, or those whose fatness is proven to be unavoidable. These women gain the benefit of moral absolution for their fat bodies because their fatness results from factors beyond their personal control.

Bias also lists the Natural Fatty, who is fat solely due to genetics and who becomes a case study in natural human diversity; she is absolved of moral failure—fatness is not chosen or due to problematic choices. We also meet the Fatshionista, the fatty within a specific size range and with impeccable fashion sense and either money or sewing skills, who serves as "an embodied argument against ideas of poor hygiene, slovenliness, and lack of desirability."[32] In a darker turn, Bias also points out that the Dead-Early Fatty operates as a "good fatty" stereotype, in that this version of fatness corroborates and justifies the medical and pharmaceutical industry and their doom prophecies. The Dead-Early Fatty in essence works to "justify social and financial exclusions, to fund research & product development, and to create oppressive legislation."[33]

Bias finally offers up the Rad Fatty, who is "the ultimate rejector of stigma, appropriating stigmatizing terms and turning them on their head, refusing conformance at every level, and often engaging in performative displays of behaviors that are discouraged in or considered stereotypical of fat people but with intention and a tone of rebellion." This fatty deeply understands fat politics, involves herself in activism, has an academic understanding of sizeism, and works to understand the radical roots of oppression while also seeking to undo hierarchies and anti-fat biases. In a final bold statement, Bias calls out the processes by which the "good fatty" archetypes often work to justify inclusion and exclusion practices, saying, "Where we create one inclusion, we often create or reinforce other exclusions. It's important to be aware of where and how we seek social capital and who we leave behind when we do so . . . LEAVE NO FATTY BEHIND!"[34]

Bias effectively illustrates the social roles assigned to fat people and captures several of the paradoxes of fat life, particularly the tensions between health and unhealth, restriction and freedom, exclusion and inclusion, morality and matter-of-factness, and more. She works in this comic zine to not only call out the various prejudices and pressures fat women experience from the outside but to question the kinds of emotional and psychological acrobatics fat women perform within themselves. The never-ending quest to be the most desirable kind of fatty captures the challenges fat women face as they move through the world, as the "bad fatty" stigma can be used to justify their lack of rights, access, or privileges. By understanding fatness as a set of moral schemas attached to bodies—with fat people needing to work hard to escape the most "immoral" version of fatness—Bias portrays here the adhesive, sticky qualities of the good and bad fatty and how these operate insidiously in many spheres of life.

In many ways, the whole movement toward body positivity has strains that connect back to the "good fatty" archetypes, complicating easy stories of progress and accomplishment for fat liberation. What does it mean that certain kinds of fat people are held in higher regard than others, who are excluded from body positivity? What kinds of fatness are unacceptable, and what stories do we tell about those people and those bodies? Is body positivity a mere extension of "fat acceptance," that lowest-common-denominator version of fat activism that suggests that merely tolerating the presence of fat people is sufficient? What does it mean to be "positive" about bodies marked as marginalized, abject, and often unworthy of rights?

While some of the fat women I interviewed outrightly rejected any fat positivity, most expressed ambivalence about the body positivity movement, seeing it as affirming of body diversity while also (in their minds) condoning or even "glorifying" unhealthy bodies. Building on the "good fatty" stereotype, many fat women believed that all fat women must be actively working to not be fat. Isabella strongly frowned upon a three-hundred-pound model on the cover of *Cosmopolitan* magazine: "It's sending a message that people from all walks of life are honored, and women might tip the scales over 300 pounds. But on the flip side I can see how someone who's that large, poor baby, like she has to do something to help herself." The clear internalization of anti-fat body rhetoric sounded all the more painful coming from fat women themselves. For most women, there was no meaningful space to simply be fat as is. Instead, the wellness rhetoric of *bettering yourself, deserving better*, and *doing self-care* becomes a cover for *lose weight, don't be pathetic*, and *get un-fat*.

FAT AND HEALTHY?

The concept that fat people could be included in notions of health and healthiness, and that they deserved access to exercise, dance, and wellness spaces, was a major accomplishment of early fat activist work. Much of this groundwork to push back against thin-as-the-only-healthy-body ideology was laid by organizations such as Health at Every Size (HAES), which began in the 1990s, along with inclusive exercise programs like gentle yoga, Fat Kid Dance Party, and No BS Active (a program codeveloped by Whitney Way Thore, star of the TLC show *My Big Fat Fabulous Life*). In particular, HAES contested notions of fat people as inherently unhealthy and excluded from fitness and wellness spaces. Its central premise argues that higher body weight does not mean a person is automatically unhealthy and that the unique challenges of weight stigma and bias require new forms of thinking about body size, health, and wellness. The program encourages weight-centered approaches to treat clients of all sizes, arguing that balanced eating, life-enhancing physical activity, and respect for bodily diversity are all necessary components of health.[35] HAES also promotes the concept that individuals are not solely responsible for their body weight and size, and that the cultural fear of fatness and problematic structural inequalities about health and food access contribute to people's relationship with fatness. Further, given that most diets fail and that long-term weight loss is almost universally unsuccessful,[36] moving toward more positive frames for fatness, weight, and body size is necessary to broaden definitions of health.[37] In contrast to medical approaches about weight management, HAES encourages a "fulfilling and meaningful lifestyle" through eating according to internally directed signals of hungers or satiety and doing a reasonable amount of physical activity and exercise.[38]

In particular, HAES challenges some of the key assumptions about body size, weight, and weight loss, including that being fat poses significant risks of death, weight loss prolongs life, anyone determined to lose weight can keep it off through diet and exercise, weight loss is a practical and positive goal, the only way for fat people to improve their health is to lose weight, and obesity-related costs place a large burden on the economic and health system. HAES also argues that traditional weight-loss approaches can cause physical, emotional, and spiritual distress, ultimately fail, and lead to discrimination, prejudice, and self-hatred that undermine fat people's quality of life.[39] Instead, HAES encourages body acceptance, intuitive eating, and active embodiment while also pushing health professionals to respond to bodily diversity more positively and constructively. The impacts of this approach have been substantial, as individual changes in eating behaviors and quality of life have been associated with a HAES approach, though improvements in health continue to be inconsistent.[40] Partly in response to HAES, certainly as a reaction to more aggressive and overt forms of fat activism, the medical world is slowly starting to change its attitudes about fatness, moving away from emphasis on unrealistic weight loss and working to reduce stigma and identify how it impacts medical treatment.[41]

While the HAES movement and the growing number of fat exercise programs have been enlivening and important, particularly in shifting public perceptions of the links between thinness and health, and fatness and unhealth, they are still burdened by the ideologies of healthism and "good fatties" and "bad fatties."[42] These programs argue that *fat people are healthy too* without challenging these fundamental premises: (1) only healthy people deserve rights, (2) only healthy people deserve dignity, and (3) healthy people are (morally) superior to unhealthy people. These programs reinforce the premise that "good" fat people constantly exercise and engage in wellness behaviors and that health is the avenue through which people gain and maintain their value. Missing from the rhetoric of "fat can be healthy too" is a more critical analysis of the moral language surrounding fatness, particularly as it applies to women. We might start to also ask: What rights, protections, and care do less-healthy fat people deserve and have access to?

No one benefits from linking morality to body size; as bodies are constructed as projects of labor, everyone is taught to see their body as deficient, and thinness is pursued relentlessly. Embedded in the concept of HAES is the silencing of the more complicated, and perhaps painful, discussions of health more broadly. Many different discourses are erased and silenced by focusing on fat-people-can-be-healthy-too discussions, including critical conversations about our profit-driven healthcare system and the affiliated pharmaceutical industry, capitalism and its relentless insistence on productivity, classist ideas about health as something only wealthier people can access, and racist and patriarchal mandates for women to take up less space than men. In essence, the relentless emphasis on health and healthiness, albeit largely well-intentioned, reinforces the way that people relate to fatness through the lens of moral failure. Thin people imagine fatness as something to avoid, dread, and stigmatize, and fat people relate to their bodies by trying to distance themselves from the "bad fatty" archetypes and stereotypes. The more radical, fundamental challenges to fatness as a kind of moral failing are left in place if the endpoint of our politics is *health at every size*.

DISCIPLINING THE FAT BODY THROUGH BARIATRIC SURGERY

Fatness is consistently pitched as something that requires work: to contain it, combat it, chip away at it, or to keep going at all. Wellness culture seduces women to frame bodily control as self-care, as this taps into long-held and deeply felt beliefs about women's bodies as in need of discipline, control, and submission. Women's bodies are constantly encouraged to be slimmer, more toned, properly groomed, more youthful, and more conventionally attractive. At its most basic level, fatness is a threat to all of these. Fatness is, at its core, a threat to traditional white, cis, heterosexual femininity. Its potential for danger is seen and experienced in the reactions thinner people have to fat bodies and in the continued pressure fat women face to shrink themselves down.

This patriarchal framing of women's diverse bodies as abhorrent—particularly along age, size, and racial lines—has long appeared throughout US culture. Increasingly narrow definitions of beauty have taken hold in popular culture, pornography, and the media.[43] Cultural pressures for women to shrink their bodies, whiten their skin, smooth any lumps and bumps, reverse the evidence of aging, and control and contain any bodily fluids have long constituted areas of feminist inquiry and critique.[44] An especially insidious thread runs through the messaging on weight loss: *You will have a new lease on life. You will experience hope for the first time. You can show yourself, not hide yourself.* This framing of fatness as prohibitive to joy, relationships, love, successful careers, or even to life itself permeates discourses about weight and body size. When I interviewed fat women across the US, the single most prominent and significant impression I got from them was that fatness prevented participation in various kinds of life practices, relationships, and experiences. They imagined their fat bodies as walling them off from many aspects of social life and opportunities that they saw thinner people having: dating, marrying, having children, eating in public, having certain kinds of jobs, feeling included in social spaces, taking pleasure in their bodies, feeling at ease in their bodies, and more. These are the vulnerabilities that diet culture takes advantage of, as fat women are sold on the story that by losing weight, they could gain access to the desirable world of thin women.

This sense of fatness-as-exclusion, largely reinforced by diet culture and the relentless linking of health and happiness to thinness and "ideal" beauty, appears at its peak intensity in the marketing and promotion of bariatric surgery, that is, surgeries designed to permanently alter the stomach and digestive system in order to induce rapid and sizeable weight loss. Many studies have examined how bariatric surgery marketing has focused on notions of the "quick fix" and have pitched bariatric surgery as the next logical step in fat women's weight-loss journeys.[45] Often couched as "no big deal" and relatively easy to obtain, bariatric surgery is a hugely profitable industry, estimated to be worth $2.41 billion in 2020 and $4.81 billion by 2028.[46] (That said, debates about whether bariatric surgery actually saves health insurance companies money are ongoing because of the high cost of repeat surgeries and medical complications.[47]) In particular, younger women, who often face more weight-related stigma than other groups, have been most aggressively targeted for bariatric surgery, frequently under the guise of avoiding future health complications and staving off the negative effects of fat stigma.[48] Embedded in the pressures to have bariatric surgery is the framework that fatness is inherently lethal and that surgery is the only way to lead a happy, healthy, and fulfilling life. Doctors often plug certain statistics to their patients, including that surgery can extend survival (implying that surviving as fat is rare and difficult), lead to long-term weight loss, and is a straightforward procedure with a high survival rate.[49]

Left out of this picture, of course, are the plethora of possible short- and long-term complications that people experience from the surgery, including leaking, bleeding, erosion of the stomach, ulcers, loose stools, feeling of sickness when eating or drinking, frequent bowel movements, vitamin and mineral deficiencies, abscesses, bowel obstruction, acid reflux and heartburn, major airway events, infection, malnutrition, rebound weight gain, organ injuries, pulmonary embolism, and death.[50] In fact, bariatric surgery has had a complication rate as high as a whopping 40 percent, though this has dropped slightly over time with increased use of laparoscopic techniques and better training of physicians.[51] Malpractice lawsuits are commonplace due to surgical complications, uneven training histories of physicians, and medical professionals not listening to or believing bariatric patients about their physical complaints.[52] A review of malpractice lawsuits related to bariatric surgeries found that 82 percent resulted from a delay in diagnosis, and 64 percent resulted from misinterpreted vital signs related to postoperative complications reported by patients.[53] The gap between the realities of bariatric surgery—it is a life-altering choice that carries serious risks like permanent disability or death—and the marketing story of bariatric surgery differ dramatically.

Themes of control and discipline of the body permeated fat women's testimonials about bariatric surgeries, suggesting that discipline and control of the body were perceived as success and joy. One woman in a bariatric testimonial recounted, "I've lost a person [meaning 150 pounds], I've also really gained a person, and that's myself." Bariatric patients reported that having imposed control and limited choice following surgery ironically led them to feeling more in control.[54] The controlled, managed, non-excessive body, then, led to psychological relief, suggesting that cultural attitudes about disciplined bodies influenced individual experiences with eating. That said, their experiences of some of the unpleasant side effects of bariatric surgery, particularly "dumping," or the violent illnesses that occur when eating too much at one time, led many women to associate eating with feeling sick and to fluctuate constantly between losing and gaining control.[55]

The construction of the "out-of-control eater" and freedom from impulses to eat also appeared in bariatric marketing. Recent studies of bariatric surgery patients, both pre- and post-surgery, found that perceptions of "troubled eating" often relied not on eating practices but on the types of bodies doing the eating; in other words, fat bodies were constructed as inherently problematic while thinner bodies became "successful" and "healthy" even when evidence showed otherwise.[56] It makes sense, then, that fat women were told messages about how much freedom they would feel after bariatric surgery, and all of the newfound life experiences they would have access to, while under constant medical surveillance and control. The permanent alteration of their stomachs required them to internalize the discourse of freedom under the guise of controlling and altering their bodies.[57] Only by occupying a thin body could fat women escape the caricature of the "troubled eater." Feminist scholar Kathryn Morgan argues that the decision to undergo bariatric surgery is "deeply embedded in extraordinarily complex neoliberal biopolitical structures and dynamics of fat hatred camouflaged by liberatory discourses that promise 'empowerment,' becoming 'normal,' and discovery of her 'real self.'"[58] She goes on to say that fat hatred stems from racialized gendered oppression and that normalizing bariatric surgery portrayed bariatric patients as legitimizing dominant obesity discourses and practices and demonstrating their status as "good American bio-citizens."[59] In essence, bariatric surgery reinforces the idea that fatness always leads to negative health outcomes and that fat women should preempt their inevitable decline in health by permanently altering their stomachs and bodies.[60]

We should continue to interrogate what it means when people move from the culturally inscribed "undisciplined" body to one of "discipline," with various patriarchal, racist, ableist, ageist, classist, and capitalistic implications clearly in tow. The post-bariatric surgery body is infused with messages about good (read: white, heterosexual, young, nondisabled, conventionally beautiful) femininity and productivity. (Never mind that this body is actually starving, losing hair, and often suffering from long-term malnutrition, poor immunity, neuromuscular dysfunctions, weakness, and anemia.)[61] Assumptions about bariatric surgery as the "savior" of fat people's dignity and quality of life often mask the reality of what post-bariatric life looks like: blending up chunks of chicken, eating only a few ounces at a time, not being able to drink water with meals, and suffering with brain fogs, bone loss and brittle hair, violent vomiting and diarrhea, depression, and insomnia.[62]

In fact, many people felt much *worse* both physically and psychologically after undergoing bariatric surgery. One study of Norwegian women found they chose surgery because of concern about future illness and stigma associated with fatness but ended up reporting chronic pain, loss of energy, feelings of shame and failure, and the self-concept of being disabled and withdrawn.[63] Another study of bariatric patients two years after surgery found that 50 percent had regained the weight, likely due to metabolic and hormonal mechanisms underlying body weight,[64] a phenomenon rarely mentioned in marketing or information sessions.

In addition, the social and psychological outcomes of bariatric surgery were often dire. Those who underwent bariatric surgery reported higher divorce rates one year after the survey, a greater fixation on how their bodies looked, and more long-term body dissatisfaction compared to those who did not have bariatric surgery.[65] A frightening study of seventeen thousand bariatric surgery patients found they had a higher death rate, including more suicides and heart disease–related deaths, than the general population, with 1 percent dying within a year of surgery and 6 percent dying within five years of surgery.[66] Suicide rates were much higher for bariatric patients compared to those who had not undergone the surgery,[67] suggesting a need for better understanding of who seeks bariatric surgery, what their particular vulnerabilities might be, and what kinds of care they need before, during, and after surgery. It is essential to critique bariatric surgery more aggressively and analyze and evaluate the differences between the outcomes promised from surgery and the lived realities of postoperative life.

Of course, reports from those who have had bariatric surgery present a vast array of reactions about what it means to become thin. Some women described it as life-changing or an entry point into the world of thinness and its accompanying privileges. Others described it as destabilizing to their sense of self, or even mournful, as they lost parts of their fatter selves. Some expressed deep satisfaction with it and others expressed regret.[68] The key message, though, is that bariatric surgery results in a messy network of reactions and complications, as drastic shifts in embodiment and a person's relationship to food require a reassembly of the self behaviorally, socially, and psychologically. Left out of these narratives are challenges to the fundamental ways that intense anti-fat stigma shapes consciousness, medical choices, and the quest for thinness.

Looking closely at bariatric surgery marketing and the pressures fat women face to get this surgery bring cultural priorities of thinness-at-any-cost into view. The fear of fatness, a key driver of these pressures, relies primarily on the erasure and invisibility of actual fat bodies. Fatness is constructed, particularly by thinner people and the medical establishment, as the antithesis of life. The incessant advertising to women in particular seems especially notable, given that bariatric surgery is allegedly about health not gendered compliance. The intensifying pressures fat women face to have bariatric surgery reveals this logic as fraudulent and faulty, showing again that making women thin, compliant, and conventionally attractive has always mattered far more than actual health. The world of bariatric surgery, and the accompanying lack of acknowledgment of anti-fat biases and terror about fatness embedded within it, reveal that the controlled and disciplined body, no matter how ill, is preferable to the fatter body, under the current terms of patriarchy and capitalism.

THE CARNIVAL TRICK OF WELLNESS

The wellness industry has couched fatness as the ultimate failure, both because doing so generates obscene amounts of profit, but also because it couches dieting, restriction, and control *as* wellness. The wellness industry thinly disguises its dieting priorities behind the rhetoric of self-actualization and self-care, painting fatness as a barrier to both. Assumptions that thin people want to stay thin and fatter people want to lose weight operate as permanent assumptions of this industry. The disturbing inability to see fatness as potentially healthy, or at least not the ultimate emblem of unhealth, is a willful ignorance created to inspire insecurities and ultimately profit from them.

In these ways, the wellness industry is an uncomplicated, albeit behemoth, entity. It wants people to feel insecure, to imagine the need to feel more confident or empowered (read: thin), and it thrives on snazzy and imaginative ways to package dieting as about fulfilling emotional needs. Becoming a "better self" by being thinner becomes an easy elision. These are griftopias of pricey wellness retreats, "clean eating" programs, and glitzy surgical centers. Bariatric surgery advertisements offer a particularly vivid example of promising the utopia of a thin future: "You're not too young for bariatric surgery" and "You will be able to get rid of your depression after surgery."[69] While somewhat clunky, these slogans summarize so much of what the wellness industry does: it promises an end to angst and suffering *if you act now!*

We've fallen deeply for the carnival trick of the wellness industry. We're all marks, easy targets, rubes. In reality, we emerge from the multibillion-dollar wellness industry often in the same-sized bodies, feeling the same complex emotions about our lives, wearing the same types of clothing (produced in faraway places that allow us not to think too much about the working conditions of those who made them) only with lighter wallets. Our participation in this industry further reaffirms the supposed moral rightness of terrorizing fat people and framing them as the ultimate symbol of failure.

Cultivating a permanent sense of opposition to the tactics of the wellness industry is an essential next step in the battle for fat justice. Rethinking bariatric surgery, especially as it is marketed to consumers and discussed in the medical community, is a good starting point. Permanent alterations to otherwise-healthy organs should instead be a last resort after all other avenues toward improved health have been exhausted. Similarly, understanding the capitalistic underpinnings of extended-sized clothing, gentle yoga, and other "inclusive" practices is important if we are to stay one step ahead of how these industries co-opt empowerment discourses and sell them back to us as products. We have to see programs like Noom for what they are: thinly veiled diet companies that equate plates of bacon with weight loss, leveraging anti-fatness while hiding behind wellness—all for a limited-time low monthly price. We must begin to see how the "good fatty" stereotypes serve to siphon the agency from fat bodies, to hollow out our complexities, to deaden any other pursuits besides becoming *un-fat*. These wellness-industry tools require fat bodies to be seen as unwell while portraying thin bodies as good bodies. If there is only joy in control and restraint, in the careful curation of the thinner body, the fat body comes to operate as its double: an excessive, unruly symbol of terror and fear. The movement from body positivity to outright fat rage, then, is a logical response to the system that has too often equated fatness with disaster and calamity.

CHAPTER 4

HEAVY LIFTING

Fatness, Capitalism, and Workplace Stigma

"**H**aven't you noticed?" my friend said over lunch the other day. "All of the fat academics are vanishing. You can get fat once you have a job, but you can't *be* fat when you want a job." It happened slowly, the disappearance of fat women from the professional sphere, the exclusion of them from potential jobs, the trivialization of their work, the erasure of them from graduate school, and the gradual attrition of fat undergraduate students. Academia is hardly alone in blocking and excluding fat bodies from the professional classes, as fat bodies are kept permanently on the margins, rendered invisible. Indeed, fat women are far less likely across the board to attend graduate school, get promoted at work, have managerial positions, get paid a fair wage, or gain entry into competitive careers compared to thinner women.[1] Being fat in public, it seems, carries a serious penalty.

Discrimination against fat people appears rampantly in employment, education, and healthcare as well as in interpersonal interactions. In fact, over 40 percent of fat people reported that they experienced stigma on a *daily* basis, a rate far higher than any other group.[2] This kind of routine stigma can dramatically impact quality of life, as fat people who experience weight discrimination live shorter lives than those who do not.[3] As we consider the impact of being fat at work, we must understand that *the negative outcomes of stigma far outweigh the negative outcomes of fatness itself.*

Stigma is a ubiquitous, overwhelmingly destructive part of the lives of fat people, particularly when they interface more with public life. In one study, 28 percent of teachers said that becoming fat was the worst thing that can happen to a person, 24 percent of nurses said that they are "repulsed" by fat people, and even when controlling for income and grades, parents provided less financial support for their fatter children than their thinner children.[4] Fat discrimination permeates jury selection, adoption proceedings, and housing decisions,[5] and leads to more concealment of weight, lower self-confidence, and poorer performance at school.[6] Given that anti-fat stigma permeates so many areas of fat people's lives, it is not surprising that workplaces have become hotbeds of discrimination and stigma for fat women.

Recently, diversity, equity, and inclusion (DEI) initiatives have attempted to systematically make workplaces more inclusive and welcoming to people with an array of identities and backgrounds. These initiatives often focus on race, gender, religion, and ability, though occasionally they have expanded to include social class and appearance.[7] Most often, these efforts are pitched at increasing diversity of the workplace rather than lessening or ending discrimination.[8] That said, inclusivity efforts in the workplace have rarely considered the needs of fat bodies, and when they have, these efforts often focused on teaching workers to not explicitly state aloud their anti-fat sentiments.[9] Inclusivity efforts have often failed to recognize the material, physical needs of fat people in workplaces, particularly in terms of structural and physical changes fat people might need to feel comfortable and safe. Fat workers more often withdraw and isolate compared to other workers, and they more often report physical and emotional strain in their work environments.[10] Actual inclusiveness, then, means that companies must move beyond buzzwords and account for the diverse bodily needs of fat people much as they do when working to accommodate disability.[11]

Ironically, workplace stigma can make different groups of people simultaneously hyper-visible and invisible. Fatness is something that draws attention from others and causes people to stand out at work, and yet, the minimal efforts companies make to accommodate fat bodies reinforces their invisibility in terms of policies and practices of workplace cultures. Marilyn Wann, author of *Fat!So?*, notes that companies create "unaccommodating to dangerous" environments for fat people, adding that "workplace culture comes from our larger culture, which certainly has a hierarchy around weight. Thinner people are seen as better."[12] And, given that the CDC estimates that 42.4 percent of Americans were "obese" and 73.6 percent were "overweight" in 2017–18, these hierarchies have a dramatic impact on a sizeable percentage of the American workforce.

A full *50 percent* of employers admitted they were less likely to hire fat workers than thin workers, as they perceived fat workers as lazy, lacking in self-discipline, less competent, less conscientious, and unmotivated.[13] (These concerns and misgivings have not borne out in real life, as personality characteristics of workers were shown to be unrelated to fatness.)[14] Further, 45 percent of employers say they are less likely to recruit fat job candidates, and fat workers are regarded less often as having leadership potential.[15] Fat women faced particular barriers and discrimination while interviewing for jobs, as they applied for more jobs and engaged in more job training compared to thinner women, yet received job offers far less often.[16] In audit studies and experimental studies where employers evaluated fictional job candidates and workers—a methodology that allowed for measuring bias and assessing the reasons for bias—employers evaluated fat workers far more negatively than thinner workers. Having a fat body when applying for jobs influenced employers' views of hiring, qualifications and suitability ratings, disciplinary decisions, salary assignments, placement decisions, and coworker ratings. Across thirty-two different experimental studies, fat applicants and workers were evaluated more negatively and had more negative employment outcomes compared to thinner applicants and employees.[17] Bias against fatness itself was the greatest physical predictor in choosing interview candidates, suggesting that thinness tops all other reasons and justifications for securing a job interview.[18]

Those tasked with interviewing consistently made hiring decisions about fat job candidates based on appearance-related criteria, especially for women.[19] Women's body image and grooming were evaluated as being linked to job competence. In one study, after five hundred hiring managers were shown a photo of a fat woman applicant, 21 percent of them described her as unprofessional despite having no other information about her.[20] Moreover, employers' feelings about their own bodies influenced hiring decisions: if employers felt satisfied with their own bodies and perceived their bodies to be important to their self-concept, they were even more likely to not hire fat workers.[21] People rated hypothetical fat women as particularly poor choices for hiring,[22] especially in more active jobs, and said that fat workers were less desirable for all kinds of occupation types—sedentary, standing, manual, and heavy manual—suggesting that there is no perceived occupation where fat workers would be well-suited or valuable.[23] Strangely, if interviewees directly acknowledged or talked about fatness or disability status, employers rated them much lower than if they were simply fat or disabled but never mentioned it aloud, suggesting again that highlighting fatness can have deleterious effects on job interviewees.[24] Even more, employers who discriminated against fat interviewees did not see this as a problem or a form of discrimination; they considered it acceptable and justified.[25]

Fatness also correlates with lower pay rates at work, making concrete the notion that fat stigma has a dollar cost or wage penalty. Fat women often are assigned lower starting salaries and ranked lower compared to thinner job candidates.[26] Consistent over several decades, fatter women earned thousands of dollars less than thinner women, according to a study at the Harvard T. H. Chan School of Public Health based on ten thousand people tracked since 1979.[27] Even after controlling for socioeconomic, family status, and health limitation variables, the wage penalty for fat men ranged from 0.7 to 3.4 percent, while the wage penalty for women ranged from 2.3 to 6.1 percent.[28] One study that looked at weight more specifically found that an increase of sixty-four pounds of body weight was associated with a 9 percent decrease in wages, approximately equivalent to the difference of one and a half years of education or three years of work experience.[29] Another study found that fat workers were paid roughly $2,500 less than thinner workers.[30] Both Black and white fat women faced significant wage penalties, even after controlling for social class.[31] Disturbingly, more educated fat women in better-paying white-collar positions had significantly lower income compared to their thinner counterparts, a finding not found for fat men.[32] Graduate admissions committees also less often admitted fat women than thin women to graduate programs in psychology,[33] and rampant discrimination has been seen online imagining fat people as inadequate graduate students.[34] Fat women also faced more discrimination in educational attainment and marriage outcomes, which only further exacerbated the overall injury to their long-term economic well-being when they faced wage discrimination at work.[35]

Along with a clear pay gap, workplace biases and discrimination have become pervasively normative. Two large-scale studies found that fatness was linked to lower workforce participation, independent of other health and sociodemographic variables, suggesting that fatness itself prohibited workplace participation.[36] In one study, 54 percent of fat employees reported weight stigma from coworkers or colleagues, and 43 percent reported weight stigma from employers or supervisors, including derogatory humor, pejorative comments, differential treatment, or even being fired because of their weight.[37] One-quarter of "overweight" and one-third of "obese" workers missed out on a promotion due to their size. More than half felt left out of their teams at work.[38] Fat women workers were less often given customer-facing jobs, particularly in more prestigious industries.[39] At least one in ten fat women reported explicit verbal abuse from coworkers about their body size.[40] Bullying and harassment were also reported as normative.[41]

Negative workplace experiences increased in severity as women's body sizes got larger. The difference between mild and severe fatness had a drastically different impact on wages, with white women experiencing a 5.8 percent decrease in wages for mild fatness and 24 percent decrease for severe fatness, and Black women experiencing a 3.3 percent decrease in wages for mild fatness and 14.6 percent decrease for severe fatness compared to thinner counterparts.[42] The fatter the workers were, the more likely they were to report discrimination in the workplace. "Overweight" workers were twelve times more likely, "obese" workers were thirty-seven times more likely, and severely obese workers were one hundred (!!) times more likely than thinner workers to have experienced employment discrimination.[43] These effects were even more severe for fat women than fat men, as fat women were sixteen times more likely to report weight-related employment discrimination.[44] Moreover, bias toward fat women workers began at lower weights and happened more aggressively than it did for men, as fat women started to face fat stigma and workplace discrimination at lower BMIs.[45] As psychotherapist Susie Orbach writes, "Men are meant to be big and strong, and women are meant to be tiny and not take up too much space. They can have everything in the world now, but they have to be slim. That's the horror of current aesthetics for women."[46]

These forms of employment discrimination are typically not isolated incidents. A study of 2,290 workers found that those who experienced weight discrimination in hiring, promotion, or wrongful termination reported that it had happened at least four times during their lifetime.[47] For women working in professional jobs, weight discrimination was especially pronounced—and occurred repeatedly—compared to those working in nonprofessional settings.[48] A study of top CEOs at Fortune 1000 companies found that fat women were remarkably underrepresented in these leadership positions, while fat men were overrepresented.[49] Fat women described discrimination that happened more formally (not being promoted) and informally (being excluded from social activities or receiving negative verbal comments).[50] Even worse, women who gained weight *during* their employment periods (that is, after they were hired) were rated by their supervisors in their annual evaluations far more negatively compared to women who stayed the same weight, suggesting that fat stigma only worsened as weight increased.[51] Employees' feelings about fat managers also reflected negative stereotypes, as thinner employees judged their fat managers more negatively for any perceived flaw in their job performance.[52] The logic becomes circular, as the culture of fat discrimination leads to more discrimination at all levels. As one journalist puts it, "As long as we are all terrified of becoming fat, this will go on. Yes, we are terrified. Because we all know how fat people are treated in this society."[53]

Fat workers are not often legally protected from these forms of discrimination, though some legal scholars argue that fat stigma will become the next major legal battle for workplace biases.[54] The legal ramifications of discriminatory practices against fat people are often murky, as no consistent federal protection against sizeism exists; rather, individual states and cities create their own standards for workplace discrimination. Washington, DC, for example, has outlawed appearance-based discrimination, while San Francisco has more pointedly outlawed discrimination based on height and weight.[55] Having a company policy that explicitly outlaws disparate treatment of workers based on weight has at times effectively lessened fat stigma and discrimination.[56] Unfortunately, few companies have adopted such policies, creating new inroads for human resource departments to consider the impact of hiring practices and decisions.[57]

Fat stigma at work had a deep impact on workers' experiences of their jobs and their perceptions of their own competencies. Fat workers engaged in numerous strategies to manage fat discrimination, including joking and using humor, demonstrating their competence and intelligence, being detail-oriented and impeccable in their work, or rebelling against fat stigma.[58] Fat women also reproduced dominant ideas about fat negativity, engaging in distraction, hiding from coworkers, concealing their bodies, making narratives about fatness to others, overcompensating, or being defensive in order to manage fat stigma.[59] Further, fat women workers often perceived the need to conceal their weight and felt less self-confident at work compared to their thinner counterparts.[60] Studies of fat university professors—who are grossly underrepresented in academia—found that they felt compelled to overperform and take on additional responsibilities in their roles at the university. In doing so, they believed they could overcompensate for the discrimination, stigma, and microaggressions they experienced in the university workplace.[61]

Fat professors less often received promotions and tenure, suggesting that their fears of being perceived as less competent were based in reality.[62] Anti-fat discrimination constitutes a pervasive, consequential, and career-altering aspect of fat workers' lives, particularly for fat women.

FAT WOMEN TALK ABOUT WORK

Most research on fat women and their workplace experiences has focused on the structural inequalities in workplaces, particularly how overt and covert forms of discrimination harm fat women. Surprisingly little qualitative research has asked fat women to narrate their experiences about work.

The fat women I interviewed perceived workplaces as spaces that engendered a great deal of self-consciousness around physical appearance, whether they worked in working-class jobs or in more professional settings. Recalling a specific incident of stigma at her delivery job, Audre (twenty-nine, African American, bisexual, 230 pounds) said, "I remember once hearing a customer say, 'Yeah, she's gotten big,' and I freaked out and started crying at work because I thought he was commenting on my weight." Audre also recalled that getting uniforms made her feel acutely self-conscious about her size: "With the job, you have to be in uniform, so you have to tell them the size pants you need. I remember telling my boss the size I needed and she's like, 'You don't wear that size,' and I was like, 'Yes I do.' It made me feel horrible, like I should be more fit or more skinny." That said, finding a job that did not require a prefabricated uniform did little to solve these problems, as Kellyann (thirty-seven, white, heterosexual, 190 pounds) felt especially self-conscious about her clothing while working in the banking industry: "Buying clothes for work was really stressful because I could never really fit into the uniform or even be able to buy nice work clothes. It's all about clothes for me!" This sense that fat women lacked access to proper-fitting uniforms, that weight gain was seen as a liability, and that access to professional clothing was an impediment to fitting in were ubiquitous aspects of fat women's work lives.

Concerns about appearance also showed up when companies formally or informally highlighted the physical appearances of employees. Professional schools sometimes discouraged fat women from joining particular trades or professions. Marge (sixty-six, white, heterosexual, 245 pounds) said she felt self-conscious about her size when she aspired to attend dental school: "I talked to one of the professors and they said, 'With your weight, we'll train you but we can't guarantee you a job because you won't be able to maneuver very fast.' I thought to myself, 'Maneuvering? Like passing tool kits?' It was absurd." She added that her waitressing jobs at classic diner-style restaurants have also inspired shame about her body: "The uniforms had to be a certain height, so many inches above your knee, and I was always self-conscious about my legs being chubby." These practices of putting fat women into uniforms that did not fit well, sidelining them from entire lines of work, and moving them from "front of house" to "back of house" jobs fit with trends in existing research about fat discrimination at work.[63]

Fat women also described feeling particularly self-conscious about their size when they interacted with larger groups of men at work. The sense of penalty for both fatness and gender while working with men suggested that the stakes of sexism appeared more acutely when fat women negotiated their bodies around male coworkers. The physical requirements of different workplaces posed a challenge for fat women, as they struggled with the physical demands of (mostly) blue-collar or lower-paying jobs. Many jobs required tasks that were physically tiresome for fat women's bodies. Yvette, who worked in medical transportation, talked about the physicality of sitting in cars and vans all day as difficult and awkward for her: "I wouldn't eat enough. I feel like I'm taking up space, so if we're in a car or something, I have to suck it in or try to not take up space because I'm massive. I just feel so uncomfortable." These narratives highlighted the importance of attribution to the source of workplace problems, as the structure of work itself was left mostly unquestioned while fatness itself became the "problem." This feeds the narrative that bodies *within* workplaces should change rather than the nature of work changing to accommodate different bodies.

Fat women also experienced direct discrimination related to getting hired, being promoted, or being fired. Esther, who worked at an electronics store, believed she was fired because of her weight: "Next thing I know, they said, 'We're done with you,' and he fired me because of my size. I told my husband that mental-health wise, I'm never going back to work for anybody." This general sense that fatness is a liability at work and can result in being passed up for promotions, not hired at all, or even fired, was regularly mentioned by fat women. Because fatness is rarely recognized as a part of DEI protections, anti-fatness goes unchecked, is unquestioned, and becomes folded into workplaces as an assumed reality. Microaggressions—commonplace verbal or behavioral slights and insensitivities that exacerbate stigma and hostility toward a devalued group—also appeared in fat women's descriptions of their workplace cultures, particularly as their bodies became targets of ridicule and underhanded comments.

The culture around food and eating at work also engendered discrimination against fat women. For example, Tahi noticed that her boss at the warehouse, who was fat herself, experienced similar anti-fat stigma at work: "I had a supervisor who was very, very large and I noticed she would never come into the room with us to eat or always felt the need to only eat a salad in there." This commonplace belief that companies can target fat women for ridicule, commentary, and explicit anti-fat attitudes reinforces the hierarchies between different body types. The viciousness of this was further reinforced by the sense—from employers, workers, and companies—that anti-fatness was somehow inevitable and justified. In this sense, fat women's work experiences were rife with emotional and structural land mines.

ACCOMMODATING FAT BODIES AT WORK

While some companies are starting to think about changes to their policies around body size, those in positions of power most often ignore body size when they make commitments to diversity and inclusion. These are missed opportunities for workers and employers alike, as numerous accommodations could be made to better meet the needs of fat workers, including prevention of discrimination and stigma in the first place, support for fat workers' physical needs, and better psychological support, particularly for those struggling with (nearly inevitable) outcomes of living in a body-shaming culture.

Within the workplace, prioritizing the prevention of anti-fat discrimination in the first place should be a key goal. Formalizing anti-harassment, anti-bullying, and anti-violence policies is a crucial step so that fat workers have some recourse if they face direct attacks or assaults at work. Training managers and supervisors on weight bias and discrimination and communicating that weight discrimination will not be tolerated can also help set a tone of anti-discrimination for fat workers. Management should ensure that supervisors treat accommodation requests sensitively and professionally and stop any of their own harassing or bullying behaviors.[64] If companies have official policies without buy-in among supervisors and employees, there is little benefit to fat workers.

More inclusive seating is a small but impactful change that employers could make. Chairs without arms and bench seating that accommodates up to 450 pounds, for example, would help to ensure that workers are comfortable

and physically supported. As activist Marilyn Wann pointed out, "When employees exceed the weight limit for furniture, the results can be dangerous."[65]
Appropriately sized uniforms and T-shirts are also critical, as many fat people
end up wearing clothing that does not fit properly. (Also, T-shirt giveaways at
work, meant to boost morale and unity, must not exclude larger-sized people.)
Beyond that, being comfortable at work increases the likelihood of workers
staying at their jobs; happy workers are more productive and content.[66]

Some specific benefits that can help fat workers include ensuring that
health insurance options have coverage for short- and long-term disability
along with avenues for workers to discuss weight-related concerns with supportive healthcare providers.[67] For those workers wanting to lose weight,
health insurance companies play a key role in decision-making and gate-
keeping when it comes to treatment. This can add tremendous stress for
fat employees, as understanding available options is often mired in anti-fat
rhetoric and assumptions (gyms assuming the only health goal is weight
loss, for example, or doctors not being aware of the latest treatment options
for weight loss). Coverage of nutrition and dietary counseling, bariatric
surgery (an enormously complicated option, per chapter 3), and gym and
fitness subsidies have direct implications on fat workers' options for addressing the needs of their bodies. Future years will likely see the need for
health insurance companies to improve coverage of weight-loss medications,
which can cost upward of $1,000 per month, putting them out of reach
for most workers.[68] Robust mental health treatment also provides another
layer of tangible support for fat employees, including Employee Assistance
Programs (EAP), which provide free psychotherapy; these programs can
help workers cope with weight-based discrimination and stigma or other
issues they face.

Wellness programs at work, which too often target weight loss as a collective and personal goal, could be rehauled to focus more on weight-neutral
goals, such as meditation, walking, improved sleep, cancer screenings, and
vaccinations and even participation in programs that sell produce boxes or
promote other ways to encourage diets with more fruits and vegetables.
While some of these goals can still be fraught with anti-fat biases, moving
away from weight loss (and especially weight-loss competitions) as the primary metric for wellness can help fat employees avoid further stigma and
reduce the perceived legitimacy of anti-fat attitudes at work.[69] Changing
workplace food culture can also help fat employees, as it directs attention

away from food talk and fat talk. Helping workers to connect over things besides eating, de-emphasizing lunchrooms as socializing sites, offering diverse foods at company functions, and creating policies prohibiting supervisors from commenting on people's eating choices can be strong first steps.

Having fat-inclusive workplaces also means assessing and changing other aspects of company structures and cultures. For companies with on-site medical care, ensuring the availability of higher weight-bearing scales, larger blood-pressure cuffs, longer needles for vaccines, and larger chairs in the medical center are crucial strides toward inclusivity. In terms of team-building exercises, companies can avoid events that exclude fatter people, such as horseback riding, zip lines, or ropes courses with a weight limit. For companies that require travel, first-class plane tickets or the extra space seats, reimbursements for more comfortable ground transportation, and accommodations for fatter people's needs at hotels and conference sites can also help. To address some of the daily needs of fat employees, offices might open an hour later to help avoid crammed morning commutes on public transportation or actively encourage workers to seek formal accommodations to increase their productivity or attend to their needs.[70] Also, given that many workers buy lunch at or near their workplaces at least twice per week,[71] healthier on-site options with organic food, salad offerings, and juice bars rather than fast food or vending machines would benefit all workers. Again, these small changes—hardly trivial for those struggling to care for their bodies at work—could build a more inclusive environment.

Focusing on workplace policies and formal accommodations, administrators might promote options for fat employees to apply for support for their physical needs at work under the Americans with Disabilities Act (ADA). Given that higher body weight can trigger a variety of associated symptoms such as joint pain, mobility difficulties, shortness of breath, and comorbidities like diabetes and sleep apnea, which can "substantially limit a major life activity" in the standard language of the ADA, fat workers may qualify for official accommodations to help lessen the burdens on their bodies. This symbolic and material link between fatness and disability might be something not all fat workers feel comfortable with, but official workplace accommodations could increase the likelihood that fat workers stay at their jobs. (A broad look at the ADA accommodation data shows workers who got an ADA accommodation were 13.2 percent more likely to work than those who were not accommodated, and 47 to 58 percent of those who need an accommodation did not have one.)[72] Notably, the ADA covers individuals for accommodations who are "regarded as disabled," even if other criteria are not met. Whether fatness qualifies as a disability itself, or as something where they are "regarded as disabled," has yet to be fully determined. That said, accommodations for fat people at workplaces have become more commonplace as awareness of fat people's embodied needs in the workplace has become more widespread.[73] During the height of the COVID-19 pandemic, many fat workers applied for ADA accommodations due to increased vulnerability to severe illness from COVID-19.[74] As long as workers can perform essential job functions with reasonable accommodation, the law says, they deserve accommodation without discrimination or fear of job loss.

How to address grievances and anti-fat discrimination remains a murky legal question with regard to workplaces. A government advisor in the UK recently proposed to the European Congress on Obesity in Vienna that obesity should be considered a "protected characteristic."[75] This status would ultimately allow workers to file lawsuits against fat-shaming colleagues and bosses, and it would give fat workers an avenue to pursue legal action about anti-fat discrimination at work.[76] Whether other parts of the world will follow suit, including the US, remains to be seen. As legal scholar Anna Kirkland points out, adding fatness to a list of protected statuses and identities requires a variety of contradictory claims that point to the difficulty of moving fatness out of a moral framework. For example, arguments for legal rights for fat workers, she argues, posit one of several, often contradictory, positions: (1) fat people are falsely discriminated against at work and can function like everyone else; (2) fat people are subject to unfair stereotypes that do not reflect the experiences of individual workers; (3) workplace standards are inherently anti-fat and constructed to maintain thin people's superiority and power; (4) fat people face discrimination similar to African Americans and have been systematically discriminated against and excluded; and (5) fat people constitute another facet of workplace diversity and fatness should be seen as an enriching part of workplace diversity.[77] Implications for workplace and legal protections based on each of these premises vary substantially and point to the reality that imagining and protecting fat rights is in its infancy.[78] Questions of how to better accommodate diverse body sizes at work and mitigate the negative impacts of workplace discrimination will require ongoing conversations and an intensified interest in how policy changes reflect underlying attitudes about fatness.

THE "INVISIBLE KNAPSACK" OF THIN PRIVILEGE

Conversations about thin privilege have emerged as an increasingly relevant, albeit controversial, subject both within and outside of academia. Attention to how thinness and fatness intersect with other social identities like race, gender, sexuality, social class, and age add to the intersectional perspectives on body size and power differentials.[79] Because thinness largely operates as a default goal in a patriarchal society—that is, women are assumed to want or need to be thin and to strive to make their bodies sexually desirable to men in these ways—examinations of privilege around thinness are often sorely lacking.

Critics of thin privilege point to its conceptual limitations and the difficulties of moving from recognizing a problem to acting on that problem. Australian feminist writer Anwyn Crawford recalls the problems of merely identifying thin privilege rather than doing anything about it: "I've lost count of the number of meetings, workshops, and protests where a checklist of privileges is 'acknowledged' at the start, as if mere words could encircle a space with magic and vanish the tangled inheritance we each bring with us."[80] Other critics of conversations about thin privilege have argued that discussions of fatness and thinness often emphasize a single dimension of oppression rather than a more full and nuanced analysis of the intersections of social identity, particularly how fat oppression operates for people of different social identities. This rhetoric can ultimately undermine social justice goals. Glib discussions of thin privilege can lead to policing and exclusion around bodies and language rather than outlining and reaching for fat activist goals.[81]

With this in mind, I have nevertheless outlined some of the ways that body size and privilege intersect in workplaces in concrete ways. In a nod to the landmark essay by Peggy McIntosh, "White Privilege: Unpacking the Invisible Knapsack,"[82] where she examines the various privileges she has as a white person that her women-of-color colleagues do not have, I outline here some of the unearned and unexamined privileges that thin women have at work. This list is not an effort to undermine the intersectional readings of bodily privilege and oppression, nor is it designed to minimize the painful ways in which *all* women face structural oppression based on their gender. Rather, this is an exercise to make concrete the costs of anti-fat practices and to locate thin privilege not in the abstract and conceptual spaces of work-places but in the tiny mundane interactions that people engage in.

1. Thin people can reasonably assume they will have "front of the house" jobs if they want them and will not be assigned to "back of the house" jobs against their will.
2. Thin people can wear a wider range of clothing at work without being accused of dressing inappropriately.
3. Thin people can generally expect that their hygiene and cleanliness will not be questioned when they interact with customers.
4. Thin people will not be the first to be accused of stealing food if someone's food goes missing from the office fridge.
5. Thin people will be labeled as more competent, likeable, social, friendly, personable, and desirable during job interviews because of their body types.
6. Thin people can assume that their bodies will not prevent them from getting promoted and will not lead to them being fired from their jobs.
7. Thin people can take the elevator or avoid stairs without coworkers assuming they are doing so because of their body weight.
8. Thin people can reasonably assume they can find plentiful clothing options for their job or fit into assigned uniforms with relative ease.
9. Thin people will not pay a surcharge for their uniform sizes at blue-collar jobs.
10. Thin people can talk about their children and partners at work without assumptions being made about their body types and sizes.
11. Thin people can talk to disgruntled customers without the threat of them insulting their weight.
12. Thin people can do physical labor without fear of people thinking they are not fit enough to do the work.
13. Thin people, especially thin men, can eat meals at work without feeling like they need to monitor how much is on their plate or how healthy the food on it is.
14. Thin doctors can give advice about health and fitness without being seen as "fraudulent" or unaccredited.

15. Thin professionals can assume that their bodies will not be used as grounds to discredit their expertise or credentials.
16. Thin teachers can work with young children without having them comment on their appearance and the size of their body.
17. Thin people can assume they will not be placed in the back of professional group photos to hide their weight.
18. Thin people can fly on airplanes for business trips without worrying about being able to sit comfortably in their seats.
19. Thin people can sit comfortably in office and conference room chairs.
20. Thin people can tell their coworkers they are exhausted after working with clients without their coworkers assuming that their weight is causing the fatigue.
21. Thin people can eat at work without their coworkers negatively evaluating their eating choices.
22. Thin people, especially thin men, can eat a lot at a company party or celebration and assume that others will find it cute, fun-loving, or quirky rather than disgusting or unhealthy.
23. Thin people can assume that company literature and promotional items will depict people of their body sizes in a positive light.
24. Thin people can sweat while at work without it reflecting negatively on them.
25. Thin people can attend medical appointments during their time off without it reflecting on them as a moral or character flaw.
26. Thin people can assume that vaccines and medications, including flu shots and COVID-19 vaccines, are properly dosed and that they will be maximally protected from disease after receiving them.
27. Thin people can have food-related hobbies that they openly discuss at work (such as being a foodie) without it reflecting on their body weight in a negative light.
28. Thin people can assume that if they are late, this will not reflect stereotypes that people have about their body size.
29. Thin people can reasonably assume they are not paid less because of their body size.
30. Thin people can expect not to be targeted and put on display during workplace "weight-loss challenges."

31. Thin people are able to not worry about their being out of breath or appearing to exert effort as a negative reflection on their body size.

32. Thin people do not have to worry about problems with their desk being an inappropriate size for their stomach.

33. Thin people can receive invitations for workplace social events, especially ones that require more physical activity, without fear of being negatively evaluated for their body size.

34. Thin people do not have to worry about coworkers' judgments when eating dessert at an office party.

35. Thin people can blatantly discuss their extremely negative feelings about their own weight gain and can expect sympathy and encouragement from coworkers.

36. Thin people can overtly discuss their diets and weight-loss techniques and can expect interest from, and conversation with, their coworkers about the topic.

37. Thin people can take a sick day and not worry that their supervisors or coworkers will attribute this to their "unhealthy lifestyle choices."

38. Thin people can expect that their body size will not be a subject of office gossip.

39. Thin people can work without worrying about how much space they take up in conference rooms, company cars, airplanes, and other small spaces.

40. If thin people need accommodations for health issues, those accommodations will not be undermined, questioned, or belittled in the same way accommodations for fatness are.

ANTI-FATNESS AND THE LOGICS OF CAPITALISM

Capitalism requires that workers become "products" that sell their labor in the marketplace, and the ideologies of capitalism assign fat women lower value on the marketplace than their thinner counterparts. Perhaps more than any other chapter in this book, the content in this chapter makes clear that fat women pay an economic price for their body size, as fatness was framed by workplaces as anti-productive, anti-efficient, and in need of discipline. In this sense, an analysis of fat women's bodies at work, and the ways that fat women were saddled with oppressive assumptions about their bodies, underscores how fatness operates as a form of structural, interpersonal, and individual liability.

The content of this chapter raises questions about the interface between neoliberalism and capitalism, particularly as they intersect and inform each other through fat women's bodies at work. While neoliberalism posits that individuals are responsible for their own wellness, advancement, and success, and thus, workplaces merely reflect the ways that individuals work to achieve certain statuses within them, capitalism has become obsessed with the surveillance, monitoring, and image of workers. Both see bodies, particularly body size, as a marker of value on the marketplace, and both reduce people to their bodies, linking value and morality to the presentation and performance of particular bodies. A key argument here is that, under capitalism, fat women's bodies are marked as particularly threatening, both to the notions of patriarchal beauty (which also allows economic control over women) and to the incessant push for particular kinds of productivity (where bodies are rendered as disposable). Who is seen, and what value those bodies have when seen, impact the logics and political practices of workplaces, severely disadvantaging fat women's bodies in particular. As Anwyn Crawford writes, "The rhetoric of visibility can be, and is, used by rulers against the ruled: to be visible is, on some level, to accede to the anti-terrorist logic that one has 'nothing to hide.'" She adds, "I am much more interested in how radicals across the world—whatever their bodies—can work together at escaping these intertwined visibilities: the image-logic of capitalism, the coercive gaze of the state."[83]

In this sense, anti-fat attitudes at work can only be dismantled through two competing frameworks. First, we must unpack and challenge the material and emotional conditions of fat stigma at work, unraveling the ways that negative emotions about fat bodies drive structural inequalities (and vice versa). Second, a broader revolt against the logics of capitalism and how they deeply impact how *all* bodies are seen, treated, objectified, monitored, and policed in relation to work and workplaces is essential. Within those efforts, fat bodies can be untethered from their status as uniquely and particularly abject and instead linked to other bodies and identities that also suffer from the burdens and intrusions of capitalism. Fat liberation requires a collective effort to resist the logics of capitalism, from the insistence that bodies are interchangeable, to the overreliance on productivity as the ultimate sign of morality, to the treatment of people's labor as detached from their humanity.

Dismantling anti-fatness at work requires attention to the tiny, mundane experiences of fat women's work lives, as stigma weaves its way into interactions that are seemingly trivial and insignificant ("You've lost weight, haven't you?" "Didn't you just eat?" "What sized uniform do you need?"). The priorities of capitalism—making bodies comply and obey, treating bodies that do not comply and obey with disdain, ensuring productivity above wellness and happiness, and so on—are revealed in fat women's experiences at work. Across all job types and fields, between coworkers of all stripes, and within the policies and practices of white-collar and blue-collar work, fat bodies are fired, blocked, refused, squeezed, ignored, sidelined, dismissed, demoted, and discarded. This mistreatment is enabled by those in power and perpetuated by those who also largely lack power. How people treat fat bodies reflects the coercive gaze of the state. The treatment of fat women's bodies in particular reveals a cautionary tale of what happens when workers' bodies are read to be outside of the framework of productivity, discipline, and control.

In essence, the intense policing of fat bodies at work should be seen as a warning sign of what is coming for us all: the treatment of our bodies as objects that are disposable, worthy of abuse, and easily discarded and maligned. The questions of how soon people will revolt, and how much they are willing to protect those made vulnerable by these logics of capitalism, are critical questions of our time.

PART THREE

FAT VULNERABILITY

CHAPTER 5

THE SPECTER OF FAT DEATH

S onya Renee Taylor defiantly titles her book *The Body Is Not an Apology* and, yet, fat bodies are constantly portrayed as apologizing, as vulnerable, as undeserving of care, as *confessing* some sort of wrongdoing. Fat people are routinely neglected, declared guilty, rendered voiceless. They are, in the starkest terms, allowed to die, made so invisible that they live in a constant state of precarity.

Some might say that the current treatment of fat people in the medical world constitutes a shirking of medical ethics and a frank violation of the medical oath "Do no harm." By rationalizing poor treatment of fat people, placing individual blame on people for being fat, and largely failing to imagine fat people as in need of protection, the current medical system has largely failed to properly care for fat people. Research on fat bias in medical settings across demographics and geographic locations in the US found an overwhelming amount of anti-fat discrimination from doctors, nurses, hospital policymakers, insurance companies, and pharmaceutical companies. This results in fat patients feeling powerless or ignored, avoiding treatment, being treated as difficult and noncompliant, lacking confidence in their medical care, seeing doctors less often and for shorter durations, and receiving different treatment options and fewer preventative measures compared to thinner people.[1] A large-scale scoping review of twenty-one studies about the relationship between fat people and the medical system revealed staggering levels of dysfunction: weight bias was identified in primary healthcare through doctors' contemptuous, patronizing, and disrespectful treatment of fat people, lack of training, ambivalence toward fat patients, and attribution and assumptions about patients' weight and health outside of the scope of the presenting symptoms and complaints. Further, fat people were pervasively impacted negatively by such treatment and avoided or delayed visiting doctors, expected differential healthcare treatment, experienced low trust and poor communication with their doctors, and felt they had to "doctor shop" to be treated with basic humanity during doctor's visits.[2] The treatment of fat people in healthcare settings can rightly be characterized as a crisis.

At the top of the list of problems with medical professionals' attitudes toward fatness: most doctors ignore evidence-based approaches to weight loss and caring for fat people. Instead, as journalist Michael Hobbes writes, "Years from now, we will look back in horror at the counterproductive ways we addressed the obesity epidemic and the barbaric ways we treated fat people—long after we knew there was a better path."[3] He traced a brief history of fatness, noting that about forty years ago, Americans started getting larger bodies as a collective whole, with nearly 80 percent of adults and a third of children now meeting the clinical definition of overweight or obese. He notes, "More Americans live with 'extreme obesity' than with breast cancer, Parkinson's, Alzheimer's and HIV put together."[4] The collision of people getting fatter along with spikes in overt and covert biases against fat people has led to the medical system framing fatness as a personal failure, giving people an excuse to lecture and harangue fat people "for their own good." These biases also help to explain why Americans spent more money on dieting every year than on entertainment or leisure activities. Forty-five percent of Americans said that they were preoccupied with their weight some or all of the time, and nearly half of girls ages three to six admitted to worrying about getting fat.[5] One can only imagine how much worse this will get with the new clinical guidelines from the American Academy of Pediatrics on treating fatness, where doctors recommend weight-loss surgery options for children as young as twelve, and dieting and behavioral modification options for children as young as two.[6]

It is hard to reconcile the fact that nearly every fat woman I have spoken with in my research studies—every fat woman I know, for that matter—has recounted horror stories of medical bullying and scolding, moral diatribes about the perils of fatness, and pressure to lose weight despite the fact that sustained weight loss occurs in less than *1 percent* of people. Medical doctors and public health researchers both know, and have known for some time, that diets do not work—Weight Watchers, Paleo, Atkins, keto, and the rest—and that between 95 and 98 percent of attempts to lose weight fail, while two-thirds of dieters gain back *more* than they lost after attempting to diet. As Hobbes points out, "The reasons are biological and irreversible. As early as 1969, research showed that lowering just 3 percent of your body weight resulted in a 17 percent slowdown in your metabolism—a body-wide starvation response that blasts you with hunger hormones and drops your internal temperature until you rise back to your highest weight. Keeping weight off means fighting your body's energy-regulation system and battling hunger all day, every day, for the rest of your life."[7]

Pressures on fat people to lose weight as a mechanism to be healthier continue in abundance even though it is a well-known fact that healthiness and thinness are not synonymous. Between one-third and three-quarters of fat people were shown to be metabolically healthy with no signs of elevated blood pressure, insulin resistance, or high cholesterol. Conversely, about a quarter of thinner people could be classified as "the lean unhealthy," and unfit thinner people were twice as likely to get diabetes than fitter fat people.[8] As Hobbes notes, "Dozens of indicators, from vegetable consumptions to regular exercise to *grip strength*, provide a better snapshot of someone's health than looking at her from across a room."[9] And yet, medical pressure to try increasingly aggressive diets, exercise more often, or eat fewer sweets and snacks continue to fail to produce sustained weight loss.

People who go to medical school are often deeply unaware of their own anti-fat biases; medical school actually *increases* doctors' anti-fat attitudes rather than decreases them.[10] Consequently, fat women have described a plethora of horrors when visiting doctors: inappropriate questions, overt contempt, treatments delayed or denied entirely, medical decisions framed in the language of "deservingness" and "worthiness," assumptions about their lack of education or inability to understand medical information, and more. (I once had a doctor describe my body to me as an "overloaded dump truck.") The medical profession has routinely dismissed fat women's complaints, minimized their symptoms, blamed any and all medical problems on fatness, and denied the very real possibilities that fat people struggled with eating disorders when they attempted to lose weight.[11] In fact, doctors often minimized the problems of fat women's eating disorders, seeing fat women's restricted eating as "helpful" to their weight-loss journeys, even when dieting itself produced eating-disordered behavior.[12]

Doctors spent less time with their fat patients compared to their thin patients, showed less emotional rapport in the time they did spend with them, and often used more negative words in their medical notes about fat patients ("noncompliant," "overindulgent," and "weak willed," for example).[13] Doctors with more weight bias gave more diet and exercise recommendations, offered more health advice about weight loss, used less teaching discourse with patients, and started them on pharmaceutical treatment options sooner than doctors with less weight bias.[14] Anesthesiologists frequently discussed anesthesia risks with fat patients by describing fat patients' bodies as high risk and "difficult," rather than giving matter-of-fact or patient-centered explanations about their care.[15] In an audit study that used patients with migraine symptoms to test doctors' reactions to them, patients described as fat were characterized by doctors as having worse attitudes and being less compliant with medical advice; in twelve out of thirteen measures, doctors described fat patients in more negative terms.[16]

Even more disturbingly, at times doctors simply chose not to treat fat patients at all. One study of ob/gyns in South Florida found that 14 percent refused to see any new patients that weighed over two hundred pounds, while another study found that doctors routinely refused to treat fat patients at all due to increased costs of larger medical equipment.[17] Many medical professionals have argued that fat people need to be "incentivized" to lose weight, even though such programs have no history of working effectively to achieve that outcome.[18] In fact, using such "tough love" tactics and overtly shaming and deriding people about their weight resulted in the opposite effect, as weight stigma and medical admonishment about fatness typically increased patients' body weight rather than reduced it.[19]

Fat patients often felt that their doctors did not understand them or, worse, felt actual contempt for them. This belief was not misguided. Medical students reported feeling that fat cadavers they worked on during gross-anatomy courses were "difficult," "unhealthy," and evoked disgust in them.[20] For fat patients seeking out surgery, they were expected to have a level of trust and vulnerability that was not compatible with doctors' actual attitudes about fat patients. As Michael Hobbes reported, surgeons routinely belittled and degraded fatter patients' bodies while they were under anesthesia: "An anesthesiologist on the West Coast tells me that as soon as a larger patient goes under, the surgeons start trading 'high school insults' about her body over the operating table." Empirical studies supported this claim, as medical students frequently encountered belittling and derogatory humor about fat patients from other medical students, residents, and faculty during their years in medical school.[21] Patients rightly worried about the lack of empathy among their physicians and surgeons, and superfat people were especially justified in worrying, as doctors' negative perceptions increased as patients' weight increased.[22] In one study, one in three surgeons delayed treatment and changed the timing of treatment for cancer based on body size in spite of no medical reasons for doing so.[23] Surgeons often felt nervous and under-trained in operating on superfat bodies, though quality care for fat patients is, according to many experts, an achievable goal.[24] The notion of whether increased usage of robotic surgery techniques, retraining of doctors, or generally lessening weight stigma will reduce fat bias in medical settings remains an open question.[25]

Doctors' offices themselves communicate messages about which bodies were valuable, accommodatable, and visible to medical professionals. Examples include hospital gowns that are too small, exam tables that don't support the patient's weight, blood pressure cuffs that don't fit around arms, and scales that don't exceed 350 or 400 pounds.[26] Fat patients heard doctors diagnose them without asking about their concerns, and they were often denied lifesaving preventative care or diagnostic procedures such as CAT scans, MRIs, even blood tests, because doctors could not see beyond fatness.[27] As scholar and activist Cat Pausé wrote, "Basing diagnosis, and subsequent treatment, on assumptions made due to an individual's body size, is not evidenced based care. Some may even call it malpractice."[28] Alarmingly, even when fat people embraced their bodies and told doctors they were happy with their size, doctors often scoffed. When fat women described healthy behaviors, doctors responded with disbelief. Pausé documents numerous stories of superfat women explaining to their doctors that they exercised and ate nutrient-diverse diets, only to have their doctors accuse them of lying or misrepresenting the truth of their eating and exercise habits.

Part of the problem was that doctors spent remarkably little time asking for any details about diet and nutrition. With appointments lasting an average of fifteen minutes and doctors receiving minimal training in medical school about nutrition, doctors typically did not ask patients much about their diet and exercise routines. They also were not incentivized by insurance companies to talk at any length about diet and exercise programs, though they *were* asked to prove that they discussed weight loss with patients, even if the visit was unrelated to weight loss.[29] These factors, along with routine biases doctors learned both in medical school and in their daily lives, exacerbated misguided assumptions about fat patients' eating practices, and it encouraged doctors to praise patients for overtly eating-disordered behavior. There is still a widespread assumption in medical communities that fat patients do not overly restrict eating (anorexia), binge and purge (bulimia), or show other signs of eating disturbances beyond overeating and overindulging in "bad" foods.[30] Sharon Maxwell, profiled in the *New York Times*, affirmed that doctors took no issue with her eating-disordered behavior, saying: "Anything that made the scale go down, I was given a pat on the back."[31] Fat women with anorexia were twice as likely to report vomiting, using laxatives, and abusing diet pills compared to thin women with anorexia, and fat women with anorexia spent an average of thirteen and a half years waiting for doctors to treat their anorexia, compared to three years for treatment of thinner women with anorexia.[32] The effects of these delays were particularly problematic for fat Latinx and African American teenagers, who suffered disproportionately from undiagnosed bulimia.[33]

Anti-fat bias in healthcare has been well documented throughout many specialties and subspecialties, including those of dieticians, psychologists, physical therapists, occupational therapists, speech pathologists, podiatrists, exercise physiologists, and more.[34] This raises questions about the quality of care fat patients receive across the board. Fat people faced a higher likelihood of both misdiagnosis and underdiagnosis. One study found that fat patients were 1.65 times more likely than thinner people to have significant undiagnosed medical conditions, such as endocarditis, ischemic bowel disease, or lung carcinoma, suggesting that misdiagnosis and inadequate access to healthcare can kill fat people.[35] Asthma, chronic obstructive pulmonary disease (COPD), and knee osteoarthritis were also vastly underdiagnosed among fat patients.[36] Perhaps even more disturbingly, mood disorders—especially bipolar disorder—among fat patients seeking bariatric surgery were both highly prevalent and underdiagnosed, and the screening tools used for pre-bariatric evaluations often failed to identify serious mood disorders.[37] Doctors also routinely recommended different treatments to patients of different sizes who presented the same symptoms. Fat patients more often heard that they must lose weight, while thinner patients received more symptoms-specific screenings and proactive medical care, such as physical therapy, blood screenings, and preventative scans.[38]

The mistreatment of fat patients was so depressingly ubiquitous as to be unremarkable and routine. A plethora of faulty or misguided treatments were often given to fat patients as "sound" medical advice: fad diets, extreme exercise plans that did not account for their current fitness levels, commentary about "willpower" and "strength," recommendations for consuming less than one thousand calories a day, advice to lose one hundred to two hundred pounds, and so on. When fat people asked earnest questions about diet and exercise plans, they were often met with reluctance, as time-crunched physicians would rather pass the buck or ignore these requests.[39] Physicians routinely chose not to build rapport with fat patients, even if that produced negative consequences for fat patients' medical care.[40] This whole process of seeking medical help and being treated poorly often exacerbated fat people's feelings of despair, hopelessness, and frustration, and sometimes resulted in the ultimate failure of healthcare: fat patients refusing to seek medical treatment at all. Fat people more often postponed or canceled doctor's appointments because they feared doctors reprimanding them about their size.[41] In this way, fat stigma and sizeism was *itself* a formidable health hazard.[42]

The consequences of fat people avoiding medical treatment—something done with remarkable consistency—were often dire. Fat women were more likely to die from breast and cervical cancers than thinner women, in part because fat women were less likely to visit doctors and get cancer screenings. For fat queer women, their avoidance of medical care further marginalized them and put them at even higher risk for serious illness and death.[43] There is widespread documentation of the risks of medical neglect in relation to fat people's healthcare: fat patients diagnosed with acid reflux when they had cancer, fat patients skipping their MRIs because the machines could not hold their weight only to later discover they had a serious (and easily discoverable) tumor, vaginal bleeding ignored as weight-related when it actually revealed cancer, and so on.[44]

The avoidance of medical care, and lack of access to a sense of collective grievance or anger about the consistently poor medical treatment fat people received, may stem from the relative lack of community that fat people have had with each other. Fat people respond to medical discrimination in their own individual ways: taking criticism, being deferential to doctors, privately feeling angry or defiant, avoiding the critical eyes of the medical world, and so on. They do this largely without community support. As Hobbes notes, "But perhaps the most unique aspect of weight stigma is how it isolates its victims from one another. For most minority groups, discrimination contributes to a sense of belongingness, a community in opposition to a majority." Fat solidarity, however, is a rarity: "Surveys of higher-weight people, however, reveal that they hold many of the same biases as the people discriminating against them." Fat people who endorsed Protestant work ethic beliefs (that is, working hard leads to success) as well as world beliefs (people deserve their fates) were especially likely to endorse anti-fat attitudes. This lack of fat community solidarity makes sense if weight operates as an individual "blemish" or a transitional, liminal, or temporary identity—something en route to a thinner self that is waiting to be revealed. How can a fat person claim a community or identity if the fundamental message is that fatness should not exist in the first place? The bedrock beliefs that fatness is repulsive, that fat people are pathetic, that weight loss is the ultimate goal, and that all people, fat people included, dislike fatness, has helped to fuel this relative lack of collectivity or solidarity around fat identity.

FAT WOMEN ON ANTI-FATNESS IN THE MEDICAL SYSTEM

More than perhaps any other subject, the discussion with fat women about their traumatic, discriminatory, and stigma-laden experiences with medical care illuminated a disdain for fatness that was structural, institutional, interpersonal, and deeply emotional. My conversations with fat women about their interactions with doctors contextualized how the specter of fat death infuses fat women's lives.

Rather than taking women's medical concerns at face value, doctors often communicated to fat women that losing weight would overwhelmingly solve all of their medical problems. Vaiana expressed anger and exasperation at how her doctor assigned responsibility to fatness for all of her unrelated medical conditions: "Even something like an ear infection, which doesn't have anything to do with your weight, he's always going to be like, 'Oh, you're not on a diet?'" Hannah felt similarly about weight being the centerpiece for every medical conversation with her doctors: "My size becomes the focus of the visit. I just want to talk about how I have a cold or whatever, but because they weigh me and talk to me about it, weight directs the conversation." Audre reflected on how doctors frequently overstepped the boundaries of the topics in the room to purposefully comment on her weight: "I went for a Pap smear and she started talking about my weight saying, 'From the last time you were here, you've gained too much weight,' and then she printed out all these packets for me about weight loss and eating healthy. I was like, 'What the hell is this? I didn't ask you for this.'" By being accosted by unwanted weight conversations, fat women came to routinely expect that any medical concern would unwittingly divert to conversations about their body size.

This sense that doctors felt entitled to discuss size on any visit led fat women to expect constant surveillance, harassment, and mistreatment about their weight. Doctors also routinely refused to acknowledge the possibility that someone could be fat *and* care deeply about their body in terms of exercising and eating well. Octavia had a combative experience with her doctor where he did not believe she could be fat and also strong and fit: "My doctor just looks at me and he's like, 'You need to lose weight, like what are you eating and what are you exercising?' I'm like, 'I've been a vegetarian for sixteen years. I know that I could take more exercise but I walked three miles to your office today. I'm not unfit!' He just didn't believe me and then said something like, 'It's easy to lose weight. Calories in, calories out.' I'm like, 'When did you go to medical school? That hasn't been the accepted consensus for twenty years!'" This relentless fixation on weight at the expense of broader health profiles, and the assumptions that fat women did not care for their bodies, led to both stigma and poorer medical care.

Fat women also encountered doctors who blatantly disrespected them by making inappropriate comments, giving bad advice, or telling them about their imminent deaths. Carrie (thirty-six, white, heterosexual, 190 pounds) was told by her doctor that her partner would not want to have sex with her anymore if she did not lose weight: "I was in a relationship and I had been trying to lose weight for that motivation. My doctor was like, 'You better not get fatter or he's not going to want to have sex with you anymore.' It was so crass and inappropriate." Isabella's doctor frequently used the term "morbidly obese" and constantly fed her the story that she would die imminently from being fat. Esther said that her doctor glibly prescribed her an all-fruit diet: "He said, 'You're too big for your size. Eat fruit. Eat only bananas. That'll make you thinner. Just eat bananas." Jayden was advised by her doctor to starve herself to lose weight: "My PCP said, 'Come on! We've gotta get serious now. You're fifty-seven. You've gotta lose weight or you're gonna have a heart attack.' And I said, 'Yeah, how do you expect me to do that?' He says, 'Well, every time you eat, just go longer and longer being hungry. Just stay hungry. You'll lose a pound a week if you keep going an hour more each time.'" This range of inappropriate, unethical, counterproductive, and unscientific doctor responses reveals some of the complications of fat women confronting a healthcare system that regularly couches anti-fat bias and stigma as sound medical advice.

Doctors not only missed a great deal of information about fat women's bodies because of anti-fat biases, but they also created conditions where fat women avoided seeking medical care altogether. Winnie (forty-nine, Native American and white, heterosexual, 260 pounds) became avoidant after stigma she faced during the weigh-in process: "I would hate to go on the scale. When I would see the gynecologist, I kind of just felt sometimes they were judging my body, like, 'You need to lose weight.' It just makes me feel sad. I hate going now." Tahi felt similarly about seeking medical care from her ob/ gyn's office after a postpartum visit: "Six weeks after I had my daughter I was going through postpartum depression and I had a sub that day at my doctor's office. He was making suggestions about how to get back into shape and, like, I just created a baby for nine months." These stigmatizing experiences reflect the importance of fat women having a voice during doctor's visits, perhaps by declining an unnecessary weigh-in or turning down weight-loss advice, though such decisions must first garner support from the medical establishment to better support fat women's health needs. Physicians need to practice empathy, improve communication about the causality of and ability to control fatness with their patients, and actively engage with patients' health goals.[45] If the ultimate goal is to encourage fat women to seek out medical care, the elimination of anti-fat discrimination is essential.

ANTI-FATNESS DURING THE COVID-19 PANDEMIC

Coverage that lambasts, berates, and degrades fat people has been a staple of mainstream news media, long before COVID-19. Fat studies scholars have criticized news organizations for using the words "epidemic," "pandemic," and "crisis" in reference to fatness, particularly given that losing weight permanently is a profound rarity.[46] Pictures of disembodied fat people appear ubiquitously on news stories and feature pieces about fatness; one study found that 60 percent of images of fat people showed them as headless torsos— suggesting that the fat *body* can be divorced from the fat *person*.[47] Headlines such as CNN's "Half of America Will Be Obese Within 10 Years, Study Says, Unless We Work Together" have appeared commonly in mainstream news coverage of fatness.[48] Solutions often center on individuals changing their behavior or bodies, or weak policy-level interventions like implementing higher taxes on "bad" foods, adding calorie counts to menus, or reforming the Supplemental Nutrition Assistance Program (SNAP).[49] Further, medical language often treats fat people as an afterthought, foregrounding their (flawed) physiology over their personhood. For example, one recent scholarly study described fat people as mere containers for an ever-expanding pathogen: "We explore how the obese host provides a unique microenvironment for disease pathogenesis."[50]

A closer look at news coverage during the pandemic about the lethality of COVID-19 shows many familiar fatness-as-risky tropes as turbocharged iterations of themselves. While the dread and terror people feel about fat bodies has long been an underlying force of American life, the pandemic ratcheted up these panics as an outright cultural phenomenon. Discussions of COVID-19 weight gain—along with memes, stories, social media posts, and news articles about thinner people gaining weight—became a ubiquitous part of the cultural zeitgeist during the early part of the pandemic. At least thirty thousand Instagram posts related to "quarantine15" appeared in the first month of lockdowns, and Twitter and Facebook were inundated with weight-gain memes and phrases.[51] Memes quipped, "So, after this quarantine . . . will the producers of *My 600 Pound Life* just find me . . . or do I call them . . . or how will this work?" Other popular memes included: "Now that I've lived during a plague, I understand why renaissance paintings are all of chubby women laying around with their boobs out."[52] Editorials and dieting advice quickly followed, with headlines like "How to NOT Gain Weight During Coronavirus Quarantine" and "You've Heard of the Freshman 15? Here's How I'm Avoiding the 'Quarantine 15.'"

Media coverage of the pandemic promoted a relentlessly anti-fat narrative about future "fat selves": new weight gain was terrifying, all people would gain weight during quarantine, and weight gain was a shared experience that exemplified the misery, dread, panic, and despair of the pandemic. In essence, panicky conversations about weight gain became a scapegoat for the experience of distress itself. People were unable to talk about the existential terror of dying from COVID-19 or the psychological pain of losing social connections at work or in their communities, so weight gain became the avenue for discussing angst. COVID-19 and fatness messaging took a familiar turn toward blaming individuals for not being thinner and thus more protected from the virus. Story after story detailed the concern about fat people's risks, coupled with messaging about how fat people were responsible for their fatness and how they should take more action to lower their weight in order to save themselves.[53]

The juxtaposition of psychological realities during the pandemic was stark: while some people overtly grappled with fears of dying and losing loved ones, far more people joked, commented, and shared their fears about fatness as a stand-in for the anxiety of living through the pandemic. It was as if fatness itself became its own disaster, and the lurking possibilities of growing fat (code for losing desirability, becoming further marginalized, and feeling "gross") became the ultimate symbol of pandemic fear.

Anti-fat content and fearmongering about fatness appeared abundantly within online content early in the pandemic, particularly as social distancing, lockdowns, and a lack of vaccines ramped up people's anxieties. As writer Renee Cafaro noted, "Even friends I feel should know better are sharing 'fat beach body' memes, counting calories or joking about 'binging' on quarantine snacks, all during a period when we should just be grateful for life and focused on beating the coronavirus."[54] Those made vulnerable by anti-fat rhetoric were subjected to repeated exposure of anti-fat content online and in the news media, often couched as humor, further exacerbating their distress. According to data on this, the majority of adolescents reported increased exposure to at least one form of weight-stigmatizing social media content during the pandemic, and pandemic-related increases in body dissatisfaction were prevalent, especially for fatter girls.[55] For adults, a longitudinal study of both pre- and post-pandemic eating behavior found that those who had reported being stigmatized for their weight pre-pandemic experienced more stress, depressive symptoms, binge eating, and eating to cope with stress during the pandemic than those not stigmatized for their weight prior to the pandemic.[56]

Research on the heightened impact of fearing weight gain during the pandemic further supported the idea that people emotionally link fatness with dread and terror. Fear of weight gain during COVID-19 impacted women of all different body weights. Fatter women exposed to weight-stigmatizing media during the pandemic increased their consumptions of calories, as exposure to negative stereotypes about fat women lessened their healthy eating habits.[57] Neuroendocrinologists argued that fat women faced a vicious cycle of hearing about weight stigma and hearing about COVID-19 risks, which resulted in higher cortisol secretion, increased eating behavior, more weight gain, and more difficulty losing weight.[58] Ironically, the more people of all sizes feared becoming fat, the more they typically ate,[59] just as being exposed to weight stigma can make people believe they weigh more than they actually do.[60] People's early pandemic media exposures contributed to distortions about food and eating that were laced with anti-fat biases and rhetoric.

Ultimately, the pandemic showcased how the fear of fatness (already a dreaded status) became the repository for so much of the surrounding social and medical trauma of the pandemic. Assumptions that fatness was linked to vulnerability to serious infections and diseases have existed for many years. In the late 2000s, when the H1N1 influenza virus circulated, fatness was linked to higher rates of hospitalization and mechanical ventilation largely due to decreased lung function in fatter people.[61] With COVID-19, fatness again predicted more susceptibility to severe infection and death.[62] Though the exact mechanisms by which fatness increased vulnerability to severe COVID-19 illness, hospitalizations, and death are still largely unknown in any definitive sense, researchers have consistently found that higher body weight is linked to higher mortality from COVID-19.[63] While the medical world proceeded cautiously, initially linking fatness to COVID-19 vulnerability in March and April 2020, the number of studies making these links increased dramatically after the first six months of the pandemic. Study after study reliably found that COVID-19 was stored in fat cells, contributed to a more aggravated inflammatory response and enhanced injury to the heart, and could result in a more intense "cytokine storm," where the lungs became particularly vulnerable when interacting with higher viral load from storage in fat cells.[64] Further, fatness tends to activate the development of gene-induced hypoxia (low oxygen levels) and can weaken the overall immune system via low-grade, persistent inflammation responses throughout the body.[65] Structurally in the body, fatness also increased risks for the lungs to be pressed and for airflow to be restricted.[66]

These particular characteristics of fatness made fat people vulnerable to the already-dangerous COVID-19, particularly if they had other diseases and conditions that further exacerbated their risks. Researchers know that hypertension, COPD, type 2 diabetes, and moderate to severe renal disease impact fat people's vulnerability to COVID-19 infections.[67] The data from hospitals are also stark: fat COVID-19 patients had longer hospital stays when admitted, experienced a more severe disease progression, and were less likely, with a five times higher risk of in-hospital mortality, to survive an ICU admission compared to thinner COVID-19 patients.[68] One study estimated that fat people were 46 percent more likely to contract COVID-19, 113 percent more likely to be hospitalized, 74 percent more likely to be admitted to the ICU, and 48 percent more likely to die of COVID-19.[69] For those under fifty years old, severe fatness substantially increased mortality risks, while for older people these risks were somewhat lower.[70] Similar data were found in other countries with disproportionately higher numbers of fatter people, including the United Kingdom, Slovenia, Belgium, Italy, and Portugal.[71]

While these data provided a stark picture of fat people's susceptibility to COVID-19, they also underscored another facet of COVID-19 care that was widely missed during the pandemic: fat people needed *different kinds of care*, given their vulnerability to severe disease and death. Some medical researchers urgently called for policy-level action to address the specific risks of COVID-19 for fatter people, arguing that without such policy interventions, fat people would be at extreme risk for mortality.[72] Many researchers also advocated for fat patients to be among the highest priorities for the initial vaccination doses, another warning that went largely unheeded.[73] Despite the calls for those with a BMI over forty to receive priority for vaccinations, fatter people were not considered high priority in at least twenty-one US states; people were grouped by age instead.[74] Only a small number of states added high BMI to their list of vulnerable populations, and even fewer states opted to prioritize high-BMI people in their first few waves of vaccinations.[75] Some researchers instead pushed for doctors to educate patients on better nutrition and diet,[76] relegating the problem to the individual rather than considering how to protect all fat people from poor outcomes from COVID-19. This failure to understand fatness as a vulnerability and to act in structural ways to prevent the severe illness and death of fat people, points to how fatness was—and remains—a key bias in public health decision-making around vaccinations.

Medical researchers also cautioned that fat people, especially severely fat people, needed more aggressive treatment and more attentive medical care when they contracted COVID-19.[77] It was yet another warning that went largely unheeded by hospital administrators and medical practitioners. Body size was considered a less significant risk factor than age in the distribution of monoclonal antibodies for COVID-19 treatment; body size was not consistently considered a condition worthy of priority for COVID-19 care.[78] For example, guidance for fat people about whether fatness constituted an "immunosuppressed condition" was not widely released, nor were instructions about whether booster shots would be uniquely helpful to fatter patients. And, despite warnings that fat people were more likely to experience long

COVID, there were no major interventions or strategies for identifying and treating fat people with long COVID that addressed their unique bodily needs. There are still no widespread public health campaigns to warn fat people of their increased risk for long COVID.[79]

Very few systematic efforts were made during the first two years of the pandemic to ensure that fat people's health vulnerabilities were recognized and addressed in their workplaces. All mitigation efforts to address links between fatness and severe COVID-19 infections were placed on individuals rather than structures. Individual fat workers concerned about their vulnerabilities had to apply for workplace accommodations, take extra precautions with masking and social distancing, switch jobs, or quit altogether, again reinforcing the idea that mitigation of COVID-19 risks fell to the level of individual responsibility. This lack of collective protection and safety only intensified as the pandemic dragged on. Ultimately, if fat people were understood in the medical community as more vulnerable to COVID-19, they were also often portrayed as *deserving* of their vulnerable status because of the moral failing of being fat in the first place. This circular logic—that fat people were more vulnerable because they made themselves more vulnerable—created a dangerous context for anti-fat sentiments to thrive.

One of the more alarming developments during the pandemic occurred around the questions of who was responsible for their own vulnerabilities to COVID-19 and what medical responses should be taken as a result. In other words, if a limited number of lifesaving vaccines were available and only certain populations could get them, which people *deserved* them and, notably, which people did *not* deserve them? If fatness followed a predictable story of being framed and shaped by stories of individual responsibility and culpability, with each person being held responsible for (poor) personal decisions and (poor) fitness and nutrition, it makes sense that fat people largely assumed the status of being undeserving of COVID-19 treatment or preventative care. And, predictably, deprioritizing fat people for vaccines and COVID-19 treatment, driven by the high demand for vaccines as scarce resources and the inability of public health officials to treat fatness as a systemic and structural issue, had intensely lethal outcomes for fat people. Essentially, fat people were cast as "undeserving" of priority treatment because of their supposed "immoral" and "lazy" personal failings. Adding fuel to the fire was that a disproportionate number of fat Americans were (and are) poor people of color, which further compounded patterns of neglect and mistreatment.[80] Notions of which bodies are worthy of saving (rich, white, thin) and which bodies are disposable (poor, of color, fat), haunt the entirety of the US COVID response.

The precedent for assumptions about fatness and medical worthiness is embedded in the logic of the medical world, already set years prior. For example, excluding fat people from early antiviral treatments has been a commonplace and widely accepted medical practice.[81] Several studies have found that vaccinations of all sorts were routinely improperly dosed for fatter patients and that severely fat patients were at a particular disadvantage due to this lack of proper dosing based on body weight.[82] When people received incorrect doses of vaccines, they were more vulnerable to contracting illnesses such as flu, pneumonia, and shingles and to having poor outcomes if they did contract them, in part because they had less robust reactions to vaccine doses at higher body weights.[83] Fat people have also typically had a poorer response to all vaccines, though reasons for this have been fiercely debated.[84] This discrimination, resulting in not addressing fat people's dosing needs, has likely cost many fat people their lives.

During the COVID-19 pandemic in particular, fat people's vaccination dosing needs were often overlooked or dismissed, even though they were clearly more vulnerable as a population. There was virtually no public discussion at the CDC, the Food and Drug Administration (FDA), or any other federal agency of dosing fatter people differently than the general adult population, despite repeated studies showing that mis-dosing vaccines continues to pose health risks for fatter people.[85] Fat people who received flu vaccines were still twice as likely to contract the flu each year compared to thinner people,[86] and fat people more often contracted hepatitis B after being vaccinated than thinner people.[87] Warnings about the risks of improper vaccinations for fat people were raised early on in the pandemic, as independent medical researchers cautioned against the "head in the sand" approach to dosing all adults with the same amount of vaccine. Recent studies have confirmed that fat people may have needed, and will continue to need, additional booster shots compared to the general population in order to achieve sufficient immune protection,[88] though no public health guidance has encouraged this thus far.

One possible reason for fat people's decreased vaccine responsiveness is that fat people far too often are vaccinated with needles that are too short for their body types. The use of needles that fail to compensate for the thickness of people's fat layers during vaccinations has been shown to occur in *75 percent* of all vaccinations of fatter people.[89] (Needle length requirements based on body size are not routinely recalibrated, nor are fat people taught by medical professionals to self-advocate for longer needles during vaccinations and, of course, they should not have to do so to get basic care.) Longer needles reach the muscle tissue and deliver the vaccine more effectively to the body. If medical professionals use too short a needle, the vaccinations become relatively ineffective, particularly for women, because the substance gets injected into the subcutaneous fat pad rather than the muscle.[90] This can also cause skin reactions and complications in addition to poorer immune responses.[91] In a study of hepatitis B vaccines, needle length accounted for a significant portion of the discrepancy in immune response to the vaccine between fatter and thinner people,[92] suggesting that longer needles would help fat people generate proper immune responses to vaccines across the board.[93] Whether vaccination clinics will stock the correct length of needles, whether they will train staff to correctly identify patients who need longer needles, and whether they can treat fat patients sensitively and without stigma when using longer needles are all open questions.[94]

Kimberly Dark has argued that these conscious and unconscious biases can be so pervasive in medical settings that doctors and nurses often unconsciously strip the humanity from fat patients. To counteract this, she advises every fat person to have a "go bag" ready in case they need to be hospitalized. The bag should include photographs of loved ones and other personal items to show doctors that fat people are fundamentally human, not simply a projection screen for medical bias and dehumanization. She framed this go bag as a necessity for operating within the anti-fat medical system we have today.[95]

The website Nobody Is Disposable also advised fat people going into the hospital to create a "connection kit" that can "help providers connect with you as a human being worthy of lifesaving treatment. You may be one of hundreds of sick people they are seeing, so try to help them see you as a unique person."[96] This kit might include a humanizing photo of yourself along with a few small pieces of information about you and a list of phone numbers and photos of your loved ones. For serious medical procedures where advanced planning is possible, they also advised considering areas where weight-based discrimination is illegal, such as Binghamton, New York; Madison, Wisconsin; or San Francisco, California.[97] That fat patients would need, in their most vulnerable periods, to consciously work to humanize themselves to avoid potentially lethal consequences, reveals just how dire the relationship is between the medical world and fatter bodies. This necessity for fat people to "market" their humanity during a medical crisis reveals not only the profound damage that anti-fatness causes, but it also exposes the utter cruelty of the entire system—medical embedded within capitalism—itself.

THE INABILITY TO COMMEMORATE FAT DEATH

The stripping away of fat people's humanity is a lifelong story, one emblematized most acutely in our fundamental inability to commemorate, mark, or grieve fat death. That fat people cannot even expect to escape anti-fat stigma *when they die* stands as testament to the deep pathologies of our cultural hatred of fatness. To reflect on this, I conclude this rather somber chapter with a consideration of this painful inability to honor fat death in a culture so appallingly hostile to fat life. Anti-fatness is, after all, so deep and so pervasive that it can lead to scorn and mockery of fat death, even (or especially) for those fat people who were bold public advocates for fat liberation and social justice.

I want to pause here and reflect on the death of fat scholar-activist Cat Pausé, who died in her sleep on March 25, 2022. Pausé had an outsize impact on the field of fat studies, forcefully advocating for fat people's rights to have dignity in institutions that often strip away fat people's humanity. Through her writings and advocacy, she pushed the medical world to accommodate, understand, and value fat people rather than shaming, ignoring, and humiliating them. Her work spanned a wide range of issues: fat stigma, the role of social media in fat scholarship and activism, fat pedagogies, medical discrimination against fat people, and fat people's experiences of COVID-19 and vaccination, among others.[98] As a public intellectual, she had a podcast called *Friend of Marilyn* and regularly contributed to the field of fat studies as a keynote speaker, an op-ed writer, a scholar, and a commentator in a number of different outlets and forums. She was, by all accounts, a force of nature as a writer and thinker, a deeply empathic and caring person, and a fierce defender of fat people's right to be recognized as fully and deeply human.

Her sudden and unexpected death ignited a firestorm of reactions from allies, friends, colleagues, critics, commentators, and online trolls. There was an instant outpouring of grief over her death from within the fat community, followed immediately by aggressive and chilling attacks and ridicule directed toward her from comments online. This juxtaposition between a community in mourning trying to grapple with profound loss and the aggressively anti-fat trolling and commentary that blamed her death on her being fat and implied that she "got what she deserved," serves as a startling reminder of the impossibility of grieving and commemorating fat death. Her family chose not to make her cause of death public. This decision not to release that information, alongside the ever-present undercurrent of overt anti-fat hatred and misogyny, spurred far-right commentators to link her death to fatness and portray her as a victim of her own ideology. "Not to be a dick but died suddenly doesn't apply here. If you choose to be dangerously overweight you're welcoming trouble," one commentator wrote.[99] Others offered even more viciousness and laughter at Pausé's death: "Glorifying obesity all the way to her XXL coffin," "Rest in Grease," "I just don't know how we can afford to lose any more of these strong womyn. I mean really, it's like we lost 3," "I wonder if these people think about the poor backs of the pallbearers at their funerals," "Fat acceptance = accepting they are going to die 40 years before the average. And I accept that."[100] Another right-wing commentator linked Pausé's death to transgender suicide rates, the "Left's" lack of desire to discipline their kids, and "creating monsters."[101] Fighting for fat liberation while living in a fat body, it seemed, only "invited" death and was tantamount to killing oneself intentionally. For the right-wing propaganda machines and online trolls, a fat woman's death, particularly for someone who dared to push back against anti-fatness, unleashed an especially virulent strand of cruelty. (Truly, it is impossible to adequately capture the feeling of this cruelty without looking at these comments yourself; almost nothing can prepare you for what it feels like to see these en masse.)

In many ways, the emotional framings of fatness repeated on loop in the broader cultural imagination has long linked it to imminent doom and imminent death. The associations between fatness and death—something that cycles through fat people's lives whether in conversations with family, visits to the doctor's office, interfacing with social media, or just being in the world—are perpetually forced upon fat people's psyches. The specter of fat death follows fat people around. These are the narratives that haunt the edges of Pausé's story. For those of us working to combat anti-fatness, what happened to Pausé after she died can happen to us all. Everything we do—as activists, scholars, humans—can be trivialized and aggressively dismissed through our own deaths. In a fundamental sense, Pausé reveals that we are not even allowed respite from anti-fatness when we die.

Still, if Pausé has taught us anything, it is that no matter how bleak the conditions of anti-fat hatred are, and no matter how dire and dangerous this all seems, the power of resistance and the necessity of revolt push fat liberation forward. Our collective fury matters, and it cannot be diminished or silenced. After all, grief is a form of ignition for transformative change, and Pausé deserved better than to be scoffed at and dismissed, ridiculed and ignored. She was an integral part of the movement to make fat people's lives better and, in death, a painful reminder of how much work there still is to do.

Fat activist Mikey Mercedes reflected on the fusion of solidarity and grief alongside the fundamental betrayal inherent in the vicious trolling around Pausé's death: "She made it so abundantly clear how much she loves fat people in everything she does. She has done so much work to make sure that fat Black people are in charge of their own narratives. She wanted to keep fat people safe. She wanted to build things for us. She wanted to make sure the work she was doing was sustainable so that it could benefit more than just the people who are around right now." The betrayal of seeing online trolls denounce Pausé felt singularly terrible to Mercedes: "I wasn't surprised when the very troll-y posts about Cat's death started to surface. I hoped and prayed that they were not going to, but they did, and that shit hurt. To see someone who's done so much work with so much care be reduced to fodder for people who don't know the value of showing up for other people, it hurt. It hurt me in a way that other fatphobic shit doesn't hurt me anymore because you see it all the time, but this one absolutely hurt." Her feeling of injury, experienced both personally and collectively, captured a sense that Pausé—and all fat activists—fundamentally deserve better.[102]

When I spoke with fat activist Aubrey Gordon, she recalled the painful contrast between how deeply Pausé was loved in the movement, and how horrible the reactions to her death had been by outside trolls: "It's deep. She was and is so loved and appreciated. It makes me really, really sad, because Cat was incredible and one of the loveliest and most unifying forces in the movement, and then it was instantaneous that she became fodder for arguments from horrible, horrible trolls. I really think that one of the wildest and worst human decisions a person can make is to mess with somebody when they're grieving, and to mess with a community when they're grieving is a monstrous thing to do." She added, "When she passed, they were just celebrating. That was all that was happening. They were only happy, and that felt like the wildest underscoring of the thing that you learn time and time again as a fat person, which is that *absolutely nothing matters as much as your body.*"[103]

Fat activist Tigress Osborn, infuriated by the dehumanization of Pausé after her death, reflected on how fat activist deaths are treated across the board, remembering someone else she knew who died and whose family wanted to distance themselves from their daughter's fatness, fat activism, and affiliations with the community. Osborn said, "I'm just mad about it and still trying to navigate how to not get pulled into some public debate with a grieving family about who's allowed to grieve and how, but also not wanting this legacy of this fat activist—who did incredible remarkable things—to go unrecognized because her family is embarrassed." The erasure of fat activists from the public eye, and the erasure of fatness itself, haunted Osborn.[104]

When I asked Osborn about the pain of feeling like fat activist work gets erased, degraded, or undermined in death, she talked about some of the painful decisions she had to make as executive director of the National Association to Advance Fat Acceptance (NAAFA): "It's horrible to know that's what your loved ones will be put through. I had those conversations with my family before I took the role of NAAFA chair, in terms of potential job loss or discrimination, but the conversation I did *not* have with them was, 'Hey, by the way, if something happens to me, people are going to publicly make fun of my death.'" Reflecting on the cruelty of this, Osborn defiantly said, "The best we can do about it is valiantly live our best lives and that is the middle finger up to them. I think about the protection of my own health now not just as my own sense of mortality versus wanting to be around a long time for my own loved ones, but also, symbolically, what it means."[105] Later, she quietly said, "It's such a trashy, disgusting human behavior to be like, 'In your face!' when someone fat dies. It's gross. If it was true that every single thing that led to their death is about them being fat, it should still be a tragedy that they died, not a tragedy that they were fat."

CHAPTER 6

ON FAT VULNERABILITY

"**I**t's a terrifying thing," a fat therapy patient of mine recently told me. "I live in a body where I never know whether I will be cared for. I can't *assume* care. I can only hope for it. I know what it means to be hated." I have worked with fat therapy patients for nearly two decades, and these are not uncommon expressions within sessions. Like many therapists, I sit with these stories both as a listener and as someone whose body is also implicated in their struggles. We rummage through the damage that anti-fatness has done, and we work on making space for looking closely at—and deeply feeling—the costs of that damage.

To understand vulnerability is a prerequisite for feeling anger about what they have endured; it also, in many cases, allows them to see their bodies as connected to larger stories and cultural patterns, to feel less alone in the struggle. Vulnerability is, after all, an openness to *seeing* injury, a window into the pain that people feel from that injury. Without understanding fat vulnerability, particularly the kinds of wounds, injuries, and assaults that fat people face, a more robust response of resistance and revolt stagnates. When cultural stories about fatness refuse to make space for fat vulnerability, we siphon off cultural expressions of fat injury and, ultimately, the humanity and humanness of living as fat. In doing so, the refusal to deal with fat vulnerability and marginalization shapes and limits the creativity of resistance to fat oppression and closes down possibilities for solidarities and connections between people. By contrast, when fat vulnerability is taken more seriously in the public consciousness, fat resistance, activism, and solidarities thrive.

Fat activists posit that we cannot talk about, over, or around fatness, but rather, that we need to understand how fatness operates as a point of vulnerability for *all* bodies, even if differently experienced or expressed. This means considering how the treatment of fat people operates as an embodied expression of misogyny, sexism, racism, ageism, ableism, and much more. Fat embodiment in this chapter works both as an ideology and as a fleshy materiality, something we imagine and something we are. By examining and understanding this duality, we can break open and rewrite the tightly controlled narratives about fat injury, vulnerability, and resilience.

To better understand how other marginalized identities like age and disability have been situated within a politics of vulnerability, it is useful to take a closer look at ideas of protection and who is considered deserving of care. Historically, ideas of "deservingness" and "worthiness" linked up with public policy in American Civil War pension law, as the US government laid out its first large-scale policy of compensation for select men and "worthy disabled" people. Thus, the system of understanding deservingness of care, and deservingness of monetary compensation, has its roots in thinking about veteran status as a protected class.[1] This history may help to explain why it has been so difficult to broaden these definitions to include other groups—historically and today. Both in a policy sense and even in social and cultural relationships, seeing other groups as vulnerable and worthy of care and protection has been difficult. Certain kinds of disabilities and statuses are deemed worthy of protection, while others are seen as byproducts of individual failure or social ills. For example, in a recent study about the deservingness of different groups for policies that would protect those groups, participants ranked elderly people as the most deserving of protection, unemployed people as deserving of less protection, and immigrants deserving the least protection.[2] It seems that the ability to recognize other people's vulnerability was often tainted by attributions for how and why people embodied certain social conditions. (This bodes particularly poorly for fat people, who mostly are seen as "doing it to themselves" and rarely as an aggregate group who might be worthy of protection.)

Tensions between seeing bodies as individuals and situating bodies in relation to social and structural contexts inform the core of disability studies and give clues to how "deserving" or "undeserving" fat bodies might be seen at a cultural level. Disability scholar Alison Kafer has carefully outlined the costs of the medical model of disability, one that "frames atypical bodies and minds as deviant, pathological, and defective, best understood and addressed in medical terms."[3] In such a framework, disability is situated as an individual malady rather than adapting social processes and policies to better accommodate, protect, and care for disabled people and their vulnerabilities. Kafer and many other disability rights activists have refuted this framing, instead calling for a better recognition of disability as a "product of social relations"[4] infused with clear hierarchies about bodies, "normality," and deservingness. She importantly argued that seeing disability through an explicitly political lens makes room for more activist responses and allows disability to be seen as a "potential site for reimagining."[5]

Social, cultural, and political values are indeed tied to bodies and embodiment, both overtly and covertly. Clearly, different values have historically been assigned to different corporeal forms, as certain kinds of embodiment become labeled as worthy or unworthy of social protection. The social model of disability casts it as a social category where disabled people often become socially isolated and excluded from full participation in society.[6] Some disabilities, for example, have been constructed as vulnerable and worthy of social protection, while others have not.[7] Even for those with bodies deemed "deserving" of protection, there is much speculation about how accommodations can be prone to abuse or misuse, including relatively small accommodations, like reserved parking spots or the option to skip a line at the Department of Motor Vehicles. People who use service dogs, receive Social Security benefits, or request academic accommodations are often viewed negatively by others, accused by some of "abusing the law."[8] Sixty percent of disabled people in the US believe that others question their disability.[9] Thus, notions of worthiness and deservingness also force disabled and vulnerable people to face questioning and harassment, and justify any accommodations they request or could benefit from. Disabled people report, for example, that even when resources are not scarce, such as ample parking spaces, they still face potential abuse from those who deem them fundamentally unworthy of having accommodations, suggesting that notions of deservingness drive these behaviors more than rational reactions to scarcity.[10]

Disability theory has begun to examine the relationship between emotions and oppression, as disgust toward disabled bodies guides much of the policy enacted around disability protections. Disabled people's rights, for example, are often mitigated by how much disgust the public feels toward their disability, with certain kinds of disabilities eliciting more or less visceral disgust.[11] When disability intersects with poverty, people often react more negatively to protecting disabled people as vulnerable citizens; conversely, when disability intersects with wealthy or middle-class status, people often consider disabled people more worthy of protection. Similarly, people believed that those with less formal education, those who were unemployed, and those with lower incomes deserved less governmental support than those with more formal education, those who were currently employed, and those with higher incomes.[12] With regard to specific disabilities that people find more or less sympathetic, a clear hierarchy appeared: wheelchair use emerged as "most deserving," followed by schizophrenia, back pain, fibromyalgia, depression, and asthma. People of color were evaluated most negatively in terms of deservingness of governmental support, particularly when evaluated by those with right-wing viewpoints.[13]

These studies set a precedent for evaluating fatness on similar terms, and in fact, researchers have consistently found that fat people were evaluated negatively along lines of deservingness and worthiness of care. If minor accommodations for the relatively small number of people with disabilities led to constructions of them as "undeserving," the vast number of fat people potentially seeking protection or accommodation would likely be seen as an even greater threat to the status quo. We are fundamentally used to fat people silently enduring poor conditions at work, in healthcare settings, and in the world at large. The recent hand-wringing about whether Medicare should cover weight-loss medications—and how such coverage would potentially catastrophically bankrupt Medicare and overwhelm the existing system—again speaks to the ways that fat people as a group are seen as threatening, pathetic, unworthy, morally failing, and disgusting.[14] (No discussion of requiring pharmaceutical companies to make these drugs available at a lower cost than the current $1,300 per month has occurred.)

Community studies scholar Julie Guthman has linked patterns of speaking about fatness to neoliberal ideas about the body and self-governance, arguing that when people imagine links between bodily control and deservingness of rights or care, they construct fatness as an individual weakness rather than a social issue.[15] One of the main barriers to seeing fat people as wholly human is the framing of them as morally and ethically "failing," which again diminishes the amount of vulnerability imagined for fat people's lives. In a comparative study of six countries (Australia, India, Poland, Turkey, the US, and Venezuela), anti-fat prejudice was predicted by cultural values that overvalued thinness as well as blamed individual people for their own fatness. Individualist cultures saw these effects amplified even more than cultures that valued collectivity.[16] The state itself engages in clear delineations between worthiness/deservingness and scorn, as efforts to link rights, such as custody, access to healthcare, and life insurance policies, to thinness perpetuate the "war on obesity" in aggressive ways. The scholar and activist Kathleen LeBesco has called for a collective revolt against such measures and a relentless attack against the harmful equation of weight and health.[17]

Along these lines, fatness and Blackness have often been cast as twin liabilities, with the intersection between the two allowing anti-fatness to reinforce racism and racism to reinforce anti-fatness. The story of how fatness absorbed immense cultural and interpersonal disdain has racialized, colonial underpinnings, particularly as Black women's bodies were cast as less attractive and appealing in comparison to white women's bodies. Within a patriarchal and racist culture, fat Black women have paid a particularly steep price emotionally, socially, financially, and materially for having bodies marked as "deviant." As feminist scholar Andrea Elizabeth Shaw writes, "The fat black woman's body poses a dual challenge to the colonially inspired dominant aesthetic norms that are instituted as a political mechanism for control; these norms symbolize the hegemonic force from which they arise. Her fat black body resists both imperatives of whiteness and slenderness as an ideal state of embodiment."[18] Building on this, sociologist Sabrina Strings explains that this marking of fat Black women's bodies as deviant arose from a collision of colonialism, whiteness, anti-fatness, and puritanical ideas about bodies: "The phobia about fat 'always already' had a racial element. And, because women are typically reduced to their bodies, fat stigma has commonly targeted women of color. Protestant moralism and the disdain of indulgence contributed to the cacophony of pro-thin, anti-fat bias. The medical field has been the most recent institution to enter the fray."[19] As a consequence of this, decisions about whose bodies are vulnerable, whose bodies deserve care and protection, and whose bodies are worthy of scorn and disdain continue to be patterned along racial lines.

Though vulnerability is experienced on a personal level, it has deep connections to political frameworks and systems. Perhaps as a response to the systemic failure to address the political ramifications of vulnerability—physical, social, and political—feminist and antiracist groups have begun to take up questions of vulnerability as having emancipatory potential. Rather than casting vulnerability and resistance as opposites, some scholars and activist groups have argued that vulnerability can generate resistance to occupation and colonial violence, gendered and racial oppression, and it can help to form bonds of solidarity between groups and across causes. For example, in response to growing patterns of disregarding women's lives, particularly poor women of color, groups like Ni Una Menos (Not One Woman Less) used vulnerability as a platform for political revolt.[20] By focusing on organizing women and trans communities, Ni Una Menos mobilized over a million women across Latin America, Spain, and Italy to protest machista violence. They did so by focusing on organizing women from different socioeconomic classes and across geographic regions. Notably, they framed violence, rape, and femicide not as individual actions against individual vulnerable people but as systemic forms of inequality worthy of collective rage.[21]

Still, some scholars have cautioned that seeing vulnerability as a precursor for a politics of resilience can draw on conservative notions of personal responsibility for overcoming structural inequalities. If a politics of vulnerability focuses overly on individualism and personal stories of overcoming obstacles, it can often fail to account for the complexity of how vulnerability can be co-opted by conservative forces.[22] Vulnerability can be used, for example, as a justification for intensifying police presence or requiring certain kinds of impositions of the state over bodies marked as vulnerable. If women's sexual violence experiences are divorced from contexts that deny or dismiss that violence, fail to prosecute and punish those who commit the violence, and systematically reinforce women's economic vulnerabilities and relationships of dependence, simply seeing women as vulnerable to violence on an individual level can be dangerous. Men may imagine that women need their protection—a phenomenon known as benevolent sexism[23]—when what women really need are systems and structures in place to allow for economic independence, freedom from violence, collectivity and solidarity, anti-patriarchal ways of imagining bodies and families, and forms of political organizing and connection. This proneness to co-optation and distortion makes it especially crucial to ask critical questions about how vulnerability is conceptualized, who constructs themselves as vulnerable (versus the state imagining them as such), and how vulnerability translates into structural critiques of systems that reinforce dominance and hierarchy.[24]

Feminist scholar Judith Butler has been particularly vocal in her assertions that a politics of bodily resistance that embraces rather than disavows collective vulnerability can advance solidarity and can serve activists in numerous liberation movements if vulnerability is not over-individualized.[25] She warns that, while anyone can be vulnerable, there is a difference between being vulnerable (perhaps temporarily) and persisting in a vulnerable condition (as a condition of your status or embodiment). More importantly, any explanation of vulnerability that reinforces individualistic or pathological rationales for making others vulnerable (for example, saying that men commit crimes against women because men have personality disorders) must be rejected in favor of more systemic approaches to violence and oppression.[26] Butler argues, crucially, that vulnerability can intersect meaningfully with political solidarity and collective rage as long as vulnerability is not separated from rage, and as long as it rejects social domination, hierarchy, and paternalism. She asks:

> What if the situation of those deemed vulnerable is, in fact, a constellation of vulnerability, rage, persistence, and resistance that emerges under these same historical conditions? It would be equally unwise to extract vulnerability from this constellation; indeed, vulnerability traverses and conditions social relations, and without that insight we stand little chance of realizing the sort of substantive equality that is desired. *Vulnerability ought not to be identified exclusively with passivity*; it only makes sense in light of an embodied set of social relations, including practices of resistance [emphasis mine].[27]

Butler goes on to emphasize how vulnerability *produces* resistance: "A view of vulnerability as part of embodied social relations and actions can help us understand how and why forms of resistance emerge as they do."[28] In this way, understanding how people are made vulnerable—in this case, how fat women in particular become burdened with cultural discourses of pathology, social injury, discrimination, and violence—is a necessary step to generating collective rage.

EXPLORING THE WOUNDS AND INJURIES OF FATNESS

It is no exaggeration to say that living as fat, particularly for women, is often an immensely difficult experience. The social wounds of fatness are felt deeply and experienced as a nearly ubiquitous facet of fat life, particularly for those who have not constructed their fat bodies as a site of resistance and revolt. (And even for those who have, the struggle against isolation, dejection, and trauma is ever-present.) In all of the conversations I had with fat women throughout the US, a constant theme wove into each interview that emphasized the anguish and injuries of fatness, particularly how they lived in a body that subjected them to relentless harm. The various forms this took—negative comments by passersby, workplace discrimination, mundane indignities, self-consciousness about food and eating, feeling degraded when speaking with doctors and nurses, and many more—spoke to how these injuries occurred both in public and private, at home and at work, with loved ones and with strangers, internally and out loud. Much of this book thus far has outlined the various forms of wounds and injuries fat people face, and the often-devastating impacts of these injuries on their sense of thriving in the world.

To further highlight issues of agency and a focus on fat activist voices imbued with collective resistance, revolt, and rage, I want to move from featuring everyday fat women to emphasizing my interviews with fat activists and their comments on how fatness can serve as a site of rebellion. I start here by drawing on their words and experiences to highlight the vulnerability they face when engaging with the world as fat people.[29] Social movement researchers have argued that people become activists when they combine a sense of collective vulnerabilities with awareness of systematic inequalities, perceptions of collective efficacy, and moral obligations to fight for the well-being of oppressed groups.[30] For these fat activists, they often drew from personal experiences of oppression and suffering to ignite a collective form of revolt. Their stories reveal how vulnerability weaves through all of our lives, including for those groups of people often constructed as less vulnerable and more able to push back against fat oppression. Indeed, fat activists had plenty to say about the indignities and injuries they have faced because of their size. I situate these as a platform to imagine links between vulnerability and resistance, between moments of injury and the necessity of revolt, particularly as the book builds toward its final two chapters on fat rage.

The ten fat activists I interviewed[31] (Stacy Bias, Barbara Bruno, Kimberly Dark, Aubrey Gordon, Da'Shaun Harrison, Caleb Luna, Mikey Mercedes, Tigress Osborn, Esther Rothblum, and Virgie Tovar), all of whom agreed to be named and quoted in this book, had much to say about the mundane qualities of fat vulnerability and how their families often exacerbated the fat vulnerabilities they felt in the world. Aubrey Gordon recalled memories of dinner with her father, feeling his intense judgment of her eating choices:

"We would sit at the dinner table and my dad would not eat while everyone else was eating. He would turn his head towards me and he would watch the fork go from the plate to my mouth, the plate to my mouth, just monitoring everything before he took a bite. He would watch me eat the entire meal in silence, so the full activity of dinner was 'Watch Aubrey eat.'"[32] Public health student and cohost of the podcast *Unsolicited: Fatties Talk Back* Mikey Mercedes recollected that her childhood vulnerabilities around fatness revolved around her mother being told and then internalizing that being a good mother meant monitoring and controlling her daughter's weight. Mercedes explained: "We were poor. I didn't get sent to fat camp. My mom wouldn't say, 'You need to lose weight because otherwise you're not going to be pretty,' or anything like that. It was instead very much like, 'I'm worried about you getting diabetes,' or 'I'm worried about you getting sick. I'm worried about you getting too fat to live a good life.' Because these were things she was being told by doctors that I saw when I was younger." Doctors relentlessly emphasized the need for her weight loss: "There was so much fearmongering. It sort of speaks to the ways in which my mom was policed in terms of her own body. My mom came to this country when she was in her teens and has always struggled with being not just a Black woman, but an immigrant Black woman, a poor immigrant Black woman. She always wanted us to try to conform in the ways we could so that we could build good lives."[33] Mercedes saw the collision of racial identity, immigrant identity, anti-fat medical systems, and fearmongering about the dangers of body weight.

Reflecting on the relationship between childhood memories and their adult experiences now, Da'Shaun Harrison, author of *Belly of the Beast*, described a layering of wounds related to living in a fat body: "I developed an eating disorder that was never diagnosed because I was fat and Black and also being socialized as a boy, and eating disorders were for thin, cis, white girls, right? I had a really tough, difficult relationship with my body." Thinking about their current struggles with their body, Harrison said, "Of course there are days when I wake up and I'm like, 'I don't like this body. I don't like this edifice. I don't want to exist in this body.' But on those days I'm always able to remind myself that those aren't the feelings that are my own. Those are the feelings that I feel because of the ways I'm treated in this world. Because if I wasn't mistreated, if I wasn't harmed, if I wasn't violated, then I wouldn't have ill feelings about my body."[34] This construction of bodily vulnerability as a consequence of living in systems that denigrate fatness, and the necessity of recognizing how deeply those negative feelings get internalized, has served as a platform for Harrison's resistance work.

As a byproduct of medical discrimination, fat people routinely face the reality that such discrimination makes them more vulnerable both physically and psychologically. Caleb Luna, author of *Revenge Body*, described how doctors assumed they would not be compliant with medical advice and so they never got proper treatment for their foot condition: "I was basically told—not that it's incurable—but the cure and the treatment requires a lot of work and rigor and therefore I should just live with it. I think there was an assumption about the kind of rigor I'm capable of based on my size. Granted, this woman never touched me. She stood on the other side of the room. It was very clear fat phobia." They reflected on the hazards of being seen only, or primarily, as fat: "There are ways that the feelings about my body are not actually about my fatness, but are prevented from treatment because of fat phobia . . . I think for a long time, I flattened everything into fatness because that's how I understood it. I do think that I have many identities, but my read of my life is that people experience me first and foremost as a fat person, and everything else comes from my fatness."[35] Fatness often becomes a primary identity that obscures, hides, and overshadows other aspects of the self.

Esther Rothblum, professor emerita at San Diego State University, editor of twenty-seven books, the *Journal of Lesbian Studies*, and *Fat Studies*, situated her experiences with fat vulnerability in the context of the ways that women are relentlessly shamed about their bodies. She recalled a childhood experience of being shamed by a teacher: "She would put candy on every child's desk except the kids she thought were too fat. She would actually say, 'I know, you won't want a sweet.' And I was drowning in shame waiting for her to make her way to me." Thinking about her adult life, Rothblum described medical settings as particularly vulnerable for her: "It doesn't matter if I've come with a sprained elbow, I'm worried they're going to tell me it's due to my weight. The gowns never fit around my hips or my waist. It's just a setting where I'm made to feel 'less than,' and I have so much privilege with my education and my whiteness, but that is where, very gratuitously, people will tell me to lose weight, no matter what."[36] These varying experiences of personal shame and discomfort layered with systems of sexism and classism reveal how she identified vulnerability across many registers, and connected her own personal experiences to broader patterns of anti-fatness in professional, medical, educational, and embodiment contexts.

The grief and harm of fat stigma also at times become more literal and material as people age. Performance artist and author of *Damaged Like Me* and *Fat, Pretty, and Soon to Be Old*—Kimberly Dark explored the complex feelings she had about aging, her changing body, and adapting to how others viewed her as she got older: "I think that post-menopause, which is where I am now, there's something new. The body changes again. It changes some more. I have developed a disability. I walk with a limp now, and that has changed how I feel about my body because I'm living with chronic pain. It hurts now and it didn't before, so that sucks, but the other thing is walking with a limp changes the way the outside world interprets me being fat because I was always a person who loved movement and athleticism. I was always a person that was strong and graceful and mobile."[37]

Dark also talked about her relationship to having a body that changes and how that made her feel more vulnerable over time: "The feeling of vulnerability is two-fold. The greater stigma I experience, the more pain in my body I experience. The vulnerability is literally physical. It's like there is a combo platter that is really hard to tease out in terms of which aspect of that is vulnerability in my body, and which aspect is coming externally." She connected feelings of vulnerability to a recognition that fat people are socially programmed to feel vulnerable and shameful.[38] This delicate interplay between feeling anti-fatness from the world, and sensing anti-fatness internally, particularly around the more vulnerable aspects of fatness like pain or loss of desirability, complicates notions of embodiment as an individual or cultural experience. Instead, vulnerability is experienced constantly both inside our heads and in relation to how the world treats us.

Building on this, Tigress Osborn, current executive director of the National Association to Advance Fat Acceptance (NAAFA), reflected on her guilt and shame for feeling conflicted about her body: "When people are longing for the body they had when they were eighteen, I'm looking for the body I had when I was thirty-eight. What I have is a shame about the shame. . . . I thought I was such a good ally but now that I have more mobility challenges, I feel bad about that, and then I feel ashamed that I feel bad about that because I shouldn't feel bad about that!" She struggled to live up to the idea of what it meant to lead a fat activist movement: "There's a sense of disappointment from people when the folks that we see as unapologetically fat express anything other than bold pride about it. That can be really difficult. You can feel like there's a loss of community if you lose weight, or a loss of community if you talk about having difficulties around that stuff."[39] The erasure of the capacity for suffering, or the minimization of the complexities of fat embodiment, carry greater salience when leading a movement that seeks to embrace and validate fatness.

Looking at how shame and vulnerability interacted, Stacy Bias, designer of the *Flying While Fat* documentary animation and "The 12 'Good Fatty' Archetypes" zine, remembered the physical and psychological pain of pushing herself too hard physically to "prove" her worth: "I had a really punitive relationship with movement where I would not do any for a long time and then go hard, so I kept hurting myself." She explained how at a doctor's office, she had a memorable interaction that underscored her physical vulnerability: "He was leaning back in his chair and he goes, 'At your size, anything you do to your body, any movement that you do in your body is going to hurt you, is damaging.' I was not in a good place mentally to hear that, and it really fucked with me. It took me five years of going to different doctors and trying different things to sort of figure out how to heal myself well enough to walk." She said, "You really have to go hard in advocating for yourself, and even someone like me with twenty years of activist experience, who has a real solid understanding of politics and has done a lot of work internally to not internalize and has the tools to deal with it—I really, really struggled."[40] This awareness that self-advocacy is a necessity to get the care she needed, and the barriers to seeing fat bodies as worthy of proper care, again showed how emotional and structural inequalities can disadvantage fat women.

Bias also reflected on the relationship between fatness and trauma, suggesting that trauma did not produce fatness, but rather, that much of her trauma resulted from her mistreatment after she became fat: "A lot of us are marginalized in many respects and trauma comes with marginalization. I don't think that we can say that we are fat *because* we are traumatized, because people deal with trauma in multiple ways, so fatness is not an inevitability of trauma and also fatness is not inherently linked to trauma." Looking at her own trauma experiences, she said, "I think that when you experience trauma, there are a couple of different ways you can go. One can be an externalization of your anger. One can be an internalization of your anger, or your fear, or your sadness. But I do think that being fat in a world that's highly consumer-driven, there's so much capitalist pressure to perform 'body' in very specific ways, so there is traumatization from being fat. Very few people in fat bodies are able to escape that. Of course, it varies in degree by size and by other privileges that you may or may not have, and other intersections that you may or may not have."[41] Again, fatness can both exacerbate feelings of marginalization and can intensify the already-punitive contexts we live in.

Virgie Tovar, author of *You Have the Right to Remain Fat* and consultant for body diversity and ending weight discrimination in workplaces, looked back on the story of her childhood to trace her vulnerabilities about fatness: "It's always important to name that the first chapter in my relationship with my body was a really positive one. I think a lot of us are born with a beautiful relationship with our body, one that is very intuitive, and very connective, and very integrated. That was my life for the first four and a half or five years." Tovar remembered how that positive relationship to her body changed abruptly when she connected her body's worth to feeling attractive to men: "I was introduced to fat phobia at around age five and started to internalize it pretty quickly. I was taught that if a boy was ever going to love or marry me, I would have to be a thin person."[42]

Taken together, fat activists have highlighted many points of injury and vulnerability from which they struggle to recover. These points of injury that have sprung up from fatness, the wounds carried from both long ago and more recent memories, infused fat identities with an essential vulnerability. As these narratives attest, these injuries derived both from the emotional experience of fat shame, and from the emotional framework of feeling trapped in a system that has little regard for fat bodies or fat lives. For fat activists, who often structure their work around combatting fat oppression, making space for vulnerability is doubly difficult. It can contradict the work they do to destigmatize fatness when they admit that they, too, struggle with the negative impacts of stigma, just as it can also serve as a counternarrative to an angry, rebellious resistance. Still, these stories also point to the ways that moving from individual vulnerability to collective solidarity is an essential part of securing power and rights. Without a deeper understanding of fat injury and fat vulnerability, the move toward more overt forms of anger is impossible. As I argued earlier, vulnerability is an openness to seeing injury in the first place, to allowing the duality of those injuries, and the often-furious rebellions that derive from those injuries, to coexist.

NAMING AND LABELING HARM, VIOLENCE, AND TERRORIZATION

In tandem with considerations of the social injuries done to fat people, looking closely at the emotional experience of terrorization that fat people bear is essential to a deeper understanding of vulnerability. After all, living as fat does not only mean enduring injury on a routine basis but also confronting intentional harm and terror about fatness. For some, these kinds of experiences catalyze their interest in collective struggles for justice, as seen with so many of the fat activists I spoke with. Their narratives point to the painful and sometimes transformational nature of naming and labeling harm, violence, and terrorization, particularly as it connects to systemic anti-fatness. These stories underscore the necessity of using experiences of being *made to be* vulnerable—often through social processes and within social systems—as platforms for developing activist impulses.

The links between family, medical, and social degradation appeared quite clearly for many fat people, particularly as they came of age. Da'Shaun Harrison remembered how they felt terrorized by their mother's insistence on losing weight: "Doctors continued to tell my mom growing up that I needed to lose weight, that I was morbidly obese, that I was going to die, all of these really horrid things that we hear as fat people, even as fat children. My mom would force me to wrap myself in those large plastic trash bags, force me to put on a sweat suit after that, and I would have to run around our neighborhood, and our neighborhood was not a space that was safe. It was at night, and I grew up very poor so I grew up in pretty unsafe areas and I was forced to run for hours at night. It was horrifying." Reflecting on the emotional consequences of this, they said, "I was continuously reminded of the way that my body did not and could not conform to what was expected of it. I felt absolutely monstrous, so when I hear the language of monstrosity when talking about Black fat folks in particular, it resonates with me because that's what I felt. I felt like a monster."[43] The transferring of panic and fear from medical doctors to parents to children, combined with living in various states of precarity already, exacerbates fat vulnerability and links fatness to experiences of humiliation and fear.

Connecting their own traumatic history with the histories of how fat Black men have been treated, Harrison worried about the objectification and "thingification" that accompanied fatness: "I want to create an understanding for why we don't get to be whole in other spaces, and create an understanding for why Eric Garner or Mike Brown would be read as 'thing,' why they are 'thingified' in the world. I think that to me it's very important because it gives room for a sort of deeper analysis around the ways that the world is structured and requires us to be compartmentalized. It requires our bodies to be separated, to be pulled apart, to be removed." Harrison linked this to feelings about the traumatic impact of anti-fatness and the lack of language surrounding it: "The trauma that you live with as a fat person feels like one of the only traumas that doesn't get taken seriously. You experience these traumas and then you have to hold on to them by yourself because no one else thinks of you and your body as something that's being oppressed or something that's experienced violence. It makes it much more difficult to consider the weight of what you are navigating because your actual experiences are not considered traumatic or violent. It's clear how detrimental fat trauma is, and how few solutions we have to take it seriously."[44] This erasure of collective suffering and collective justice-making gives fatness a quality of isolation and aloneness, making it all the more prone to the vicious cycles of oppression.

Fat bodies are constantly being cast as expendable and laced with stories about mortality, risk, and imminent death. For example, Kimberly Dark discovered that her son was being warned that she would imminently die from her fatness, marking yet another kind of violence and terrorization that extended to family members.[45] The belief that fat people are ticking time bombs waiting to implode—particularly as communicated to family members of fat people—laces anti-fat rhetoric with medical "expertise," however flimsy the basis for it may be.

In a related sense, the willingness to subject fat people to medical surgeries that are permanent and risky speaks to the shifting metrics for what is considered "acceptable risk" for fat people to become thinner. Esther Rothblum situated bariatric surgery as a kind of violence and terrorization of fat bodies, particularly in the lack of recognition of the long-term impacts and risks.[46] The dearth of critical voices warning of the dangers of bariatric surgery contrasts sharply with the incessant rhetoric of weight-loss surgery as safe, easy, and a universal solution to the "problem" of fatness, again revealing a cultural willingness to subject fat people to the kinds of medical procedures that most people would deem unthinkable and brutal.

While fat people have endless stories about medical negligence, discrimination, hostility, and indignities, these experiences are often compounded even further by racism and classism. Caleb Luna remembered the terrorization around medical problems and disability and how medical neglect interfaced with their other vulnerable identities: "My primary entry into the medical world was my injury in sixth grade when my hip socket slipped out of place in my pelvis. That started with pain in my ankle and moved to pain in my knee and then moved to pain in my hip." After delaying surgery and finally getting surgery, Luna reflected on how these delays harmed them: "I was further injured because I had a surgery to repair the initial injury, and it didn't heal well, and then I had another surgery to remove the pin, and then the injury happened again. That felt very much about race and class as a child. I remember my parents and my family talking about being vulnerable, not just as fat people but I had a working-class single mother who is hard of hearing, short, and fat herself and seemed like a very easy target for predatory practitioners. And now I'm disabled."[47] The refusal to take fat people's medical problems seriously, particularly within a healthcare system that designates certain people and certain bodies as disposable, can create and maintain health disparities that disproportionately harm fat children of color and fat poor children.

Fat activists also described feeling vulnerable and violated in medical settings, noting that anti-fatness had dire consequences for them. Mikey Mercedes remembered seeking therapy after a sexual assault experience and hearing more about weight loss than trauma recovery: "I remember speaking to a psychiatrist and I was like, 'It gives me a lot of anxiety to eat dinner. Sometimes I get so anxious to eat dinner that I won't eat, and then later on I'll eat a whole bunch after everybody's asleep, like I'll sit on the floor of the kitchen and eat cold food out of the fridge and I feel like I can't stop, and that's after maybe a day or two of trying my best not to eat anything and then feeling uncontrollable hunger and panic.' My psychiatrist was like, 'Okay, so is there a way for you to not get to the point where you feel like you're eating uncontrollably? If you're eating less, then you'll lose weight.' He just continued to see it as an asset that I was restricting food."[48] Pressures to lose weight mattered more than recognizing her traumatic reactions or imagining eating in a more holistic way.

At times the terrorization of fat bodies moved to an internal state of self-loathing and self-destruction that was fed by social feedback. Aubrey Gordon linked this to the constant onslaught of trying to lose weight, talking to her loved ones about it, and being blamed for fatness: "Even the most lovely and supportive people in my life, I would go to them and be like, 'This diet isn't doing it. My doctor told me to do this thing and that's not making me thin, and this isn't making me thin, and that's not either.' They would very kindly, very gently tell me all the reasons I was wrong, I was to blame, and that I must not be doing it right." In reaction to this, Gordon realized there was no stopgap to work against this kind of fat terrorization: "The hardest part wasn't feeling so low about my body image. The hardest part was abso-fucking-lutely no one to go to with it who would just hear it out. That's gruesome. That's socially gruesome behavior from a bunch of really good, thoughtful, kind, wonderful people who were villains in this part of the story. Heroes in, like, every other chapter, and then in this one, just like gremlins."[49] The lack of nuance and visibility of fat suffering—particularly what it means to negotiate living in a fat body within an anti-fat world—alongside the pain of supposedly well-intentioned thin people continuing to push weight loss at all costs ultimately saddles fat women with no space to process poor body image on its own terms.

Fat people live in a world designed to normalize shame and self-loathing as they endure violence and scorn directed at them. As Stacy Bias noted, "We have to acknowledge that the world that we live in, everything in it, is set up to make ourselves feel bad and so that is a natural, normal, expected, and entirely rational reaction to our existence. Not liking our bodies every day is really fucking normal, because there's nothing in the world that's set up to support us in liking our bodies and that indoctrination starts early."[50] It can be a revelation to understand that disliking (or even frankly hating) one's own body is no inevitability; those impulses came from somewhere, and in this way, they reflect a system that is both relentless and fragile, dogmatic and underminable. The problem, then, lies in destabilizing the normalization of suffering while also recognizing how mundane and routine fat suffering is. We must somehow engage with fat vulnerability not by minimizing or erasing the experiences of terrorization, but by foregrounding them in order to build solidarity and community, and ultimately, forge ways to fight back.

IMAGINING COMFORTABLE FAT EMBODIMENT

In contrast to these stories about the mistreatment, injuries, and harms done to fat people, an understanding of fat vulnerability also necessitates more familiarity with how people strive for a *comfortable* fat embodiment. Learning how to resist is not merely a set of loud, persistent, and rebellious actions (though many of these will be considered in the next two chapters) but also an openness to allowing fatness the space to exist as mundane and normative. Striving toward comfort and moving toward self-acceptance is envisioned here as an early part of seeing the vulnerability in resistance itself.

For Virgie Tovar, fat activism itself made space not only for a more comfortable embodiment but for broader recognition of the links between fat oppression and other social identities, life experiences, and social processes. She said, "Fat activism gave me language to understand what fat phobia was and it was really powerful. That was kind of the beginning of healing the relationship. It's really incredible to see how my relationship to my body changed. It kind of went from a very adversarial relationship to my body as an art object, my body as a political object, my body as a site of abjection, and a site of repudiating cultural expectations, a site of aggressively affirming my gender." She noted that her body has given her more insights about different types of institutional oppressions.[51] Re-situating fatness not as a reservoir for all sorts of other traumas and identities opens up space for thinking about the body in complex ways and understanding the body as political.

When envisioning her movement toward body satisfaction, Tovar marks fat activist spaces as producing comfort through community: "When I think about the most comfortable spaces, I can think of very early fat activist spaces, where I was just around all fat people, and it was so nonjudgmental, and everybody was just so unapologetically fat. We were all wearing bikinis and lingerie and tight clothes and short shorts. We were just eating food and just being fat and being honest about being fat, and not having to hide parts of being fat. Not just being fat and cute, but like, fat and chub rub, fat and rejection, fat and loneliness, fat and caring for your fat rolls, those kinds of things. I would say those have been some of my most comfortable moments." When reflecting on her attitudes about her body now, Tovar embraced the idea of growing old as a fat person and being more confident in her aging fat body: "I don't look at thin people and wish I had their lives. I don't look at clothes that don't fit me and blame myself. When I think about myself in the future and getting old, I am fat and it makes me happy. I think there's this very deep level of acceptance that is so liberating and beautiful."[52] The sense of building community around fatness and seeking relationships that affirm fatness seems to open up space for simply *being* fat in a more assured way.

In essence, comfortable fat embodiment was deeply connected to developing and sustaining fat community and collectivity. Tigress Osborn remembered her early days of fat activism: "In the Bay Area, where I came of age as an activist, I started a nightclub event in Oakland. It wasn't an exclusively Black space, but it was a really Black-centered space, a space that was centered around fat Black femmes. When I see pictures of us all dancing together, people who are in these bright colors, in these fun outfits, made-up and stylish and having a great time, I feel a lot of joy in those memories."[53] As an antidote to the aloneness and isolation fat women often feel, discussing shared grievances and nurturing the bonds of community and working to combat anti-fatness as a collective body was a powerfully healing force.

Comfortable fat embodiment also related to appreciating the strengths of a fat body or imagining it as sexual and joyful. Barbara Bruno, who helped to found Health at Every Size (HAES), identified comfortable fat embodiment with sexual joy: "Having good sex is a great way to have a more positive relationship to your body."[54] Caleb Luna also linked comfort about fatness to comfort with nudity: "I did figure modeling for the first time this week and it was one of the first times I was nonsexually nude in front of others. Before the pandemic I would also walk around my gym's locker room naked at different points. I would do it intentionally to help me with my comfort around it, to varying degrees of success. But I found this figure modeling experience to be really empowering and lovely and helped me kind of feel comfortable in my nude body in this way that I had never been before."[55] Again, opening up space to experience the fat body as partially free from the relentless narratives of anti-fatness, whether through a scientific appreciation of the body, experiences of sex, or comfort with nudity, highlights the social and political importance of the fat body simply being allowed to *exist*.

These descriptions of fatness and comfort also complicate the idea that fatness is inherently uncomfortable, traumatic, or difficult; rather, these expectations are *imposed upon* fat bodies. Though fat activism presented one avenue for people to feel more comfortable in their bodies, many other aspects of life offered the chance for comfort, matter-of-fact living, and just existing. Positive romantic relationships, new thinking about aging, linking fatness to other experiences and identities, sexuality, nonsexual nudity, taking space away from the demands of the gaze, and finding spaces for collective joy all constituted ways that fat people made space for more comfortable embodiment. This is not to say that comfortable embodiment is an invulnerable experience, but rather, that when we make space for bodies to rest, play, and breathe, we can better understand the costs and losses of what happens when they are taxed, mocked, burdened, squeezed, belittled, and degraded.

THE UNEQUAL DISTRIBUTION OF VULNERABILITY

Vulnerability is at once a sticky and slippery topic, something that often works simultaneously as projected onto the bodies of others (and thus we become invulnerable) or claimed as something we are (and stripped away from others). In a political sense, when groups mark and claim their vulnerability, they often do so at the expense of recognizing others as vulnerable too. There are some complex and contradictory politics at play when looking at the experiences of fat vulnerability. For example, by marking the injuries of fatness and the wounds fat people experience when moving through the world, it is tempting to portray thin people as invulnerable, or incapable of experiencing injury. Of course, they are not. Thin women in particular simultaneously perpetuate patriarchal ideas about thinness and *are subjected to them.* Patriarchal systems dictate that women's value is largely defined by their sexual appeal to men, and anything that exists outside of that—bodies that are too large, too dark-skinned, too explicitly sexual, not sexual enough, and so on—is punished, sometimes harshly. Similarly, if fat people resist their oppression and fight for their liberation, they can project onto others a vulnerability that they then disavow in themselves; sometimes activists feel pressured to renounce vulnerability in order to claim power. Fat people should be allowed to fight for a world that treats them better and makes space for their own struggles and suffering. They can work on making a different world and feel overwhelmed, exhausted, even defeated by its cruelty.

Fat vulnerability is unique and important and not exclusionary to other modes of bodily vulnerability. In fact, we can easily argue that *all* bodies are made vulnerable by fat oppression, that *all* bodies are drawn into the sticky trap of body-shaming and degradation that is most fully realized in the fat embodied experience. Even among fat people, experiences of fat vulnerability vary dramatically in relation to actual body size and shape, not to mention how race, class, and ability stratify and influence experiences of fat vulnerability. As the gender theorist Judith Butler and colleagues argue, "[V]ulnerability and invulnerability have to be understood as politically produced, unequally distributed through and by a differential operation of power. . . . [O]ne of the main reasons why there is opposition to (if not an outright denial of) vulnerability is that vulnerability has not been adequately related to the existing practices of resistance."[56] As such, if we are to understand the kinds of political revolt made possible when people are forced to be exceptionally vulnerable, and if we are to validate the resistance and resilience that occurs when people experience immense distress in relation to systems and structures of power, it is essential to examine fat resistance in tandem with fat vulnerability. Fat people are not asking for paternal protection by admitting their vulnerability; they are, in essence, mobilizing their vulnerability to rebel against violence and subjugation. Like consciousness-raising groups during the second wave of the women's movement, which aimed to mobilize people to engage in political activism based on their own experiences with oppression, domination, and subjugation,[57] efforts to mobilize fat vulnerability also have explicitly political intentions. Vulnerability in this sense becomes a resource, a mode of understanding the conditions that led to the necessity for freedom and rebellion in the first place.

In this way, we would do well to consider how the "unequal distribution of vulnerability"[58] works in relation to fatness and fat injury, and how naming and marking this can perhaps alleviate some of the signifiers attached to vulnerability (that is, fat people as "damaged," fat people as "pathetic," fat people as in need of management and concern by others). We should continue to ask: If we work not to overcome vulnerability, but rather to mobilize it as an act of resistance, how can we undermine some of the power exerted upon fat bodies? How does vulnerability move between registers as individual and collective experiences, as intrapsychic and social at the same time? What forms of power and freedom do fat people need, and how might they secure those without disavowing their vulnerability? To highlight a trickier point, I ask in the next two chapters a question that has been building throughout this book: If fat people have been made pervasively vulnerable—through discrimination, humiliation, workplace biases, media representations, attacks on their health and well-being, refusal to commemorate their deaths, and more—how can this vulnerability translate into a capacity to act politically, to rage against oppression, to enact the practices of revolt?

PART FOUR

THE NECESSITY OF FAT FURY

CHAPTER 7

GUTTURAL RESISTANCE

Ranting About Fatness While Poor,
Black, Disabled, or Queer

S ometimes you just have to scream.

The history of feminist, antiracist, queer, and working-class rebellions brim with tales of rage and refusal, fury and ferocity, sometimes hiding in plain sight, most often obscured by the more "respectable" and palatable stories of resistance. It is hard to tell the story of anger, and even harder to tell the truth about the immense power that anger can have. Fury pushes against mainstream narratives and draws in the marginalized. It reshapes neat-and-tidy histories and stories, so often overly sanitized, that typically narrate social progress. Anger ignites things, lights fires, explodes.

In her book on women's rage, Rebecca Traister recounts the story that most people know about Mrs. Rosa Parks—the "perfectly demure" woman whose refusal to surrender her seat ignited the Montgomery bus boycott of 1955–56—and what the story often left out, that Parks could more accurately be described as "a fervent antirape activist who had once told a would-be attacker that she'd rather die than be raped by him and who, at ten years old, threatened by a white boy, picked up a piece of brick and drew it back to strike him if he approached."[1] Rosa Parks later told her terrified grandmother, "I would rather be lynched than live to be mistreated and not be allowed to say 'I don't like it.'"[2] To redraw the caricature of the quietly refusing Rosa Parks as a brick-wielding, full-throttled, wrath-filled activist is jarring but necessary.

Anger is, after all, a catalyst for change. As Traister writes, "It can be a communicative tool, a call to action, engagement, and collaboration between ideological compatriots, who, without first having made their ire loud and public, would not have known that they had the numbers to form an army, or see past difference and toward peaceful cooperation."[3] Anger provides the necessary underpinnings of social change, particularly as it links people together in shared solidarity and mutual expressions of rebellion. Through these connections, powerful institutions and systems of oppression become fragile and breakable. As Traister notes, "We have known all along that with [women's anger] came the explosive power to upturn the very systems that have sought to contain it."[4]

It is not surprising, then, that the story of fat fury has largely been dismissed and overshadowed by other kinds of stories—fat people as "normal," fat people as assimilating, fat people as friendly and jovial, fat people as quietly and passively hidden away. Fury might imply, quite dangerously, a recognition of injustice, a refusal to quietly endure impossibly poor treatment, and the threat of collective revolt. It is, at once, born of suffering and cruelty, but it is also, as Traister says, "an exuberant expression."[5] Fury creates things, produces joy and energy, and, in the best scenarios, makes life more livable and survivable. Fat fury is essentially a refusal to exist within the necropolitics of death and despair, instead directing energy toward demanding and imagining more.

In this chapter, I work to map the margins of fat experiences, featuring a critical analysis of interviews from fat people all-too-often left out of mainstream narratives about fatness. In particular, I draw on my interviews with fat activists (who are also poor, Black, disabled, and/or queer) to build a case for why personal and collective anger is a necessary antidote to the oppressive practices they endure as multi-marginalized people living in fat bodies. I also trace how fat activism itself has emerged from these very spaces, driven largely by those who have collectively refused silence, shame, and isolation. Drawing from the traditions of the politics of marginalization, working-class studies, and feminist analyses of precarity, guttural resistance reimagines an angry politics that prizes abject bodies and those cast out or excluded from institutions like academia, systems of wealth and privilege, and the middle class. As Black feminist writer and poet Audre Lorde wrote, "[A]nger expressed and translated into action in the service of our vision and our future is a liberating and strengthening act of clarification, for it is in the painful process of this translation that we identify who are our allies with whom we have grave differences, and who are our genuine enemies."[6]

CONFRONTING THE LIMITS OF BODY POSITIVITY

While body positivity has offered new lenses and approaches through which to view and confront normative body shame (see chapter 3 for a fuller examination), fat activists have expressed serious reservations about the liberatory potential of "love your body" rhetoric. As something easily distorted by the logics of capitalism, neoliberalism, and the wellness industry, body positivity is often imagined by thin people and companies seeking to capitalize on normative body hatred as the endpoint of the struggle for fat inclusion. As long as everyone "loves" their body, no structural critiques or changes are needed. Further, those targeted by body positivity are typically thinner white women rather than a more diverse array of identities and body types. I include here fat activists' critiques of body positivity in an effort to provide a springboard to the more rambunctious, rebellious, and radical versions of fat liberation they envision. These critiques also serve as a reminder to confront systematic and institutionalized fat phobia while taking care not to allow fat liberation politics to be appropriated in service of thin people affirming thin bodies. Taking seriously the struggles of fat embodiment means better understanding and critiquing the limited avenues fat people have for feeling good about their bodies; the limitations of these approaches point to the necessity of full-blown revolt.

Fat activist Stacy Bias recognized the value of body positivity but worried about its limitations in terms of structural critiques of fat oppression. She said, "Body positivity absolutely has its place. It's a doorway through which people can enter, but when it stops there, that's when I have a bit of a problem. I think fat liberation work is more action-oriented, more solution-driven, more focused on inequities and inequalities in the world. It's more systemic, addressing actual access issues and things like that, and it prioritizes the people who are most marginalized, at least when it's done well." Reflecting on the different needs of fatter people and body positivity and the centrality of systemic change, Bias said, "I think we have a tougher road in terms of loving our bodies, or the 'love your body' mandate that the body positivity movement brings. I think that process, especially for someone who has trauma, which is something I navigate, is complicated and lifelong, so I am definitely in a more 'body neutrality' camp, where my relationship with my individual body is very private and personal and individual and irrelevant to the work I do in the world because, independent of how I feel, how you feel, we *all* deserve access to things like medical help, jobs, housing, furniture that doesn't collapse beneath us, air travel, and stuff."[7]

Fat activist Mikey Mercedes also worried about the hyper-individualistic nature of body positivity at the expense of bigger critiques of fat oppression. She had a particularly searing critique of body positivity as linked to capitalism: "Body positivity—it's individualizing. It assumes autonomy in making decisions about accepting the body, caring for the body, and helping your body thrive, when in reality fat people don't have that autonomy most of the fucking time. Body positivity shifts blame and energy. There's this very capitalist-agnostic component to body positivity that I really hate, like the notion that we can get further to self-love through things like rapid consumerism and just adorning our bodies with different things that make us happy. It's like this endless pit to nowhere that just enriches capitalistic entities that want to make money." Her astute analysis that body positivity is so popular in part because it serves the needs and interests of capitalism again foregrounds a distrust toward the popularity of body positivity as a stand-in for fat liberation.

Mercedes also critiqued the links between body positivity and white privilege, particularly how it supplanted fat rage with ignorance toward systemic inequality: "There's also this other part where I don't like the political movements that are afraid of rage. Political work that is placating or intentionally shying away from the anger of marginalized people is bullshit. It's not real. And body positivity space is so filled with thin white women in particular who are so uncomfortable with the notion that their work or existence has political implications for people more marginalized than them." For Mercedes, her fat activism focused on systemic mistreatment of marginalized people: "My fat activism specifically centers fat people of color, specifically fat Black people, especially those who are impacted by ableism, poverty, and transphobia. Those are the people I care about. Our existences live in the political. Other people have the options of declining to live politically, really that's them just being ignorant of the ways they impact other people through their existence, or the ways that they feed into and reinforce things that are harmful."[8] This sense of fat activism as intentionally targeting other kinds of marginalization, and holding privileged people accountable for how they perpetuate inequality, reinforces how more radical fat activism is deeply intersectional.

The necessity of fat activism and the limitations of body positivity often went hand in hand. The movement away from individualizing the affirmation of fat bodies and instead recognizing the power of building a social movement was key for the fat activist Esther Rothblum. She added that, unlike the corporate appropriation of queer liberation (largely seen in gay pride parades now), corporations often see fat people organizing as a fundamental threat: "With fat stuff it's the opposite because a lot of these corporations are selling weight-loss products, so in a way having people be more satisfied in any way with their bodies is very threatening to the corporate sector."[9] Fat liberation was both threatening to capitalism and necessary to move people from individualistic to collective solutions to social problems.

Fat activist Caleb Luna lamented the limitations of body positivity as refusing to make coalitions across populations: "A lot of the conversation has been on really individualistic facets of the fat experience in terms of self-esteem and body image, and not about interconnective struggle, or thinking historically or globally, trying to make connections to other movements. A lot of people come to the movement because they want to feel better about themselves, and I don't think that's a bad goal. I see the value in that. I just think it can't be the *end* goal."[10] Kimberly Dark likened body positivity to other half-hearted and limited solutions to fat oppression: "The idea of body positivity as the holy grail does not change political circumstances. The idea, somehow, that if we just get clothing manufacturers to create a broader line of sizes, that's some kind of win, well, it's like letting a slightly larger group of people into a nightclub when actually what I want is the club burned down." She added, "The fact that white supremacist hegemony is still driving the corporate focus of body inclusivity upsets me. How long should a slender white person be the voice of Health at Every Size or fat activism?"[11] In essence, if body positivity is positioned as a starting point rather than an ending point, it can have a place in building a movement, but it can be destructive when it becomes the endpoint of fat politics.

In her robust critique of body positivity, Aubrey Gordon honed in on the problems and limitations of allowing space for more people to simply feel beautiful: "I am not interested in a system that preserves beauty as a metric for humanity, or as the yardstick for someone's dignity or access to services or any of that kind of stuff. I don't really need people to tell me in movement spaces, 'You're beautiful.' That's not a thing that I am desiring of. I would rather that we just said, 'I think you deserve a place here as much as anyone else and I'm going to help you make that place.' It feels like body positivity is still walking through the door of marketing beauty to get some kind of humanity or dignity, and I don't care about that. I want somebody to take the big TNT plunger and blow up that door. I don't feel like we need that door. I don't feel like it's serving anything. What it does serve is misogyny and white supremacy, a bunch of classism, a bunch of that shit." In other words, feeling beautiful, if not situated in more political terms, matters little to the project of liberation. Lamenting the corporate takeover of body positivity, Gordon added, "Way more people saw the Dove ads than read the Fat Underground's *Fat Liberation Manifesto*. There's a flood of completely depoliticizing people going, 'I also want to feel good about my body,' but they didn't want to interrogate any of their biases, so a bunch of people who were already pretty well-affirmed by the beauty standard came in and were like, 'But I don't feel affirmed enough,' and then closed the door behind them for fat people, for disabled people, for the kind of people who started the thing."[12] This shift toward fat activism as rebellious, explicitly in-your-face, and away from the limitations of body positivity also positions fat liberation as rambunctious and ambitious rather than catering only to thin women's needs for reassurance.

Building on these critiques, in their book *Belly of the Beast*, Da'Shaun Harrison lays out a scathing critique of body positivity as a way for thin people to maintain their power over fat people, writing: "This is what is violent about 'body positivity'; it is benevolent anti-fatness in that it is masqueraded as some sort of semblance of acceptance for fat people, when it is instead an opportunity for Thinness to reroute, but not give up, its hold on fat people's collective liberation. As a politic, Thinness is a system that seeks to subjugate and ultimately eradicate fatness and fat people."[13] For Harrison, body positivity has a politics so watered down and appropriated that it actively works *against* fat liberation by instead prioritizing the eradication of fat people altogether.

POLITICAL SOLIDARITY ACROSS SIZES

The problems the fat activists outlined about body positivity point to a broader question: How do we build solidarity between fatter and thinner people without prioritizing thin people's needs, erasing the complexity of fat embodiment, or requiring certain kinds of emotional experiences of embodiment that foreclose possibilities for intersectional engagement with the world? What could solidarity across body sizes look like?

One key part of solidarity across body sizes involves the recognition that nobody wins when women are pitted against each other and when bodies are subjected to control, discipline, or hierarchical valuation. Caleb Luna suggested that people with different body types—particularly very tall people and very thin people—can relate to some of the struggles fat people endure: "It's so funny that we have these shared experiences of having a hard time finding clothes or not really fitting comfortably on planes. We have these kind of quirky accommodations that we need. We all suffer because of these arbitrary metrics of what a standard, normal human body is, and we all fall outside of it. For tall people, and extremely thin people, it's not easy, but they're not pathologized for it. So I think we could all just see that being outside of this constructed norm is the issue and not actually the way that our bodies are."[14] In this way, harnessing people's recognition of arbitrary definitions of "normal" bodies, and their understanding that those metrics are the problem rather than individual bodies being the problem, could facilitate more movement toward solidarity across sizes. After all, thin people also lose when bodies are tightly controlled and regulated, and when access and privilege is assigned only to an extremely narrow group of people with certain kinds of bodies. Similarly, Barbara Bruno argued that solidarity could occur by uniting against the powers that dictate what kinds of bodies people can and should have: "There are still inspections on how women are supposed to dress and what she's allowed to do as her occupation. Uniting against body size tyranny would be one way to have solidarity, and body color tyranny and body sexuality tyranny. This is the way people are. They don't fit into this narrow mold and a lot of people are afraid. There's so much that has to do with fear."[15] By recognizing the patriarchal, white supremacist, classist, and heterosexist roots of defining bodily norms, people can unite to make space for more bodily differences.

Nuancing the differences between fatter and thinner people could also help build solidarity, as there are differences between emotional discomfort or disliking one's body versus real structural accommodation problems. Stacy Bias described the importance of solidarity with regard to plane seating, and how emotional versus structural differences deserve recognition: "Up to a size 24, most people don't start facing real access issues on planes. It's more discomfort or stigma or experiencing judgment or discrimination or looks or whatever, which is real and a struggle. We all deserve to have space to air that and get support for navigating the emotional aspects of being in a space that hasn't been designed for your body. . . . But then there are superfat folks who can't physically fit in a seat, who might struggle with airplane or airport seating, or with long stretches between gates. They have real, physical access issues. It can be a struggle in a group to understand the difference between emotional access and physical access, to ask them not to take up more space with anxieties that are not super relevant to the physical access issues people are having." She added, "If people could do some emotional labor—which would take looking beyond themselves and putting themselves in the shoes of people who are a different size and are facing different levels of access issues—then that would be a kinder, more compassionate, gentler world. It takes a lot of compassion to have a movement where everybody gets heard."[16] By validating everyone's emotional needs but differentiating issues of access based on size, a broader movement that coalesces around culture of access (for fat, disabled, or older people, and so on) could emerge.

While most fat activists envisioned some ways to have solidarity with thinner people, a few fat activists were more critical about the possibilities of solidarity across body sizes. Mikey Mercedes argued that real solidarity involves those who have power understanding that they must lose or surrender some of it to allow those without as much power to live better lives: "There are a lot of thinner people who are only comfortable supporting fat people insomuch as they can get something out of it. That's not a new thing. White people have been doing that in struggles for Black liberation forever. It isn't a thing they do to enrich themselves. It's a thing they should do because it's the right thing to do." The surrendering of privilege, or operating on a more principled basis rather than a self-serving basis, was a necessity in order to have real solidarity between fatter and thinner people. Mercedes also said fatter people needed to shift their mindsets away from accommodating thin people's needs: "Fat people need to make fewer concessions. We need to have standards, because that's how we've gotten ourselves into this mess. We don't have the collective fervor yet because of decades of doing work with people like thin allies who just want to capitalize off of our oppression."[17] Da'Shaun Harrison also felt skeptical of working in solidarity with thinner people: "Of course, I have thin friends and we build solidarity with one another, but I'm not entirely sure that I want to build solidarity with others. I guess I'll say this. I think that thin people have a much greater responsibility than they believe to be true, and I think until they are willing to give up their resources, to give up their access, give up their lives, give up their spaces to us, care for us, everything that they do will fall short of what is required of them. I think that thin folks have very little interest in doing what's required of them to destroy anti-fatness as a concept."[18] In this way, understanding the futility of full solidarity while still working to build a different world was a key principle of radical fat activism.

THE ROOTS OF FAT OPPRESSION

As a major tension in all activist work, the struggle between working on within-system change (the more liberal approach) and enacting more sweeping radical change ("going to the roots") stands at the core of how activists work toward their goals. Within-system changes are more open to policy and legislative change and have the benefit of modifying and working within existing structures. However, within-system changes can validate the existing systems of power and hierarchy, thus leaving in place systems that disadvantage marginalized people. The types of changes possible are often less ambitious in nature and less able to address the larger structures of power inequity. Within-system changes can also be easily chipped away at and rolled back (such as the loss of federally recognized abortion rights in the US). Radical change, on the other hand, takes an ambitious stance of looking at the core or root issues of inequality, and often seeks more structural, sweeping change based on its analysis of the root causes of oppression. That said, radical change often seeks to undermine systems rather than work within them, which can alienate potential allies and reject more measured ways of engaging in social change.[19]

This same tension between within-system and radical social change informs the core of how fat activists have imagined their work, particularly as they struggle for concrete, material change for fat people while also sharpening their analysis of why fat people suffer and are discriminated against. Certainly, we should not approach liberal and radical activism as opposites per se, but as substantially different approaches to solving social problems and addressing inequality. Still, thinking in radical ways, and imagining avenues to enact radical shifts to thinking about fatness, is a key component of any kind of long-lasting improvement to fat people's lives. One of the most compelling conversations I had with these fat activists centered on the more radical question of what lies at the root of anti-fatness. I asked them to consider the basis for fat oppression at its deepest level. Their responses revealed a commitment to connecting the struggles around body size to the histories of patriarchy, colonialism, imperialism, anti-Blackness, and settler-colonialist modes of thought.

Stacy Bias linked fat oppression to both capitalism and patriarchy, particularly in terms of how bodies are framed as productive or nonproductive. She worried about the fundamental capitalist assumption that fat bodies were nonproductive and therefore not valuable: "If it's about being a productive citizen, if we're just revenue-generating plebs, then a fat body is not great. Certainly, patriarchal society has relied on having the free labor of women. It's all very Marxist."[20] This connection between the bodies that labor (and thus have value) and bodies that do not (and thus have no value) frames fatness as a threat to a capitalist-patriarchal state. In a similar way, Esther Rothblum connected fat oppression to misogyny and the hatred of women more broadly: "I think a lot of it has to do with hating women. Women's bodies are rounder, have more fat, and even for men who are fat there's a part of it that's sort of feminizing because men should be lean and muscular and not in any way look female." She linked this to associations between hyper-thinness and reactivity to women gaining power: "It's interesting that when women want more rights, when they gain more rights, they are suddenly told to take up less space, to be really small." She also linked anti-fatness to the US history of puritanism: "The US has this history of puritanism, that you can't have pleasure. You need to deny yourself and have this protestant work ethic. How dare you be happy with your body or tell people that they don't need to [hate themselves]?"[21] These links between the patriarchal mandate that women's bodies take up less space, the denigration of rounder and more feminized bodies, and the puritanical message that pleasure, play, and excess are fundamentally immoral underlie the cultural hatred of fatness, particularly for fat women.

Kimberly Dark identified links between anti-fatness, antipoverty attitudes, and anti-immigrant sentiments, particularly as all of these connected to experiences of marginalization more broadly: "We need a greater focus on the needs of humanity and all people. Here's this whole government and corporate healthcare–driven machine that insists, 'But we want you to be healthy!' If that's the thing, then we have to do something about poverty. There's no route to population-level health without handling poverty and all that goes along with it in our country." She added, "You can look at the anti-immigrant sentiment in the turn of the last century and see the same goddamn thing: 'These fat immigrants are so lazy. Look at them, eating up all your stuff!'" Dark linked these experiences of marginalization to the necessity of solidarity: "Who is *not* marginalized is a tiny, tiny group of people at this point, and so how we get a more radical outcome for fat liberation is by making sure that people understand there's solidarity. The way to get un-fucked-over is to stop fucking over somebody else! How do you acknowledge the humanity of everyone everywhere?"[22] The insistence that fatness is not seen as an isolated identity but as one of many marginalized identities frames fatness as necessarily intersectional, particularly for radical critiques of the roots of anti-fatness.

Aubrey Gordon broadened this focus on marginalized groups to include a variety of other systems of power and hierarchy when analyzing the roots of anti-fatness: "I think there are three things: white supremacy, misogyny, and ableism. Anti-fatness is an interesting thing in that it is both a system of oppression unto itself, but it's also a system of oppression that's largely there to prop up other systems of oppression." Taking a similarly broad approach to the roots of fat oppression, Caleb Luna linked anti-fatness to systems of hierarchy with gender, race, class, and ability: "In the struggle for power, humans have had to divide each other into different categories in order to empower one and disempower others, and we see this across gender most evidently. We see it across race, class, ability. These are all modes of trying to shape and define and empower others and disempower others." These hierarchical dichotomies—between men and women, white people and people of color, fat and thin people—consistently served the interests of the powerful and denigrated the less powerful. Luna added, "I just see that fat stigma comes out of that need to try to produce another category of empowering and disempowering people, but it also feels very directly connected to the moment of Western empire, colonization, and the moment that racial categories that exist today were being defined and developed. Fat bias, fat stigma, anti-fatness, fat phobia, whatever we call it, was developed as part of that, as part of trying to dehumanize Black and Indigenous people and trying to empower white people, the colonizers and settlers. Fatness has gotten weaponized in that process."[23] These strong racialized roots of anti-fatness point to the ways that white supremacy, colonialism, and misogyny have intersected both historically and today.

These critiques have certainly been validated by recent scholarly work that links colonialism, anti-Blackness, and the emergence of anti-fatness. Sociologist Sabrina Strings has compellingly argued that, prior to the mid-twentieth century, white femininity was situated in opposition to Black femininity such that thinness was applauded in part because it positioned white women apart from their Black counterparts. She argues,

> The image of the fat black woman as "savage" and "barbarous" in art, philosophy, and science, and as "diseased" in medicine has been used to both degrade black women *and* discipline white women. For decades, white feminist scholars and historians focused largely on the impact of the "thin ideal" on middle- and upper-class white women. They claimed that the thin ideal was oppressive, but also suggested that they did not know how it developed. . . . The fear of the black body was integral to the creation of the slender aesthetic among fashionable white Americans.[24]

In this sense, thinness and whiteness became inseparable, particularly as thinness became weaponized as a way to cement hierarchies between white and Black women.

Responding to Strings's work, Da'Shaun Harrison linked anti-Blackness and anti-fatness together at the point where bodies become targets of moral evaluations. When I asked Harrison what was at the root of fat oppression, they responded: "Desire. Part of what leads to the making of anti-fatness as an ideology was white Europeans witnessing fatness on African bodies and attributing it to greed and unrighteousness and sinfulness. That, for me, indicates that the heart of what made them want to create this ideology was the fact that they didn't desire Black folks. I think a lot about what that means in modern times. What does that look like now?" Harrison went on,

> It looks like fat folks being the target audience for McDonald's commercials, filled with people who are desirable, politically beautiful, politically pretty, and what that means for the ways that things are sold and marketed. It looks like fat folks experiencing disproportionate rates of unemployment because they can be fired just because they're fat, or also could just not be hired just because they're fat, and then that leading to homelessness, and that leading to fat folks being put into these positions that the rest of society sees as like the lowest rung. So many fat folks are forced into survival sex work, work that we understand is real work, but the rest of society understands as bottom-of-the-barrel.

They added, "It looks like the creation of a beauty standard that outright dismisses the lives of fat Black folks in particular, even as it borrows from what parts of our bodies look like, depending on the context of the beauty standard. Discursively, this desire to have a 'thick body' where you have fatness in certain areas that don't show up in other areas, that's compartmentalizing fatness. It's borrowing from our bodies while noting that the rest of those bodies are just undesirable."[25]

Labeling the impacts of these biases, Harrison laid out the stakes of anti-fatness in terms of unabashed racism: "It looks like police being able to murder us in the streets and then use our bodies, our animality, our monstrosity, as justification for why the murder was okay. It looks like Cook County prosecutors and judges in the 1990s and 2000s being able to play a game called 'Niggers by the Pound,' where they're able to try to see who can incarcerate the most fat Black folks the quickest, to reach four thousand pounds the quickest. It looks like fat Black trans people not being able to have access to gender-affirming care and, when they do gain access to it, having to pay two to three times the amount of their thin counterparts to be able to affirm their body and their existence. These are all things that are directly correlated to desire for me." Taking a broader view of their critique, Harrison situated desire and anti-fatness together:

> Desire is not just about who you do and do not have sex with. That's part of it, but that's not what it's all about. It's also about determining whether or not a person you wouldn't have sex with deserves to have access to the resources of power. . . . Desire is, just with any other economy, a thing to be bought and traded, and it determines large-scale how the rest of the world functions and who in the world gets to have access to power and authority, resources, care, love, durability, etc., and fat Black folks are always removed from those possibilities.[26]

This analysis also points to how desirability becomes equated with survivability, who is put in precarious positions, and who is deemed unworthy and undeserving of care.

Building on these sentiments, fat activist Virgie Tovar, in her interview with me, connected anti-fatness to the logics of colonialism and neoliberalism: "Diet culture literally is colonialism. It literally is turning the body into the racialized other and the mind into the white colonizing male, and the mind governs the body which must be controlled and dominated according to colonial ideology. And neoliberalism is really the cornerstone of American pathology and American ideology."[27] She also connected anti-fatness to eugenics, the end of slavery, and the industrial revolution:

> Essentially one type of body—the white masculinist able-bodied body— becomes the ideal, and that body becomes the prototype against which all other people are compared. Then that bootstrap neoliberalism is totally connected to the end of slavery, and all of a sudden the United States is very, very wealthy. We have the industrial revolution and all of a sudden the body goes from this sort of spiritual thing to the machine, which I see as connected to the denial of slavery and the disassociation with that history. Bodies become extensions of machines at that time.

This treatment of bodies as machines, and the subsequent links to slavery, suggest that certain bodies (particularly bodies racialized through associations to Blackness) become associated with labor, sexual availability, exploitation, and humiliation. She added that power and dominance is embedded in anti-fat ideologies: "It all just feels very connected to the idea of dominion over the body and understanding that the body is an entry point for sin, for deviation, so you have to have this governing policy over the body, and that has to do with racialized bodies, it has to do with land itself, and it has to do with animals." The sense that we psychologically despise fatness because we associate fat bodies with something in need of dominance and control (in reference to slavery and human/animal dominion) showed yet another avenue to thinking about anti-fatness in much deeper, radical terms than mere superficial aesthetics.

Linking anti-fatness to anti-Blackness and settler colonial logics, Tigress Osborn described how every fat person is affiliated with the legacies of racism and imperialism: "The historical connection between white purity and thinness is really important to understand, because even for white people who could say, 'What does that have to do with me though? If fat phobia is only about racism, then I don't experience fat phobia? Yes I do!' No, that's not what we're saying. We're saying that you experience fat phobia because of racism, and you experience anti-fatness because we have defined fatness as being 'like those savages,' whether we're talking about Black folks or

Indigenous folks. We have defined a certain kind of body as being 'like those savages,' and you're acting like one of those savages by being in that kind of body." In this way, the fat body is always already read through the lens of racialization and colonialism. She also critiqued white people who fail to see anti-fatness as having racial implications: "In even more complicated ways, we have defined thinness in opposition to 'those immigrants,' because 'those immigrants' weren't considered white men. I understand why people are like, 'But that's historical. Today, it's just that people hate me because I'm fat,' yeah, except no, they actually hate you partly because you're a race traitor and you're not being a good enough white person, and part of what you're mad about is that you're not getting the shit that comes from being a good enough white person. The rest of us—we weren't going to get that shit anyway." Osborn linked anti-fatness to gender and its intersections with race: "There is gender hatred involved in anti-fatness, and that gender hatred is connected again to white purity in a lot of ways. Ideas about masculinity and femininity have always had some connections to race, so they're all connected to this discussion."[28] This unraveling of anti-fatness as connected to patriarchal, colonial, anti-Black, anti-immigrant, and antipoverty positions individual experiences of fat bodies as in need of more radical critiques. When people read their bodies as experiencing discrimination in more isolated, individualist ways, they miss the broader analysis of the more radical upheavals needed to achieve fat justice.

IMAGINING INTER-MOVEMENT STRUGGLE

As a movement, fat liberation, which later evolved into the more formally recognized "fat studies" and the contemporary manifestations of fat activism, emerged in the late 1960s and early 1970s as an outgrowth of the civil rights and women's liberation movements. Fat activists, who had by the early 1970s learned about consciousness-raising as a key part of the era's radical feminist movement, began to form their own groups to address issues left out of view by mainstream feminism. As communications scholar Jackie Wykes writes, "These groups later evolved into fat activist collectives such as the Fat Liberation Front and the Fat Underground, and developed insightful critiques of the connections between women's oppression, fat oppression, the medicalization of the fat body, and the interests of capital vis-à-vis multimillion dollar dieting and body-modification industries."[29] These groups distributed pamphlets, wrote manifestos, and enacted various kinds of troublemaking aimed at moving fat from an individual and personal experience to a collective, highly politicized identity. Then, with the introduction of the "obesity epidemic" in public discourse, combined with the emphasis on the body as a political entity within cultural studies work, fat studies emerged as an institutional area of academic inquiry that worked in tandem with the social movement of fat activism and fat liberation.[30]

This history of fat activism and fat liberation as a social movement points to the central importance of solidarity both in the founding of the movement and in its ongoing successes today. Like many other movements that use the body as a site of resistance—particularly movements like menstrual activism, HIV activism, and disability justice—understanding linkages between different groups, and prioritizing overlaps with other marginalized communities, has allowed fat activism to gain momentum, visibility, and power. Having broader critiques—for example, understanding that fat activism must take actions to lessen poverty and make equal access to medical care a priority—is a requirement for social movements to succeed. Similarly, working with allies to join in mutual struggles for justice, and seeing movement work as both intersectional and connected to larger projects of dismantling inequitable power structures, provides necessary fuel for the difficult work of activism. As trans activist Leslie Feinberg writes, "I believe that this is the only nobility to which we should aspire—that is, to be the best fighters against each other's oppression, and in doing so, build links of solidarity and trust that will forge an invincible movement against all forms of injustice and inequality."[31]

Efforts to map fat activism as an inter-movement struggle that has worked with other social movements to forge solidarity have often failed to ask fat activists for their own perspectives about the strengths and limitations of fat activism as a movement thus far. Better understanding solidarity and work across and between social movements is a key part of understanding how fat activists mobilize their own, and others', anger and sense of injustice about fat oppression. Part of the work of understanding inter-movement struggle is identifying the people who have too often remained hidden within various social movements. Caleb Luna identified fat people at the core of all social movements, even though they often were not recognized as such. Speaking about the origins of fat liberation and its more radical inter-movement roots, Luna said, "Fatness is my primal experience in the world. The original members of the formal fat activist movement were veterans of, and inspired by, these other movements, and a lot of them were fat lesbians and queer women. I imagine most of them were white and they had a lot of experience as allies of other movements. I think that's really legible in the *Fat Liberation Manifesto*, where they name their ally status. There's certainly an awareness and a reverence for being allied with these other movements around race, gender, class, colonization, and imperialism."[32]

Luna also identified fat lesbian feminists as at the core of the fat liberation struggle: "The first fat activists were often lesbian feminists. They knew that people say anti-fatness is about health and shit, but we know it's about aesthetics. We know that fat stigma exists because men think they don't find it attractive, or white men specifically. White men don't find it attractive on white women, and so lesbian feminists were like, 'We don't really give a fuck what men want and find attractive because that really isn't how we organize our lives, and we don't need to!' I think that gave a lot of space to make that challenge, whereas a straight woman who had to be reliant on her husband might not have been able to because she had a fucking home to run and because her livelihood was attached to her husband's satisfaction with her appearance." In this way, Luna cast queer women as catalyzing the early fat activist movement through a defiance of patriarchal control of desirability, sexuality, and attractiveness. Luna again emphasized the centrality of rebelling against heterosexist modes of economic dependence: "I think feminism opens up a lot of space for just emphasizing that women can be outside of the economic control of men." They also linked anti-fatness to disability struggles, though often found that overlap more painful to accept: "As a fat person, I was really afraid to embrace disability because the only ways that I could maintain any sort of fucking dignity or self-esteem or keep my head above water was telling myself that at least my body was not disabled and that was fine and made fatness okay. I didn't allow myself to think about, 'Well maybe my body is disabled, and is that okay?' I realized later that the larger ableism of the fat activist community as well as the fat phobia in the disability community was really a problem, so these are two minoritized struggling communities that are often overlapping but put into conflict with each other because of that fear. I think bridges are being built and people are working together more, and disabled people are getting fat and fat people are becoming disabled and we're all kind of chilling together."[33] Seeing the intertwining of social movements as essential to fat activism reinforces the deeply politicized roots of connecting fatness to analyses of power while honoring allies in the process.

Inter-movement building provides the essential structure for anti-fatness work to exist. Stacy Bias attributed the roots of social justice work to the labor of marginalized people, something the Black Lives Matter movement has been particularly good at highlighting: "Everything we have in the world that's socially-justice-based comes from the labor of marginalized people and the most marginalized people in American society are Black folks. Their labor is invaluable to us. Precious. Priceless. And I'm glad that they're finally being centered. It's certainly not enough yet, but those conversations are happening in ways that they weren't before, so I'm grateful for that." She also felt that feminism allowed space for critiquing gendered understandings of fat embodiment: "Men in our society are socialized to take up space in ways that women aren't, culturally speaking. It's a socialization issue in terms of taking up space and the expectations of doing so. I think a feminist understanding is really key to developing any sort of tools for not internalizing the message that women shouldn't take up space. It's essential to fat activism."[34] Tracing the recognition of marginalized people's labor, the insistence on taking up space, and the insistence on questioning hierarchy and revolting against oppression all influenced fat activism and laid the groundwork for fat rebellions.

Bias highlighted the conflicts, contradictions, and overlaps between the fat and disabled communities, particularly in terms of how justice projects are imagined: "There's a tension between disabled folks and fat folks because, like in *Flying While Fat*, fat people can put on the protection of disability temporarily and then take it off again, and they might not do any of the labor that people in disability justice have to do in order to create a world that is accessible to them. The disabled community is not a monolith and there are people in the disability community that feel that fat people could choose not to be fat, whereas an impairment you can't choose to not have is different. There's fat phobia in the disability community and there's ableism within the fat community." She also talked about the necessity for not moralizing each other's embodiments, and the potential of alliances if each group did so: "The argument for universal accessibility, tools, venues, seating, whatever, this is a shared argument that we can make if we can take morality out of it, if we can take this idea that fat is mutable out of it and just really look at the fact that all bodies are deserving of access. But that is really an anti-capitalist sentiment because space is commodified and serves those in power, so creating a universally acceptable space means you can't cram ten thousand people into that same space. Together, those groups could do a lot to push back on this."[35] To join forces between movements, people not only have to align their goals and values, but they also have to not participate in "othering" and further marginalizing their allies. Reinforcing hierarchy is an easy reflex to have in a culture that teaches people to fight each other for scraps while ultimately ignoring how power is maintained at the top.

In essence, fat activists have to continue to *build* inter-movement solidarity in an active way, as such overlaps are not an inevitable outcome of social movements. Aubrey Gordon emphasized that inter-movement work also required staffed and funded movements along with fat leadership in other movements.[36] Gordon noted that building a more visible and impactful fat activist movement may also require creative and ambitious thinking and strategizing about how to fund the movement outside of foundation funding avenues, even if that results in less money but more autonomy.

Because fat people have a different level of visibility than other marginalized communities, fat activism has different challenges of how to reach people. Mikey Mercedes drew connections between the disability justice movement and fat activism as intuitive allies in this regard: "I feel like fat activism is really special in the way that it lacks the things that people have used to identify social movements in the past—like very large hyper-visible organizations, marches, demonstrations, specific figures—but fat activism has mostly operated without those. A lot of fat activism happens online, a lot of fat community happens online. It's a very particular way to try and organize and build community and I think there's a lot of potential for reaching people that you wouldn't otherwise reach, who are isolated or aren't allowed to be visible in the ways that other marginalized groups are. It's very aligned in that way with disability justice work."[37]

The avoidance of talking about fatness appears as a major barrier to inter-movement building between fat activism and other social movements. Tigress Osborn worried that fat activism ignored other movements, and that other movements avoided fatness because of deep-seated anti-fat biases.[38] Pushing for social movements to be more self-reflexive, radical, and intersectional opens up space for solidarity and alliances across many identities, and social movements also overlap in the particularities of how certain bodies and identities acquire a marginalized status. The necessity of recognizing and revolting against the racist, classist, heterosexist, and misogynistic roots of anti-fatness works not only to strengthen the work of fat liberation but to reinforce inter-movement solidarity and allyship. Even more, understanding the roots of anti-fatness strengthens the theoretical underpinnings of other social justice movements, as revolting against the tyranny of thinness helps to unravel the premises of many different systems of power.

A CALL FOR GUTTURAL RESISTANCE

In its current iterations, fat activism has launched aggressive campaigns to change the conversation about bodies and identities, work toward building inter-movement solidarity and alliances, and better understand the ways that the roots of anti-fatness link up with other identities and justice projects. Notably, fat activism and fat liberation have worked against the trap of prioritizing respectability politics over more radical understandings of fat oppression. They have done so by positioning fat activism as an *inherently* radical movement, indebted not only to the struggles of Black Lives Matter, feminism, disability justice, reproductive rights, and queer liberation but also to the broader analysis of anti-fatness as connected to the way American culture, via capitalism, denigrates and disposes of so many kinds of marginalized embodiment. Fat activists understand the unacceptable costs of lowering their ambitions and accepting the existing terms of embodied inequality. Most importantly, they have embraced anger and fury at the forefront of the movement, insisting on increased rights and access *and* the shared experience of righteous rage.

This shift away from respectability politics is never an inevitability; many social movements have defaulted toward assimilative politics as their ultimate endgame. Many feminist and anti-racist scholars have criticized respectability politics, which "refers to efforts to hold marginalized people to hegemonic standards of so-called propriety" and, essentially, to clamp down on physical and emotional displays of resistance and revolt among marginalized people.[39] Such politics insist that those who play by the rules and accommodate existing power structures gain advantages by doing so, and that assimilation is the mode by which disadvantaged groups gain access to power. Challenges to respectability politics have appeared abundantly in feminist and anti-racist scholarship and activism, particularly as people have better recognized the central importance of radical social change. Fundamentally, when movements choose respectability over radicalism, many of the important complexities disappear, marginalized groups largely get expelled, and the goals become smaller and more incremental rather than larger and more ambitious.

For fat activism, respectability politics might easily worm their way into the core of the movement if not for the great efforts that more radical fat activists have made to resist them. Respectability politics might argue that small fat and medium fat people, who have closer proximity to norms of thinness and conventional beauty standards of mainstream upper-class, white, cisgender, heterosexual people, are better spokespeople for the movement than superfat and infinifat people. Similarly, respectability politics might dictate that fat people continue pushing for the same priorities as thinner people in order to gain power—feeling good about their individual bodies, diet culture and weight-loss efforts, equating weight loss with moral success and weight gain with moral failure, endorsing cultural narratives that thinner people deserve love, money, access, power, better healthcare, and so on. A fat activism closely aligned with respectability politics would insist that fat people assimilate into the norms and cultural priorities of thinner people, and that fat people do not overtly "make a fuss" about how fat people are mistreated. But fat activists have squarely refuted such claims, arguing instead for the necessity of solidarity, inter-movement building, and thinking deeply about the conflicts between social justice movements. They have posited that radical critiques of the power structures that maintain anti-fatness are required in order for fat liberation to thrive. They have made a case for ranting and raving over silence and compliance.

Fat activism reminds us of the dire stakes of prioritizing the needs and practices of dominant and hegemonic groups over those with less power and status. For example, pushing to adopt the body shapes, styles, and sizes of thin, white, upper-class women, as has been imposed on women for generations has ultimately denigrated communities of color and rendered fatter bodies as "inferior" to thinner bodies. It reinforces a politics of assimilation over diversification, compliance over revolt. It justifies and rationalizes harm and violence done to fat people. The mapping of desirability, power, hierarchy, health, and wellness onto thinness—emphasized in both diet culture and discourses of anti-fatness—is not merely a push for a particular aesthetic. Rather, it fuses together sinister histories of colonial conquest, economic dependencies imposed upon women by men, deep-seated racism embedded in desire capital, and ableist notions of morally good and bad bodies. It actively discards fat people as unworthy of even the most basic rights or the most fundamental forms of care.

Building on fat activists' calls to grow fat activism in tandem with other movements and to think about fatness in relation to race, anti-colonialism, class, sexuality, queerness, ability, and gender, I end this chapter with a call to embrace *guttural resistance*. I imagine this term as something that encompasses both the expression of rage—a guttural call to anger, for example—and as something derived from a politics of and from the gutter—that is, deeply and ideologically opposed to the politics and priorities of respectability politics. Guttural resistance reimagines a politics that prizes marginalized bodies and those cast out or excluded by systems of wealth and power. It does not seek out validation and approval, assimilation and endorsement. Most fundamentally, guttural resistance comes from experiences—however hard-earned, desperate, angry, or even pathetic—of being fundamentally discarded and disregarded, and it uses these to formulate a different, more furious kind of politics. Guttural resistance is resistance rooted in a deep understanding of the power of embracing the margins, the edges, the *madness* of living in a body that is left for dead. It is concerned more with survival than show business. Guttural resistance is grounded rather than cerebral, intentional rather than "done to," crafty rather than passive. It is deeply disinterested in ideological posturing and empty promises.

Guttural resistance insists on finding its way to freedom. Such resistance inverts systems that have denigrated and violated bodies marked as deviant and undesirable, fomenting clear allegiances between movements that have at times been seemingly at odds, such as disability justice and fat liberation. If the logic of assimilation is disrupted and bodies are imagined as inherently deserving of rights, access, and care, fat liberation—the epitome of guttural resistance—can link arms with other movements to fight more strategically and forcefully. Guttural resistance draws on the legacies of queer rebellion, working-class revolt, feminist revolution, and embodied resistance. It is not afraid of vulnerability, of taking power, of a good fight. It fundamentally seeks to reorient social movements toward the "primal scream," where fury is no longer a liability but a necessary expression to create a new and better world.

CHAPTER 8

FAT FURY

*Transforming Rage
into Radical Fat Resistance*

O ver dinner, a thin friend of mine recently recounted growing tensions between her and her partner over their child's weight. Her eight-year-old daughter—that age when the weight of the world is about to bear down upon her—has become fat. The child's father has expressed fear and apprehension about what it will mean if she moves through the world as a fat child. He worries about bullying from others, lack of self-confidence, loss of traditional standards of beauty, and the difficulties she will face because of her weight. He has begun to punish the child's eating, regulate her food intake, force more exercise, ridicule her for lack of willpower, and push her to see a behavioral therapist. The child's mother, on the other hand, aspires to create an environment at home where the girl feels loved, safe, nurtured, and good about her body. She does not want her daughter associating food with emotional land mines; she wants to encourage her to eat a diverse array of food, feel joyful about movement, and understand her body as beautiful and acceptable regardless of its size. This tension between these parents— one that plays out in countless households and upon the bodies of countless children—mirrors a core tension of this book: should we work to mitigate the damage that the world can do to fat people by forcing them to assimilate into thin people's body norms—an ideology embraced by a myriad of individuals and institutions—or, as fat activists have argued, do we work on creating a different world where many different types of bodies can be loved, desired, accommodated, and appreciated?

It is, in many ways, an infuriating question, one that has great resonance for so many people struggling to merely survive: The Black child who learns from his parents to acquiesce to white police officers. The queer child who hears her parents lament that her life will be *so much harder this way*. The disabled child whose mother fears for her vulnerability to other kids when she goes to school. Assimilation feels like protection, a shelter from the full impact of what the world can do to someone. Marginalized people learn to simply endure it, and they understand, sometimes painfully early in life, that their survivability depends on this ability. Entire social systems have been designed around the enforcement of deference and compliance with systems of power in this way. Within those systems, people cling to the elusive idea of safety even when it fragments them and breaks them away from possibilities of community and resistance. For fat people, they learn, often during childhood, that the way to survive fatness is to *stop being fat*.

And yet, like so many activists have urgently reminded us, there is another way. We do not have to accept the world on these terms. Systems are fragile and mutable. *The way things are* is no inevitability. As a marked contrast to the deference and assimilation pushed onto fat people by so many aspects of their social worlds—friends and family, romantic relationships, places of worship, schools, medical institutions, sports teams, workplaces, media, and more—a spirit of resistance and revolt awaits. To work for real structural change requires fury and collectivity. This righteous anger takes us down a different path, toward creating the world we want rather than enduring the one we have. As author and activist Soraya Chemaly writes:

> How much anger is too much? Certainly not the anger that, for many of us, is a remembering of a self we learned to hide and quiet. It is willful and disobedient. It is survival, liberation, creativity, urgency, and vibrancy. It is a statement of need. An insistence of acknowledgment. Anger is a boundary. Anger is boundless. An opportunity for contemplation and self-awareness. It is commitment. Empathy. Self-love. Social responsibility. If it is a poison, it is also the antidote. The anger we have as women is an act of radical imagination. Angry women burn brighter than the sun.[1]

The political utility of anger has long been diminished and underestimated by those seeking to push social movements toward respectability

politics and away from its more radical analysis. This containment of affect—the silencing of rage that so often accompanies the shutting down of
more radical critiques—implies that rage itself is tainting or undermining the
political goals of a movement. These pressures exist both subtly and more
overtly, from the push to be moderate and "play nice" to the trivialization
of anger and the outright squashing of collective responses of anger. There
is, of course, a deep incentive to keeping people—both fatter and thinner—
engaged in self-loathing and a perpetual fear of fatness. If people are busy
hating themselves, they have less ability to recognize the suffering of others
alongside them and cannot then redirect their energies toward a sense of
collective revolt. Fear and shame are conduits for isolation and complacency;
anger is transformative and agitated, creative and world-making.

As this book comes to a close, I want to offer readers an argument for
pushing fat studies, fat activism, and fat writing in more radical directions,
particularly harnessing the central importance of fat fury and fat rage. More
precisely, I argue that fury and rage can operate as a means to smash the cycle
of shame and terror, deeply interrogate individual and institutional complicity
with fat misogyny, form new alliances and solidarities with others, unravel
some of the structural forms of fat oppression, and reveal new possibilities
for fat liberation beyond the limited options offered in mainstream spaces
thus far. Fury operates as a missing link between the terror of fatness and the
activation of fat liberation actions and sentiments. Rage and fat fury become
the necessary antidotes to the powerlessness that is otherwise engendered
by fat misogyny, anti-fat ableism, and anti-fat racism. I advocate for the
necessity of collective resistance as a vehicle for social change and a form
of fundamental survival for those invested in fat liberation, and I draw on
the insights of fat activists to guide the way. I discuss the tensions between
anger and pleasure, activism and complicity, bodies and the social world, and
I argue for a vision of radical embodiment that maintains rather than erases
narrative, subjectivity, and emotionality as political work.

In essence, fat-shaming and the degrading of fat bodies operate both
as an affective and emotional form of control and as a means to regulate
bodies. Fat shame circulates and maintains misogyny and the control of
women, foregrounds racist ideologies about beautiful bodies, and constructs
and maintains structural forms of oppression. By limiting the creative forms
of resistance that people can imagine and enact, fat shame perpetuates

the inaccessibility of anger and centers the individual and her body as the "problem."

A new fat politics must first center on a deep understanding of how emotions—felt individually, socially, and culturally—regulate, punish, and control bodies through the circulation of shame and fear about fatness. Fat terror lives in the space of affect and is communicated to women particularly in a multitude of ways that have been considered in this book so far—wellness businesses, medical institutions, the fashion industry, workplaces, the media, and more. Fat oppression could not thrive without the continued regeneration of negative emotions linked to fatness: dread, terror, shame, avoidance, fear, loathing, contempt, apathy, neglect, and sadness.

Michel Foucault has argued that resistance must mimic the transmission of power.[2] The tools that we use to revolt are most effective when we understand and mimic how power operates and is exerted upon different bodies and identities. *If fat oppression lives and thrives in the space of affect and emotion, so too do the tools of resistance and revolt.* Fat fury is not a frivolous temper tantrum of a response to anti-fatness; it is a core element of countering, reducing, and upending the terrorization of fat bodies. A new kind of fat fury can, and perhaps *must*, emerge in this moment. Fat fury can help to examine how and why our families, colleagues, comrades, and fellow feminists and radicals have largely failed to shift their own discourses about body size and have stifled early efforts to stop perpetuating fat shame, fat misogyny, and anti-fat racism. Fat fury is also aimed at the social and political systems that have framed fatness as a repository for other kinds of anxiety-inducing problems largely perpetuated within the public sphere, including widespread poverty and racism, a horrifically biased and callous for-profit medical system, a gaslighting and lying governmental system, intensifying political repression, the meaninglessness induced by hyper-consumerism, expanding mechanisms of confinement, the capitalistic contexts for "self-care," and the deeply painful practices and behaviors that continually degrade, humiliate, and scapegoat women because of their bodies and body sizes.

Making space for fat fury—that avalanche of anger that emerges from a lifetime of wrestling with fat shame—must become a priority of fat activism as it moves into its next iteration. Fat fury is an individual catharsis, a collective response to oppression, and, in many ways, a fantasy of a future just starting to form.

HOW ANGER AND DEFIANCE PROPEL FAT ACTIVISM

A commonly held set of beliefs about anger is that it impedes social progress, makes lower-status groups look bad, is "unfitting" to express, and masks underlying sadness. Women's anger in particular has received a bad rap, as women's right to feel and express their anger has been suppressed for generations, centuries even. And yet, as Soraya Chemaly points out, "[Anger] is actually one of the most hopeful and forward thinking of all our emotions. It begets transformation, manifesting our passion *and* keeping us invested in the world. It is a rational *and* emotional response to trespass, violation, and moral disorder. It bridges the divide between what 'is' and what 'ought' to be, between a difficult past and an improved possibility. Anger warns us viscerally of violation, threat, and insult."[3] At its core, anger pushes the convergence of the real and the possible, the reality we live within and the future we want and need.

Anger can be a springboard into both the recognition of inequalities and oppression and the refusal to internalize those things as individual problems. Anger is, most essentially, an emotion that breeds collective resistance by reframing something painful as directed *outward* rather than inward. (Leading theories of women's increased rates of depression posit that, in addition to the overwhelming weight of misogyny and the difficulties of living as a woman in our culture, women also learn early on to direct anger inward toward the self. This ultimately results in more depression and less outwardly directed anger, particularly compared to how boys and men are socialized.)[4] In this sense, anger has political utility because it moves people toward the social, cultural, and structural reasons for their distress by activating a sense of wrongdoing rather than self-loathing. Anger is an essential antecedent for, and driver of, activist impulses, an ignition switch and, most fundamentally, the engine that keeps the fire burning.

Activists I spoke to clearly drew upon their feelings of anger to propel them toward spaces of collective fat resistance and to catalyze thinking about underexamined areas of fat oppression. Virgie Tovar used her own embodiment as a way of channeling anger, both in confronting others and in choices she made about fashion and dress: "I think about early fat activism. Anger was such a powerful emotion, so healing for me to express. I'm thinking about moments on the commuter train when people would say something about my body or what I was wearing, and I would get in their faces, stare them down. Just that whole period of realizing I had the right to defend my body was deeply characterized by anger." This sense that anger operated as transformational catharsis was echoed frequently in conversations with fat activists. Tovar also remembered a time when she went to a museum opening dressed in a way that felt openly defiant of typical fashion norms for fat women: "When I think of defiance, I think specifically about this period where I was doing over-the-top, hyperbolic, almost like monstrous femininity, just to articulate my gender very aggressively as a fat woman to absurdly create discomfort. . . . I'm here with my fat brown body, and my socks and my sandals and my cleavage and my fatness and my mustache that I've drawn on, and you can't do anything because your respectability demands that you keep it together."[5] The direct sense of using the body to express outrage and defiance, and using the fat body to purposefully break rules, gave angry fat embodiment a concrete form.

Similarly, Tigress Osborn felt that framing her body as an explicit form of rebellion helped her to link together fatness, anger, and defiance: "I saw this saying, 'When people tell me that I'm brave, I'm not brave. I'm rebellious.' That is one of those things I always want to remind myself of that empowers me, that even when I am afraid of something around showing my body, or being in a place with this body, or being the only person in a place with a body like this, that sort of ownership of that rebellious identity is radical in a political sense. I always feel inspired by the rad fatties in my life who know that rebellion and nonconformity go together." For Osborn, inserting her fat body into public spaces was itself a radical act. She also elaborated that she had multiple targets for her anger when she reflected on the mistreatment of fat people: "I stay mad at the state of the world, and I tend to be a smart-ass around the things I'm most angry about. I sound like I'm laughing, but I'm mad." She constructed anger as a necessity for those being subjected to mistreatment: "Fat people *should* be angry! And Black people should be angry, and people who can't handle that anger should be looking at themselves, not the angry people. I'm a fat Black woman. When I tell you I stay mad, I want people to know that!"[6] This insistence on the politically transformative power of anger, and the necessity of not surrendering or blunting the impact of that anger, drove her ability to both see and enact social change.

Basing anger and defiance on embodiment and feeling pushed out of view, Caleb Luna focused on how few clothing options were available to them and how clothing sizes prioritized certain bodies and denigrated others.

Reacting to the metric of normality set by clothing manufacturers, Luna became aware of their body as devalued and unrecognizable to the fashion world. They sometimes intentionally used too-small clothing as a point of defiance: "When the 2X shirt would no longer fully cover my belly, I would just let my belly hang out underneath and walk around that way being like, 'I don't know what else to do. If you want me to cover my body, you have to provide resources for me to cover my body.' But also, I was just like, 'Fuck you!' This is an accessory and that's kind of how I would like to treat it." Commenting on how people reacted, Luna said, "People were very upset when I would just let my belly hang out. I found it to be such an empowering move to remind people that (a.) There's a person on the other side of your gaze, and (b.) Fuck you. I would just return eye contact and stare them down."[7] This transformation from seeing the fat body as *subjected to* the whims of the fashion world to intentionally defying and challenging it, even at great social and personal cost, moved Luna from internalized shame to externally based anger.

For Luna, they also channeled anger through their experiences with the medical system, particularly in its lethal treatment of fat people: "It's all a capitalist farce. When I made the connection that somebody else is profiting off of me feeling bad about myself and they're making me feel bad about myself so they can profit, that's when I was just like, 'Fuck you. No, you don't get to do that.' I just have ongoing anger about the way fat people are treated and especially in terms of the way that healthcare gets weaponized so regularly, easily, without any sort of awareness that we live in a deeply unhealthy world." The recognition of the capitalist motive to profit off of fat suffering, and to perpetuate and exacerbate the shame and loathing of fat bodies, drove Luna's activism. They also felt transformed by personal experiences with medical mistreatment: "As somebody who became more disabled through medical malpractice that was fueled by fat phobia, seeing the ways that fat phobia was a danger to my health specifically and then to have that turned around as if health is something solely within my control and my responsibility to be blamed and punished for, that is something that makes me fucking furious."[8] The shirking of responsibility from larger institutions, particularly the medical world, and the impact of that on individual and collective fat lives, sparked activist sensibilities as well.

In a similar way, Da'Shaun Harrison also talked about how their experiences with feeling defiant about their body as a teenager in response to medical mistreatment catalyzed their later anger about fat phobia. They recalled meeting with a guidance counselor: "I remember sitting in her office and going off on her too because I just couldn't believe that I was being treated in such a way. At the time I chalked it up to racism alone, but I know now that so much about that was because I was not just Black but also because I was fat and disabled." Harrison felt proud of pushing back against those forces, even as a child: "To be able to show up in that space, while I had doctors who were antagonizing me, while I had teachers and school leadership who were antagonizing me, I was able to show up for myself and my body to be able to advocate on behalf of myself and my body in ways that lots of folks who are adults are not able to do. I definitely think of those moments as both anger and defiance."[9] For Harrison and other fat activists, the recognition of inequality and mistreatment started early on and required defiance not only against individual people but entire institutions.

Stacy Bias felt that the stakes of fat activism had a life-and-death quality, and that anger had a central (but sometimes confusing) role in that: "I struggle with anger. The most angry I have ever been around bodies was when my friend [burlesque performer and fat activist] Heather MacAllister died because she was misdiagnosed due to her fatness. They missed her cancer after multiple doctors' visits and she died, and it was a quite painful death. She had gone to the doctors complaining about different symptoms and they had just been like, 'Lose weight,' and didn't do anything and then her cancer got more advanced. She was stage four by the time she was diagnosed. There are all sorts of injustices that happen but that one happened right up close, and watching what she went through unnecessarily and just how vibrant she was and how much I miss her, how much she would have given and continued to give to the world." This understanding that antifatness can and does kill fat people drove intense fat rage. Bias also felt angry in a broader way about the treatment of fat bodies: "There's a willful lack of understanding about fat bodies. This individualizing the response to a lack of wellness in general, the lack of understanding of systemic inequality and oppression and marginalization and the impact that has on individual health bothers me. That is infuriating and intentional and cruel and it benefits only the most privileged in society but is perpetuated by everyone because we're so indoctrinated. That lack of awareness is devastating."[10] The seriousness of the stakes of neglecting, ignoring, and mistreating fat people, particularly due to ignorance about medical treatment, catalyzed fat activist sentiments.

Fat activists also expressed anger about the ways that people made assumptions about fat people and why they became fat. Esther Rothblum felt angry at the attributions people made about fatness, particularly as they assumed that poverty *caused* fatness when data showed the exact opposite: "When I tell students there's a very strong relationship between weight and income, the richer you are, the thinner you are, I ask them why. They will always say something like, 'Well, fat people are poor because they eat food that's high in calories because they can't afford any vegetables,' or 'They eat macaroni and cheese, which is cheaper,' or 'Fat people are poor because they can't afford to join fitness clubs, which are very expensive,' or 'Poor people work several jobs so they can't exercise.' What they're saying is: First you are poor, and because you are poor, you become fat. The data show the opposite, that fatness *causes* poverty. There is so much employment discrimination, including discrimination getting into elite colleges even. Fatter people drift into lower incomes. I guess that's an example of the assumption that fat people are lazy."[11] Rothblum's activist sensibilities showed up in the classroom, particularly as she worked to rewrite the story of fatness more accurately while challenging faulty assumptions about fat oppression.

Fat activists nurtured a perpetual sense of anger that drove their thinking about fatness and their priorities for activist work. Aubrey Gordon felt angry that fat people encountered such ubiquitous hostility in the world, which ultimately altered their social reality: "Just fucking everything makes me angry. It makes me angry that we can't get on a plane. It makes me angry that we can't go to a doctor's office. It makes me angry that we can't go to a restaurant. All of those things that thin people do every fucking day and don't have to think about, we have to fight for and then when we fight for it, we get mocked or ridiculed or downplayed or whatever, and there isn't really a track record of anybody taking that shit seriously! It makes me mad that the rational thing for fat people to do is to shrink our worlds into nothingness, knowing that the rest of the world is so fucking hostile." The sense that fat people had to struggle for things that thin people took for granted inspired deep anger for Gordon. She also felt explosive rage at the media's treatment of fat people, willingly humiliating fat bodies: "I would say the stuff that I feel most angry about is media portrayals of fat people. I don't know if there's anything that makes me angrier than *The Biggest Loser*. That is an evil fucking show! Just to have an entire show on national television in front of billions of people, that is stomach-churning, grotesque behavior."[12] In this sense, the hyper-normalization of fat humiliation sparked fury and recognition of systemic inequalities, and pushed for the necessity of collective social revolt.

MANIFESTING FAT ACTIVISM

Anger and fury, as well as a pivot from individual experiences to collective experiences, have ignited fat activism itself. The story of how people came to fat activism, and what ignited their interest in it, shows how people's entry points into resistance movements can be sudden or prolonged, explosive or slow-burning, immediate or evolving over time. Fat activists joined the work through a multitude of different channels, finding each other through networking or by accident, though knowing other fat activists was a crucial reason why many joined the movement.[13] While many were involved during a time when fat activism was more limited in scope, fat activists have also identified the ways that the world of fat activism has had explosive growth. Their stories serve as a reminder that the road into activism is complex and diverse, and that the work that matters spans a huge range of topics, subjects, and areas of focus.

Virgie Tovar talked about how she stumbled into fat activism through social networking: "Fat activism at that time was really small, really insular, so you kind of got word of it from somebody. Somebody would hear about you doing work in that area and would bring you in, they would initiate you. That's what happened to me. I got an email one day, and then I would meet [one of the founders of fat activism] Marilyn Wann. That was my whole world, very quickly. I didn't know fat activism existed. I didn't know how to look for it. I just heard about it through the grapevine and then I was there." This initiation into a community doing powerful new work around fat embodiment was a game-changer for Tovar, something many of us have felt when becoming newly acquainted with fat activism and its politics. Sensing its potential as fresh, scrappy, and explosive, Tovar felt emboldened by a collective sense of revolt that she found in queer fat activism: "I don't need your acceptance. I don't want your fucking boring-ass acceptance. I don't want to be 'normal' because 'normal' is complicit. Normal is boring. Normal is oppressive. I'm building something else. I'm building something you can't even imagine. It's so magical that you can't even imagine it!"[14] Like other movements built around anti-assimilation, fat activism has also reoriented toward fat bodies as emblems of resistance to patriarchal and heteronormative body norms.

About her recent transition to paid work in fat activism and advocacy, Tovar said, "I went from an activist to a business person, like an entrepreneur, unintentionally. I was being invited to lecture at universities. I was monetizing right out of grad school. . . . I've moved from an explicit 'fuck you' activist who's just super emotionally dysregulated, super broke, super deep in my feelings that I had been wronged by everyone and everything, to someone who is fairly emotionally self-regulated, who's in therapy, who teaches people how not to be a fat phobe at a tech company or something like that, the stuff that excites me has changed." The conflicts between grassroots fat activism and making money doing fat advocacy is still a tension for Tovar. She felt excited about the proliferation of fat activism far beyond the boundaries of when she started working in the community ten years ago: "I think it's extraordinary to see that fat activism has proliferated to the point that there are people doing fat work who have never heard of Marilyn Wann. The fact that you wouldn't have known who that person was ten years ago is unthinkable. Everybody knew who everybody was, and everybody was kind of on the same page. Now there's a proliferation of dozens of types of activism."[15] This expansion of fat activism, and the shift away from a monolithic set of goals, made space for fat activists who disagreed about the key issues but shared a common goal of ending anti-fat discrimination and harm.

In this sense, some fat activism has focused less on policy changes and aesthetics and more on play and fun through marginality. Tigress Osborn started engaging with fat activism through her nightclub event: "I decided to do my party so that the fat community would have more options. Everybody is welcome here, but I am unapologetic about marketing it towards people of color. As folks got that sense of 'This is something different than what these other nightclub folks have been doing,' it grew. I feel proud about having helped make those connections, an environment to foster those connections." The making of space for lively fat embodiment and fat joy was crucial to being able to do other fat activist work. Osborn also talked about how she dialed in with more fat activist circles after that: "When you're in the bay, if you start going to fat stuff, you're interacting with this sort of multigenerational fat activism community because people who were part of the Fat Underground were in the bay, and people who were in the early days of NAAFA were in the bay, and these other fat feminist collectives were all there."[16] While most places are just starting to have the first traces of fat activism, places like the San Francisco Bay Area and Portland, Oregon, have nurtured fat activism for far longer.

Other fat activists jumped into fat activist work through online spaces. Stacy Bias came to fat activism through her work on a website, which then blossomed into work with the fat community: "I used to run a website called TechnoDyke.com and it started in 1998 at the dawn of when people were using the internet for social reasons. This was in the first wave of queer websites so there were quite a few of us starting these little mini online empires. It became a big thing, like fifty thousand people a month coming on and two million page views. I hid myself within it."[17] Bias went to an event for the website and received more information about the emerging fat community there. From that point, Bias worked to create a new addition to the fat activist world: "That was sort of the moment when Fat Girl Speaks [an annual Portland-based day-long event with workshops, fashion shows, and fat-inclusive performances] sprung to mind, not born of any political understanding because I didn't know that fat activism existed, but I was doing something that I needed for myself. I didn't know that there was a whole historical movement attached to what I was doing and that's when I learned about the NAAFA conference." This momentum that built from fat activism online—something that would greatly impact later iterations of fat activism—began in the early days of the internet, showing again how new mediums can be leveraged for cutting-edge political work and community building, even as the movement continues to evolve and grow in and out of new spaces.

Bias has worked to create entire new online communities that coalesce around different fat activist goals. Reflecting on the activism that matters most to her, Bias talked about issues of access and her project of addressing stigma for fat people while flying on airplanes: "*Flying While Fat* is my primary activism right now. It started as a blog post because of dating long distance." Remembering how she went on a family trip during which she was handed a second plane ticket to sit more comfortably, Bias said, "I was not ready for somebody to tell me I was two seats worth of fat, and so I refused to sit in it for the entire flight, and then I just didn't fly again for a really long time. It ruined me for flying."[18] Building on that blog post, she developed a Facebook group, a *Flying While Fat* animation, and fat activist interest groups online that work on consciousness-raising and public-policy pressures.

Others came into fat activism through research and university teaching, particularly when fatness was continually left out of conversations about oppression and marginalization. Esther Rothblum remembers that she was initially hired to do research on lesbians and LGBT people but later transitioned to fat studies. Remembering how almost no one researched fatness in those days, Rothblum recalled connecting with the early iterations of fat activism in the San Francisco Bay Area: "There was NAAFA, there was the Fat Underground, but there were few people doing work back then. I was kind of working this area in isolation. It was very hard to get published. . . . When I did stuff on fat studies, I had a slideshow of what the reviewers would say and it would be one rejection after another, one journal after another, including one editor who once said, 'Whereas I normally encourage authors to keep writing in their area, in this case I would actually suggest you do something else.'"[19] The fight against the anti-fat tendencies of academia has been a tall order for many fat activists, particularly those like Rothblum at the forefront of establishing fat studies as a field.

Mikey Mercedes came to fat activism by noticing the problematic rhetoric around fatness in her public health PhD program: "I'm the only fat PhD student who's ever been in my program as far as I know. People in my department are very into 'obesity' prevention. The students who come in are very much like the professors. . . . The first fat studies article I read was Cat Pausé's 'Borderline' article, which was such a perfect one because it's specifically about stigma in public health campaigns, and I remember reading it, and it just blew my fucking mind. I felt like nothing else is real. This is real. It was just amazing, like someone had ripped words out of my head and put them together and then put them on paper but so much more beautifully than I could have managed because at that point I didn't have the language that Cat did."[20] This discovery of fat activist writing propelled her toward doing more radical work of her own. Reflecting on the fat activism she is most proud of and drawn to, Mercedes said, "I am definitely happy that more people are paying attention to the specific overlap between anti-Blackness and anti-fatness as it exists. I know that victory is happening right now because there's so much fucking backlash each and every day to every small thing that a fat person points out or says or analyzes regardless of the lens of fat liberation or fat studies. People get so shook! I can see that shift happening in real time and it's exciting." The movement toward a more radical fat activism—one where analyses of oppression happen on a more structural and emotional level—energized many fat activists.

In a related way, fat activists have used their own pain to catalyze a shift toward activist work. Aubrey Gordon felt drawn to the work of other fat writers and activists who understood the fusion of anger and sadness: "The thing that's always under anger for me is hurt, because anger just always comes from hurt, and it felt really important and meaningful to have someone speak to both of those places at once." She also appreciated the move in fat activism away from self-love rhetoric and more toward transformative social change. Gordon wanted a more grounded, concrete, material shift in how fatness was treated by activists. As such, in her own work, she wanted to target well-intentioned thin people to help them understand the ways they were hurting fat people: "There was something about writing in this direct [way] 'You're my friend and I love you, and that's why I need you to know that you're really hurting me. I just want you to stop doing this thing because it's really, really hurtful.' There's nothing that will make thin people hear all of it, but it felt like, 'Okay, you're hearing 3 percent more of it. I'll take it!' It felt both important and extremely taxing to write in a way that held thin people's humanity while talking about how hurtful it can be. That's a big task, and that's a thing I largely avoid doing in my own personal life." She added, "I wanted to tell the truth in its fullness and also speak from a place of hurt, the vulnerable emotion underneath, where anger is like the armor emotion and hurt is the softness that armor is protecting."[21] Gordon's work has solidified a recognition of fat activism as a movement that draws from both vulnerability and anger.

Fat activists also arrived at fat activism by connecting to its militant, defiant, in-your-face spirit. Caleb Luna came to fat activism by watching the comedian Margaret Cho and her outlandish and audacious embodiment during her stand-up specials: "It's so racist and misogynist the way she was treated, but hearing her process it and refuse it, make space for it, made me wonder, 'What if I stopped worrying about losing weight? How much time would I have in my life? What would that open up for me?' Hearing Cho talk about women's magazines and how they are trying to teach women how to position their bodies during sex so that they look less fat, and her saying, 'If you care about what I look like when you're fucking me, then you shouldn't be fucking me in the first place!' It seeped into my brain and gave me all these nuggets of refusal and empowerment and comfort with my body, especially her also being queer, slutty, and a person of color."[22]

Speaking of their current work, Luna focused on how they currently embrace fat embodiment, teach differently about fatness, and work on making more public space for fat resistance: "I feel very fat positive and I'm always trying to uplift fatness holistically and visually." They added, "I also teach fat studies classes which has been a real challenge especially at UC Berkeley because there are almost no fat undergrads and that is not seen as weird. That's seen as something where obviously there are no fat undergrads because fat people aren't smart because they aren't rigorous because they couldn't have made it to this space, or because they're too dumb and poor and that's why they're fat, or they're too Black or Brown and poor and that's why they're fat, and all of those categories of people are excluded from the university setting. I realized teaching these thin undergrads that everyone is so traumatized by fatness and so many of them have histories of disordered eating or body dysmorphia or colorism from their family, or experiencing some sort of body shame from their family that fatness offers an entry point for."[23] This awareness of who is excluded and who is included, and the stakes of anti-fatness for all bodies, has pushed Luna toward more explicit acts of defiance both personally and professionally, such as their podcast and social media activism.

As fat activism spawns new cohorts, leaders, and voices, the sense of fat activism as having generative power has also increased. Da'Shaun Harrison discovered fat activism through the fat activists Caleb Luna and Aubrey Gordon, building on the genealogy of fat activists who came before them: "I found all these works mesmerizing because there was a language to describe my experience. It changed everything about how I was engaging my body and engaging fatness. I was just so intrigued and so grateful for having found language that honored my reality, but I also felt very excluded because it was also very white and very specific to cis women and that's not who I am: cis, white, or woman. It led me to do more writing about my experience as a Black, fat, non-binary trans person and what that looks like and what that means and how that experience happens in life, and now here I am. . . . I think the years 2017–19 were foundational for me and determining what my fat politics were, what it looked like, and what *Belly of the Beast* would become."[24] As more fat activists work to expand the movement and include more diverse perspectives and experiences, the goals, tactics, priorities, and critiques sometimes get pushed toward more robust and subversive analyses of anti-fat oppression.

Ultimately, fat activism may have started as a movement that pushed for people to feel better in their bodies, but it has evolved far beyond self-love in its current iterations. Kimberly Dark said her entry into fat activism came when she stopped dieting and went into performance work: "Once I started reading about and learning about the embodied storyteller on stage, it was complicated. If I never talked about being fat, I am still visibly fat on the stage, just like if I never talked about being queer, I am still visibly queer in one embodiment of queerness on the stage." Based on this, she began to write and perform about multiple identities at once: "This is part of the book that I wrote, *Fat, Pretty, and Soon to Be Old*, because 'fat' and 'old' are words that we think of as insults even though they are neutral kind of descriptions, and 'pretty' is something you're supposed to strive for but you're never supposed to say about yourself. Pretty mitigates fat or old, or fat or old could ease pretty, right? We're constantly in this, 'Do I have enough of this to erase that, or is there more of this now? If folks do not start to understand the way that hidden architecture of everyday life works, we have no prayer of dismantling things like white supremacy and sexism." She also situated the benefits of fat activism as needing to reach beyond those who already have power wanting to feel better about their bodies: "Fat activism is part of a broader agenda to help people understand that hierarchy based on appearance and privilege is fucked up, and maybe the goal is not to eradicate it, because I don't think that's possible among humans, but we can certainly diminish its impact by a lot before we start having conversations about whether we can get rid of it entirely. Because, fuck me, if somebody had told me thirty years ago that a whole lot of my life would be spent on college campuses hugging slender white blonde women while they cry about their appearance at the end of my shows, I would have been like, 'How did this happen?!' Those are the women who feel entitled to come and show their emotion, but that can't be the goal of our work can't be to make slender blonde white girls feel better about themselves. There's got to be a crushing of the system of hierarchy at some point that actually benefits people of color and women and disabled and fat people first!"[25] In many ways, this self-reflexivity of fat activists has itself pushed fat activism to do far more than mere body positivity work.

Reflecting on what fat activism can do, Dark talked energetically about the evidence of how social norms are already changing: "I think things can change more easily than we think they do. They change with things like Lizzo's new show about fat dancers. They change with think pieces about people's cherished family members they've lost. They change with images in media. We're not trying to pry loose the natural order. We're just trying to shift cultural views and that happens all the time, *all the time.*" She mused: "I think that we keep doing our thing. You don't know when the lynchpin gets pulled. You don't know."[26]

CHANGING THE SYSTEM, OR BURNING IT DOWN?

This radical sense of working to destabilize norms, unsettle structures of power, and dismantle the frameworks that drive the mistreatment of fat people pushed fat activism toward both nuance and expansion. While much of this work focused on more radical, sweeping, *burn-it-down* type of macro goals, some fat activist work looked at the smaller micro-level aspects of fat oppression such as antidiscrimination laws. While not all fat activists felt energized by within-system, policy-level changes to how fat people were treated in the public sphere, many felt that policy changes could have material impacts on fat people's lives and could interface well with more radical visions for fat liberation. The question of whether incremental changes mattered, and what specific changes could have an impact, speaks to the more micro-level, on-the-ground, could-happen-now style of changes that fat activists wanted. When I asked fat activists what policy changes they would like to see that could improve fat people's lives, most eagerly offered ideas based on the work they had done and the changes they saw as possible and much needed.

Many fat activists listed a number of policy and legislative changes they supported, namely around banning weight discrimination. Barbara Bruno felt that our government needed to enact weight discrimination bans immediately: "There's only Michigan, Santa Cruz, and San Francisco that have banned it. Having size and weight discrimination illegal across the US is very important."[27] Esther Rothblum noted that policy changes mattered because they start to feel normal and inevitable once they are put into law: "When laws change, people tend to act like those laws have always been there, like with same-sex marriage. That's why it was so threatening to the conservatives. They knew once it happened people would just act like it's always been there. That's why ending *Roe v. Wade* is going to be such a terrible thing, because people just assumed abortions were legal. I think that having more states have weight legislation on nondiscrimination would be great. That would be a really big one, and then hopefully it would filter down to these nondiscrimination statements that universities and hospitals have."[28] Banning weight discrimination could build quick momentum and retrain people's thinking about the supposed acceptability of anti-fat biases.

Virgie Tovar wanted, in addition to banning weight discrimination, more accountability in fashion, healthcare, and other settings that oppress fat people: "I think that it should be mandatory in medical school to understand the actual reality of weight science and the fact that fat people don't become dead people. I think they need to be taught that. I think we need to get rid of BMI completely. I think we need to adopt Health at Every Size in all settings and weight neutrality in all settings. I think that fashion companies need to undergo changes where fatness and anti-fat phobia need to become part of DEI work across the board. I think we need to reorient the entire system of sizing so that fashion companies make extended sizing. Universal standard actually kind of does something. If the average American woman is a size 18, then that's a medium because that's what medium comes from. Plus-size fashion isn't really even taught in fashion school. It needs to be taught and there needs to be campaigns that normalize being fat." She added, "I think the entire diet industry needs to be eradicated. I think that if we just decided that we were going to require every company that is trying to promote weight loss to show the evidence that this works at any kind of scalable size or proportion, it would instantly fold overnight. That's just the beginning of what I'm thinking!"[29] These ambitious within-system goals also show that once certain kinds of thinking change—for example, the belief that fat people could just lose weight if they tried harder—many parts of the systems that entrench anti-fatness could topple.

Reflecting on the more minute and mundane forms of discrimination, Kimberly Dark recalled being blocked from becoming a Jazzercise instructor because of weight and knowing a woman who filed a lawsuit against Jazzercise for size discrimination. She also was denied long-term disability insurance because of her size. Dark felt that chipping away at the norms of weight discrimination eventually accumulated into larger-scale changes: "I do think that all these tiny little things that we do, that all of us can do, are somehow important because the whole social change thing is like water seeping into granite, and granite is strong. At some point, though, the water starts to get into the rock and at some point, inexplicably, giant boulders break off." Each small battle matters, though she also argued for striving toward bigger and more extensive changes: "Bigger policies are also super important. Anything that reaffirms our humanity and redirects the discussion on health to environmental factors rather than personal behavior is powerfully important because we are dying on the altar of personal behavioral change. That is harmful to everybody, but for fat people it's super, super harmful. Your doctor can ignore any goddamn thing that's wrong with you and tell you to go and lose weight, and so anything that brings a focus back on poverty, clean water, genetic propensities to weight gain, is good. It doesn't matter what made you fat. You're fat, so what?"[30] This refusal to allow etiological discussions to govern fat people's rights also drew a boundary against the "Fat people deserve it!" rhetoric that often limited broader changes in anti-fat discrimination.

Stacy Bias agreed, adding that policies preventing medical discrimination are essential to fat activism: "I think that we just need to fucking understand biology and medical school is a really good place to start. This narrative of long-term sustained weight loss should get truly and finally challenged. We really need to stop pushing surgeries for weight loss and then denying fat people for surgeries they need, like a knee replacement. We need to stop allowing doctors to deny services because they don't want to deal with anesthesia. Maybe you just need to train the anesthesiologist better! There needs to be better solutions than just making fat people suffer."[31] Again, the view of smaller policy-level changes, such as better anesthesiologist training, driving the more ambitious goals of widespread attitude changes toward fat people showed how and why policy and education matter in the struggle for fat people to win rights, recognition, and access to good medical care.

Touting the harm-reduction model of social change, Aubrey Gordon imagined a litany of policies that could quickly improve fat people's lives, particularly by reducing immediate harm: "We could just do so many things! We could add fat people and size to the list of protected classes that are protected from discrimination. That's a really easy thing we could do *today*. Lots and lots of communities and movements run those campaigns. It's not hard to do. It's just political will and there's zero political will to stand up for fat people." She went on, "I think the Seat Act [that would expand airplane seat sizes] is a really interesting bill that keeps getting stalled out even though people are furious at the airlines. People are more mad at airlines than they are invested in scapegoating fat people! I think the patient's Bill of Rights on fat stuff would be huge. I think that even outside of public policy, campaigns around reorganizing medical school curricula and advising against counseling fat patients about weight loss every visit (which is their current instruction) could help a lot. Doctors are being taught to ask *every visit* about weight loss. If we get them off of that, that would be a huge win. Also, every state has a list of things that can't be considered conditions for removing a child from their home, and I think it would be a very good and easy thing to do to add that kids' weight should not be a reason. A kid's body size is not a reason to take them away from their parents." Thinking about the difference between policy changes and radical social change, Gordon said, "All of those things fit under the header, to me, of harm reduction. None of those fit under the header of liberation. All of those are just like, 'How do we get our basic needs met?'"[32] As Gordon senses, getting access to basic needs, and being able to interface with institutions without constantly experiencing discrimination, have the potential to shift the structures that currently enshrine anti-fatness as normal and pervasive.

Tigress Osborn struggled between her impulses toward harm reduction and policy changes, and more radical critiques of anti-fat rhetoric: "I believe policy can work. We want to see federal changes to the Civil Rights Act to include weight discrimination. Policy helps with recourse when someone is mistreated and it helps to prevent mistreatment, at least in certain areas. It's kind of the best system we have right now. I'm not always like, 'Burn down the whole system,' as some of my most radicalized friends are. I'm much more of, 'Okay but this is harm reduction, working within the system is a type of harm reduction.' But I still have a lot of 'Burn it down' too! I still think it's worthwhile to pursue civil rights legislation at a state and federal level." Osborn also wanted activists to think more about how people use their money as a form of power.[33] This effort to try to do both harm reduction and sweeping changes was a common thread in many fat activists' narratives.

Pushing against policy-only changes, some fat activists felt that policy changes left anti-fatness intact and did not challenge the fundamentally destructive qualities that drove those belief systems. Da'Shaun Harrison expressed skepticism about policy implementation and whether anyone would actually uphold anti-fat policies as long as the ideology of anti-fatness guided the culture at large: "I don't think any policy change will have an immediate effect on fat people's lives. I wish it did, but I think that the last few years have made very clear to me that policy doesn't really matter and that lawmakers and folks with authority in the world will do what they want to do, and so I'm not convinced that any policy would actually directly or immediately benefit fat folks. It would be nice to be able to have some legal protections to not be fired just because we're fat, but who's to say that a judge will actually care if that goes to court? I think it would be nice to have legal protections against misdiagnosing us or un-diagnosing us, but who's to say that a judge will care if it goes to court? So little policy seems to matter ever."[34] Similarly, Caleb Luna laid out their belief that empire and colonialism drove anti-fatness and needed to be abolished before policy-level changes could matter: "The only policy change I'm interested in is the United States to dissolve itself. What the world needs is for this empire to collapse in on itself, but being in the middle of it when it's happening is sure not fun. We need to scale back this hugely shitty society that has been forced on all of us. It has to go."[35] In this sense, fat activists felt impatient about the dominance of within-system changes at the expense of more radical activist work to dismantle systems in their entirety.

The problems of anti-fatness felt vast and often infuriating and, as such, not prone to easy fixes through policy-level changes. Mikey Mercedes struggled to reconcile how policy changes could equitably impact fat people when so many fat people faced other kinds of marginalization that also needed addressing: "I don't have any hope in size discrimination laws, mostly because the current laws we have don't do what they're supposed to do. There are plenty of people who cannot access the protection of these discrimination laws and I don't really see why we should be putting any time or attention into getting something like size recognized as a protected characteristic if the other protected characteristics we have belong to marginalized people who are still marginalized by the fucking system. There's also a lot of the weight-loss industry that is using things like size-based discrimination and policy advocacy to sell weight-loss products to us!" Mercedes worried about the lack of efficacy in existing systems of antidiscrimination laws. Further, she adamantly wanted more radical critiques and transformative change: "The best things that could help fat people are the things that help all people. We need things like universal healthcare. We need reparations. We need policies that shift the balance of wealth and power towards people who are the most marginalized. We need to pay attention to things like labor rights, particularly the literal environments in which people work that are shitty and exploitative and sickening and dangerous that plenty of the poorest, fattest, Blackest people in this country have to work in and are regularly exploited in. That is the reason that we don't get to thrive, because we're stuck in these incredibly exploitative positions to fund our survival and the survival of our families and communities. I think that the policies we should be advocating for are policies that get material, tangible benefits into the hands of fat people, and not any of this other shit that's feel-goody-goody but doesn't actually do anything."[36] The focus on efficacy, vision, intersectional analysis, and challenges to institutions that ignore and degrade so many people (fat or otherwise) has revealed the range of priorities for fat activists, both within and outside of existing systems.

THE FUTURE OF FAT ACTIVISM

While much fat activist work has been rooted in anger and driven by the recognition of structural inequality, there is also a deep level of hope that informs activist work. Without a vision for a better world, for what could be possible, activists would languish in despair at the inadequacy and unevenness of the work they do. Looking to the future of fat activism, fat activists talked about their vision for a world yet to come. Possibilities were envisioned as both small and large, manageable and ambitious, within-system and more fundamental. Many focused on changes they wanted to see in their lifetimes, though some imagined the world of fat activism far beyond those boundaries.

Reflecting on the future, Stacy Bias envisioned a fat activism where people's needs connect them immediately with resources and people who can help, and where access issues have made huge strides: "I would love to see more engagement with science, education, fat people in science, medicine, engineering, in all the jobs where access issues are decided. I want to see fat folks have equal opportunity in educational settings, even fitting into a seat at the university. Even the level of just physically going to university, there needs to be changes. We really need systematic change in terms of access at every point. I would love to see fat activism addressing and creating a mentoring system. If I was to start another fat activist project with infinite energy, which I do not have, and infinite resources, which none of us have, it would be to create a sort of mentorship umbrella organization which is tasked entirely with city by city, state by state, country by country, creating and mentoring individuals to enter fights at various levels and training and education."[37] Imagining how to more efficiently and effectively connect fat people to those who could meet their access needs would create a world where individual fat people do not flounder within (or get crushed by) systems that fail them.

Also wanting to ground future activist work in the material realities of fat people's lives, Aubrey Gordon wanted future fat activists to concretely make fat people's lives better and more livable: "In my dream world, fat activism is continuing to hammer on institutional decision-making, like the size of airplane seats. Continuing to hammer on those kinds of institutional policies all the way up to nutritional guidance for schools, all the way up to the food pyramid and MyPlate, to addressing the 'obesity' epidemic—big and small—I would like to see us continue to hammer on that. I would love to see us continue on this path of chasing down the roots of anti-fatness, from histories of dieting to histories of anti-Blackness to histories of ableism and all of that. I think that picture is still snapping into focus in ways that feel really fruitful and good." She also wanted people to connect their anger and fury about anti-fatness to community-level activist work: "The other thing I hope for is real, meaningful, and effective accountability for people who are actively engaged in anti-fatness, whether or not they think they are. I would love to see work more as a movement. What ends up happening often now is that fat people rightly have a lot of anger about the ways that we've been treated, and we lead with that anger. For some people that works and for others it doesn't work. We're just not being totally thoughtful about it because we don't have any fucking resources, and we don't have any people to talk to! I would love for us to get to a point where folks feel resourced and supported enough to be thoughtful about meeting their own needs versus engaging in change work. You're allowed to do both and you're allowed to do neither. We need to have conversations about what to do with very real, very deep feelings, and how to tend to those for yourself, and then, once you've done that, maybe you feel like doing more change work with other individual people in your life. That's the point at which you really start making some meaningful dents."[38] Transforming rage into action, anger into solidarity, would make fat activism even more powerful and impactful.

Focusing on within-system changes, Esther Rothblum wanted to keep focusing on publishing as an avenue to extend fat activist work, but she also worried about future crises that would generate a greater need for bolder fat activism: "Because my activism is getting people to publish, I think it's fabulous that there is so much being published all over the world and in many different journals and disciplines and books, because really the written word is hard to destroy. It will be there long after our lifetimes, so that's really important. I'm just happy that that is happening. Unfortunately, it often takes a real crisis to move things. Black Lives Matter really started with this horrible murder of George Floyd. The #MeToo movement started, obviously, with women being raped or assaulted. I'm just hoping really there won't be some major murder or issue for fat activism."[39] This fear that social movements require violent crises in order to move the dial was rooted in the lessons of these adjacent movements. In a related way, Kimberly Dark wanted fat activism to continue its push to value intersectionality and to center those on the margins: "The future of fat activism is intersectional. It has to be. We have to learn solidarity across issues. We have to take our personal experiences with marginalization and apply them everywhere they are relevant, and that means fighting the urge to say you are better than somebody else."[40] This reminder of solidarity as a growing necessity, and crisis as a catalyst for more visibility and change, was a double-edged sword for imagining fat activist futures.

In many ways, the future of fat activism coalesces around imagining new freedoms—to live well, get proper care, and thrive. Caleb Luna wanted the future of fat activism to upend common medical assumptions about fat bodies in more aggressive ways: "I would love for it to actually focus on the medical industrial complex and to break down the ways that our bodies are medicalized, and the ways that bariatric surgery is prescribed and recommended alongside all forms of weight-loss fucking bullshit."[41] To imagine a medical language of health and well-being that does not involve treating fat bodies as inherent failures would be a notable step toward a different future.

The belief that anger could transform how fat people saw themselves, and what they expected from systems and institutions, also generated a strong sense of hope. Virgie Tovar believed that many improvements were in reach in her immediate lifetime and imagined that fat activism would be transformative in many arenas, particularly if powerful entities admitted culpability and wrongdoing: "The big thing that's much harder to legislate is the healing part. I'd really like to see that and it's really hard to know how to do that because everybody needs a little something slightly different to heal. I don't know yet what that looks like on a culture-wide scale. What's really hard is that a lot of fat people feel gaslit right now, like they can't even access anger because they really do believe that it's their fault that they're fat because that's what they've been taught. They feel they don't have the right to be angry, and I think we need to change that. At some point, important powerful people need to do some course correcting. I'm thinking of the American Medical Association going on the record saying that they were wrong and they harmed people and they're going to do everything they can to right the ship. That would be massive for people!"[42] If fat people can move from blaming themselves and seeing themselves as the problem to understanding that their bodies exist in systems that have largely failed them, their anger could transform the experience of fat embodiment.

The future of fat activism might mean juggling the need to survive and the need to thrive. Mikey Mercedes also felt that changes to healthcare were crucial for fat justice: "I really want us to start a campaign to abolish the BMI. It is the most popular tool for rationing care in our healthcare system. It kills us. It literally endangers our lives and gives doctors a starting-off point with which to admonish and discriminate against us and to deny us lifesaving procedures, treatments, and services." She qualified this by saying that within-system changes are not usually her forte: "I don't have a ton of hope in changing the healthcare system as it is. I'm very much a 'Let's burn this down and then start over from anew' kind of girl, but there *are* things we can do in order to increase the chances of fat people surviving in the system that we have. I want us to establish more direct-aid networks. I want fat people making art, creating things, creating organizations, building community and amongst one another, doing our thing. It's not fast work, but it's important work and it needs to be done. I want us to have places to come together to do political education. I just want us to be present and visible, and visibility isn't the mark of how successful something is, but I feel like fat activism has hidden for so long and it's not getting us anywhere. My biggest goal, at least before I'm dead, is just that I want people to be aware of fat activism on a grand scale, and I want people to know that it is okay and acceptable and almost paramount for them to accept their fatness as an identity. That really impacts the way that they move throughout the world and it's okay to be proud of it!"[43] The process of building community, destigmatizing fat bodies, and working to topple dangerous and destructive systems would, in this future vision, become turbocharged.

As the fat activist movement grows larger and garners more successes, there is also the risk of being appropriated and distorted. Tigress Osborn imagined the future of fat activism as one where we have to get smarter and savvier about the co-optation of fat liberation rhetoric: "The biggest challenge facing fat liberation is the way in which other forces have gotten really smart about co-opting the language of fat liberation. Some of the most visible work around weight stigma in medical care, which is one of the biggest challenges that fat people face, is from anti-obesity groups who are running these weight stigma campaigns! You want to talk about being mad? The Obesity Action Coalition is running a stop weight stigma campaign. *You are weight stigma.* You are definitely weight stigma. You are wolves in sheep's clothing, running the fucking world. Fucking Noom and Weight Watchers. Even if you're the best of diet culture, we know you're diet culture. These medical organizations that claim to be doing things in the best interest of fat people when what they mean is doing things in the best interest of *eliminating* fat people, they are infuriating and powerful. Internet trolls are one thing—they're louder than us and they don't have pharmaceutical money. These people in the medical industry have billions and billions of dollars and claim to be for us and have our best interest at heart, when really, they are underscoring and funding things that kill us. That's the danger to the future of the movement."[44] Building new ways to challenge and combat these forms of co-optation and appropriation underscores the need for more critical education, stronger community ties, and finding ways to stay one step ahead of the grasp of capitalism.

The future of fat activism may also use anger, fury, and rage to destroy systems that harm fat people. Da'Shaun Harrison wanted to move far beyond within-system changes and instead focus on radical transformation of how fat bodies are seen and treated: "I think that so much fat activism right now on a mainstream level is so wrapped up in body positivity, and I think it's moving toward body neutrality, but even those fall significantly short for me. I have been referring to myself as a fat destructionist. It's very to-the-point about what my desires are and that is destruction of anti-fatness, of the structures in place that harm us, that violate us, that subjugate us, that objectify us. That's where I want us to go." Harrison assigned power to those efforts that tried to deeply understand vulnerability, protection, and care via destruction: "I think we have done enough of trying to wrap up our experiences in pretty, careful language for thin people to be able to understand, and I'm not interested in that. I think the fat activism that matters will have to move towards a fat destructionist lens that caters to, centers, and is thoughtful of the most vulnerable fat experiences with a radical analysis around it, and not something that softens the blow or doesn't really hold those of us who are actually fat in the ways that it should."[45] In this sense, the future of fat activism might be one that destroys in order to protect, that combats harm through militant protection of fat bodies and fat communities.

A FINAL MEDITATION ON FAT FURY

As a university student many years ago, I had a deep curiosity about many different subjects and areas of study. A lifelong music lover, I joined the university choir and started taking voice lessons to see if I could learn how to perform a proper aria. I worked with a vocal coach for six months when, one day, he declared to me, "Remember, it doesn't matter how talented you are if you're not thin. No one like you will ever make it in the music world with the body you have. If you want to succeed, you better lose weight." To add a final punch to this statement, he said, "The whole thing about the 'It ain't over until the fat lady sings' is just pure mythology." I recount this story not because it squashed my lifelong dream of being a professional singer (it didn't) or because it was particularly unique or memorable to me (it wasn't) or because it was especially cruel (in the scheme of other injuries and insults, it was fairly mellow). It did, however, epitomize the way that fat people's lives—particularly women's lives—are shaped by a gradual foreclosure of possibilities, a tamping down on different stories of the future. I remember hearing those comments and immediately just *accepting* that I would never sing professionally, with no questions asked. I just deleted it as an option, simply and unremarkably.

It is hard to do those kinds of inventories and reflections now. I like to think of myself as someone who has pounded down many doors, insisted radically on being myself, and worked hard to keep possibilities open. I want to understand myself as tenacious and strong, persistent and bold, shameless and risk-taking. And yet, it is impossible to fully understand how many parts of myself—how many parts of *ourselves*—simply comply with what the world has decided are the outer limits for fat people. It is a mournful thought, but also an infuriating one. I see in this book so many fat women struggling to make their way in a world that despises and limits them, that sees their bodies as pure liability. Many can barely imagine their bodies without shame and terror, and they sense, rightly, the stakes of it all: survival, dignity, care, affirmation. I hear the fat activists say how hard they have worked, and how much work there still is to do. Their fury is intoxicating and important, transformative even, and beneath it lies a yearning for a gentler world. They want to make space that can hold fat people's dignity and complexity, one that offers us so much more than we have now. It is their fury that creates this vision of gentleness, their anger that wants to soften some of this hardness. Their vision, too, is an electric, crackling yearning for a more vibrant, just, and righteous world, full of expanding possibilities, powerful new alliances, and outright embodied revolt. They are inviting us to join them in the struggle, knowing how much we all stand to gain by cultivating our collective fat fury.

Novelist Salman Rushdie, who has faced death threats and physical assaults for his work, writes of the paradoxes of fury itself: "Life is fury, he'd thought. Fury—sexual, Oedipal, political, magical, brutal—drives us to our finest heights and coarsest depths. Out of furia comes creation, inspiration, originality, passion, but also violence, pain, pure unafraid destruction, the giving and receiving of blows from which we never recover. The Furies pursue us; Shiva dances his furious dance to create and also to destroy."[46] Here, destruction and creation are synonymous. We destroy in order to create something new. At the center of this is fury, blazing forward, refusing any modicum of *Wait and see* and *Be patient* and *Small changes are best*. Fury is impatient and urgent, shattering the barriers of language and geography. It resists the simplicity and self-indulgence of despair. Fury is a relentless yearning—an expectation, a *demand*—that we can do better. It offers a way out from *the way it is*, paving the way toward *what could be*. It is passionate and inspired, unafraid of blowback, and full of fire. Fat fury, too, is a force, a momentum, a way through, pushing into a future only beginning to take shape.

ACKNOWLEDGMENTS

A book as painful and infuriating as this could never exist without others holding space for me to write it. They have nurtured and loved me, shared in my outrage and despair, and helped to build a world where we can understand and imagine fatness differently. I have felt during these years of writing that this book is made of my skin, that it is more than a cerebral exercise to take on the weighty and explosive topics that this book engages. In this way, the book has been a wound, a catharsis, a transformative process, and one that has called upon an unusual amount of heavy lifting from the circles of friends, family, and comrades around me.

First and foremost, I want to thank the people I interviewed for this book. Speaking first with fat women from around the country about their intimate experiences of their bodies provided such illuminating, maddening, and necessary stories of what fatness feels like for women as they move through the world. While they remain anonymous, I thank them again and again. Having the opportunity to then interview ten prominent fat activists—in their radical, wild, awe-inspiring modes of resistance and revolt—provided a pivotal shift to the arc of this book and to my own sense of fat community and fat possibilities. Thanks to Stacy Bias, Barbara Bruno, Kimberly Dark, Aubrey Gordon, Da'Shaun Harrison, Caleb Luna, Mikey Mercedes, Tigress Osborn, Esther Rothblum, and Virgie Tovar. They are the embodiment of hope and fury, and I am forever in their debt.

I could never have written a book about fatness without a community of feminist thinkers and scholars around me who value and prioritize feminist solidarity and the politics of the body. They understand the dialectic between struggle and joy, and have informed so much of who I am and how I write. Thank you to Jane Caputi, Abby Stewart, Ti-Grace Atkinson, Roxanne Dunbar-Ortiz, Jessa Crispin, Virginia Braun, Ela Przybylo, Leonore Tiefer,

Jane Ussher, Janette Perz, Inga Winkler, Tomi-Ann Roberts, Alex Hawkey, Marlene Tromp, Michelle Tea, Soraya Chemaly, Rebecca Plante, Deborah Tolman, Carla Golden, Phyllis Chesler, Jill Wood, Larin McLaughlin, Jessie Kindig, Amy Scholder, and Monica Casper. I am also grateful to the Society for Menstrual Cycle Research and the Menstruation and Society Seminar at Columbia University for creating space to think about abjection, embodiment, intersectionality, and resistance. Most especially, I thank Adrielle Munger, who read every word of this book and whose edits and feedback have felt like a love letter to a long-standing feminist friendship.

I owe a special debt to the Feminist Research on Gender and Sexuality Group—the FROGS—who have supported this book from day one. We have grappled together with the overarching frameworks and the nitty-gritty details of this book, and many of them lent a hand with transcribing interviews, finding research articles, editing chapters, and thinking together about how to speak about fatness to multiple audiences. I am particularly humbled by the unfaltering support of Mikhail "Micah" Collins, whose generosity of spirit and time, sharp mind, and unfailing kindness have fueled me along. A heartfelt thanks to the whole team who worked on this book: Kasey Kutcher, Kiley Romano, Felicya Ptak, Serenity Garcia, Lily Moskowitz, Audrey Zelinka, Kaitlyn Bowe, Ana Ruiz, Isabella Boker, Alyssa Gerkin, Farhat Ali, Caroline Rudel, Loralei Cook, Morgan Lucero, Marli Mayon, Sydnee Carey, and Tess Clark. Thanks also to the rest of the FROGS, all of whom embody that wonderful mix of goodwill and a spirit of resistance: Claire Halling, Alexis Starks, Rachel Caldwell, Jakob Salazar, Decker Dunlop, Michael Karger, Stephanie Voelker, Laisa Schweigert, Madison Carlyle, Laura Martinez, Carolyn Anh Thu Dang, Atlas Pillar, Emma DiFrancesco, Crys Zaragoza, Natali Blazevic, Jax Gonzalez, Kimberly Koerth, Chelsea Pixler Charbonneau, Corie Cisco, Camille Edelstein, John Payton, Tatiana Crespo, Mam Marie Sanyang, Nic Santos, and Jennifer Bertagni.

Thank you to Arizona State University for the Scholarship, Research, and Creative Activities Grant, and to the Humanities Institute Subvention Grant, which helped move this project forward. I also thank my colleagues who cheered me on through the writing of this book: Sharon Kirsch, Majia Nadesan, Tracy Encizo, Eduardo Pagán, Patrick Bixby, Rachel Corbman, Aaron Allen, and Charles Eppley. I am grateful to the journal and book editors who identified early on that work on fatness matters and that it deserves a wider platform. Note that parts of an earlier version of chapter 1 appeared as Breanne Fahs, "Imagining Ugliness: Failed Femininities, Shame, and Disgust Written onto the 'Other' Body," in *On the Politics of Ugliness*, ed. Ela Przybylo and Sara Rodrigues (London: Palgrave, 2018), 237–58. Another part of an earlier version of chapter 1 appeared as Breanne Fahs and Eric Swank, "Exploring Stigma of 'Extreme' Weight Gain: The Terror of Fat Possible Selves in Women's Responses to Hypothetically Gaining One Hundred Pounds," *Women's Studies International Forum* 61 (2017): 1–8. A huge thanks also to my fabulous, intrepid editor, Joanna Green, and the entire Beacon Press team, especially Alison Rodriguez, Susan Lumenello, Marcy Barnes, and Emily Dolbear. I am so grateful to Micah Collins for helping to index the book and to Carol Chu for designing the book's cover.

The four years of working on this book were the most difficult and challenging of my life. I have never felt more grateful for the people I love and all of the ways they have rallied behind me, particularly Mary Dudy, Sarah Stage, Sara McClelland, Clare Croft, Chris Bobel, Connie Hardesty, Katie Goldey, Lori Errico-Seaman, Sean Seaman, Steff Du Bois, Jennifer Tamir, Elizabeth Brake, Jan Habarth, Annika Mann, Garyn Tsuru, Elaine Boyd, Cathy Wertis, Karen Swank-Fitch, Joe Fitch, Marcy Winokur, Diana Álvarez, Patrick Grzanka, Rose Carlson, Denise Delgado, Pat Hart, Damon Whitaker, Lucy Phelps, and Sadie Mohler. I attribute the guts of this book to Elmer Griffin, who taught me how to say hard things, renounce fear, and read and listen closely. To my family, my tribe—especially Kristen, Simon, Ryan, and Fiona—I love you. So much of this book is written through and because of my mom, whose body I carry and whose love and courage are in my flesh and bones. Finally, I dedicate this book to Eric Swank, whose wit, humor, and intelligence are only matched by his capacity for unfailing generosity and abundant love. You fill my life with joy, kindness, beauty, adventure, and possibility—this one's for you.

NOTES

INTRODUCTION

1. Tracy Royce, "Fat Invisibility, Fat Hate: Towards a Progressive Pedagogy of Size," *Counterpoints* 467 (2016): 21–29.
2. Aubrey Gordon, *"You Just Need to Lose Weight" and 19 Other Myths About Fat People* (Boston: Beacon Press, 2023).
3. Julie A. Brunson, Camilla S. Øverup, Mai-Ly Nguyen, Sarah A. Novak, and C. Veronica Smith, "Good Intentions Gone Awry? Effects of Weight-Related Social Control on Health and Well-Being," *Body Image* 11, no. 1 (2014): 1–10.
4. Amy Erdman Farrell, *Fat Shame: Stigma and the Fat Body in American Culture* (New York: New York University Press, 2011); Aubrey Gordon, *What We Don't Talk About When We Talk About Fat* (Boston: Beacon Press, 2020).
5. Da'Shaun L. Harrison, *Belly of the Beast: The Politics of Anti-Fatness as Anti-Blackness* (Berkeley, CA: North Atlantic Books, 2021); Sabrina Strings, *Fearing the Black Body: The Racial Origins of Fat Phobia* (New York: New York University Press, 2019).

CHAPTER 1: THE TERROR OF FAT FUTURES

1. Luce Irigaray, "Women on the Market," in *The Logic of the Gift: Toward an Ethic of Generosity*, ed. Alan D. Schrift (New York: Routledge, 1997), 174–89.
2. Michael Wenzel, Amélie Mummendey, and Sven Waldzus, "Superordinate Identities and Intergroup Conflict: The Ingroup Projection Model," *European Review of Social Psychology* 18, no. 1 (2008): 331–72.
3. Sara Ahmed, "Affective Economies," *Social Text* 22, no. 2 (2004): 117–39.
4. David Crawford, Robert W. Jeffery, and Simone A. French, "Can Anyone Successfully Control Their Weight? Findings of a Three Year Community-Based Study of Men and Women," *International Journal of Obesity* 24, no. 9 (2000): 1107–10.
5. "Data & Statistics," Centers for Disease Control and Prevention, https://www.cdc .gov/obesity/data/index.html, accessed January 27, 2023; "Overweight and Obesity Statistics," September 2021, https://www.niddk.nih.gov/health-information/health -statistics/overweight-obesity. See also A. Sharma, "Trends in the Distribution of Body Mass Index Among Women of Reproductive Age," presentation to the Institute of Medicine of the National Academies and National Research Council (2015).

6. Dan Wessels, medically reviewed by Stacy Sampson, "What Is the Average Weight for Women?" *Medical News Today*, January 8, 2020, https://www.medicalnewstoday .com/articles/321003#average-weight.

7. Susan Bordo, "Anorexia Nervosa: Psychopathology as the Crystallization of Culture," in *Food and Culture: A Reader*, eds. Carole Counihan and Penny Van Esterik (New York: Routledge, 2008), 162–86; "Study: 94% of Teenage Girls Have Been Body Shamed," WCNC Charlotte, May 2, 2017, https://www.wcnc.com/article /news/features/study-94-of-teenage-girls-have-been-body-shamed/436143277.

8. American Psychological Association (APA), *Report of the APA Task Force on the Sexualization of Girls* (Washington, DC: APA, 2007), http://www.apa.org/pi/wpo /sexualization.html; Amy Slater and Marika Tiggemann, "Body Image and Disordered Eating in Adolescent Girls and Boys: A Test of Objectification Theory," *Sex Roles* 63, no. 1 (2010): 42–49; Ilyssa Salomon and Christia Spears Brown, "The Selfie Generation: Examining the Relationship Between Social Media Use and Early Adolescent Body Image," *Journal of Early Adolescence* 39, no. 4 (2019): 539–60.

9. Charlotte N. Markey, "Invited Commentary: Why Body Image Is Important to Adolescent Development," *Journal of Youth and Adolescence* 39 (2010): 1387–91; Dana K. Voelker, Justine J. Reel, and Christy Greenleaf, "Weight Status and Body Image Perceptions in Adolescents: Current Perspectives," *Adolescent Health, Medicine and Therapeutics* 6 (2015): 149–58.

10. Sarah Trainer, Alexandra Brewis, Deborah Williams, and Jose Rosales Chavez, "Obese, Fat, or 'Just Big'? Young Adult Deployment of and Reactions to Weight Terms," *Human Organization* 74, no. 3 (2015): 266–75; Timothy J. Halliday and Sally Kwak, "Weight Gain in Adolescents and Their Peers," *Economics & Human Biology* 7, no. 2 (2009): 181–90.

11. Davide Marengo, Claudio Longobardi, Matteo Angelo Fabris, and Michele Settanni, "Highly-Visual Social Media and Internalizing Symptoms in Adolescence: The Mediating Role of Body Image Concerns," *Computers in Human Behavior* 82 (2018): 63–69; Thomas F. Cash, Julie R. Ancis, and Melissa D. Strachan, "Gender Attitudes, Feminist Identity, and Body Images Among College Women," *Sex Roles* 36, no. 7–8 (1997): 433–47; Sherry L. Turner, Heather Hamilton, Meija Jacobs, Laurie M. Angood, and Deanne Hovde Dwyer, "The Influence of Fashion Magazines on the Body Image Satisfaction of College Women: An Exploratory Analysis," *Adolescence* 32, no. 127 (1997): 603–14.

12. Isabelle Guelinckx, Roland Devlieger, Kristine Beckers, and Greet Vansant, "Maternal Obesity: Pregnancy Complications, Gestational Weight Gain and Nutrition," *Obesity Reviews* 9, no. 2 (2008): 140–50; Ushma J. Mehta, Anna Maria Siega-Riz, and Amy H. Herring, "Effect of Body Image on Pregnancy Weight Gain," *Maternal and Child Health Journal* 15, no. 3 (2011): 324–32; Alison Tovar, Lisa Chasan-Taber, Odilia I. Bermudez, Raymond R. Hyatt, and Aviva Must, "Knowledge, Attitudes, and Beliefs Regarding Weight Gain During Pregnancy Among Hispanic Women," *Maternal and Child Health Journal* 14, no. 6 (2010): 938–49; Monica L. Wang, Julie Arroyo, Susan Druker, Heather Z. Sankey, and Milagros C. Rosal, "Knowledge, Attitudes and Provider Advice by Pre-Pregnancy Weight Status: A Qualitative Study

of Pregnant Latinas with Excessive Gestational Weight Gain," *Women & Health* 55, no. 7 (2015): 805–28.

13. Susan W. Groth and Margaret H. Kearney, "Diverse Women's Beliefs About Weight Gain in Pregnancy," *Journal of Midwifery & Women's Health* 54, no. 6 (2009): 452–57; Susan W. Groth, Dianne Morrison-Beedy, and Ying Meng, "How Pregnant African American Women View Pregnancy Weight Gain," *Journal of Obstetric, Gynecologic & Neonatal Nursing* 41, no. 6 (2012): 798–808.

14. E. Jean Carroll, "The Future of American Womanhood," *Esquire*, February 1994, https://classic.esquire.com/article/1994/2/1/the-future-of-american-womanhood; Margo Maine, *Body Wars: Making Peace with Women's Bodies (An Activist's Guide)* (Carlsbad, CA: Gurze Books, 2011).

15. Stacey DeAnn McKay, "Prevalence of Disordered Eating Among Sorority Members in Texas," master's thesis, Lamar University, 2001; Jessie L. Miller, Tracy Vaillancourt, and Steven E. Hanna, "The Measurement of 'Eating-Disorder-Thoughts' and 'Eating-Disorder-Behaviors': Implications for Assessment and Detection of Eating Disorders in Epidemiological Studies," *Eating Behaviors* 10, no. 2 (2009): 89–96.

16. Steven Seidman, "Defilement and Disgust: Theorizing the Other," *American Journal of Cultural Sociology* 1, no. 1 (2013): 3–25; Morgan Windram-Geddes, "Fearing Fatness and Feeling Fat: Encountering Affective Spaces of Physical Activity," *Emotion, Space and Society* 9 (2013): 42–49; Christian S. Crandall, "Prejudice Against Fat People: Ideology and Self-Interest," *Journal of Personality and Social Psychology* 66, no. 5 (1994): 882–94.

17. Nola Rushford, "Fear of Gaining Weight: Its Validity as a Visual Analogue Scale in Anorexia Nervosa," *European Eating Disorders Review: The Professional Journal of the Eating Disorders Association* 14, no. 2 (2006): 104–10.

18. Sophie S. Banfield and Marita McCabe, "An Evaluation of the Construct of Body Image," *Adolescence* 37, no. 146 (2002): 373–93.

19. Lenny R. Vartanian, C. Peter Herman, and Janet Polivy, "Implicit and Explicit Attitudes Toward Fatness and Thinness: The Role of the Internalization of Societal Standards," *Body Image* 2, no. 4 (2005): 373–81.

20. Sonya Satinsky, Barbara Dennis, Michael Reece, Stephanie Sanders, and Shaowen Bardzell, "My 'Fat Girl Complex': A Preliminary Investigation of Sexual Health and Body Image in Women of Size," *Culture, Health & Sexuality* 15, no. 6 (2013): 710–25.

21. Douglas Degher and Gerald Hughes, "The Adoption and Management of a 'Fat' Identity," in *Interpreting Weight: The Social Management of Fatness and Thinness*, ed. Jeffery Sobal (New York: Routledge, 1999), 11–27; Michael L. Silk, Jessica Francombe, and Faye Bachelor, "The Biggest Loser: The Discursive Constitution of Fatness," *Interactions: Studies in Communication & Culture* 1, no. 3 (2011): 369–89.

22. Christian S. Crandall and April Horstman Reser, "Attributions and Weight-Based Prejudice," in *Weight Bias: Nature, Consequences, and Remedies*, ed. Kelly D. Brownell, Rebecca M. Puhl, Marelene B. Schwartz, and Leslie Rudd (New York: Guilford, 2005), 83–96.

23. Christian S. Crandall, Nuray Sakalli D'Anello, Eleana Lazarus, Grazyna Wieczorkowska Nejtardt, and N. T. Feather, "An Attribution-Value Model of Prejudice: Anti-Fat Attitudes in Six Nations," *Personality and Social Psychology Bulletin* 27, no. 1 (2001): 30–37.

24. Alison J. Cullen, Anthony Barnett, Paul A. Komesaroff, Wendy Brown, Kerry S. O'Brien, Wayne Hall, and Adrian Carter, "A Qualitative Study of Overweight and Obese Australians' Views of Food Addiction," *Appetite* 115 (2017): 62–70.

25. Nicolas Rasmussen, "Weight Stigma, Addiction, Science, and the Medication of Fatness in Mid-Twentieth Century America," *Sociology of Health & Illness* 34, no. 6 (2012): 880–95; Nicolas Rasmussen, *Fat in the Fifties: America's First Obesity Crisis* (Baltimore: Johns Hopkins University Press, 2019).

26. Sarah Vaillancourt and Ginny Moore, "Fat Stigma in Women's Health," *Journal for Nurse Practitioners* 15, no. 2 (2019): 207–8.

27. Mark L. Hatzenbuehler, Katherine M. Keyes, and Deborah S. Hasin, "Associations Between Perceived Weight Discrimination and the Prevalence of Psychiatric Disorders in the General Population," *Obesity* 17, no. 11 (2009): 2033–39.

28. Simon E. Dalley, Thomas V. Pollet, and Jose Vidal, "Body Size and Body Esteem in Women: The Mediating Role of Possible Self Expectancy," *Body Image* 10, no. 3 (2013): 411–14; Dana Heller Levitt, "Drive for Thinness and Fear of Fat Among College Women: Implications for Practice and Assessment," *Journal of College Counseling* 7, no. 2 (2004): 109–17; Tim Woodman and Rebecca Steer, "Body Self-Discrepancies and Women's Social Physique Anxiety: The Moderating Role of the Feared Body," *British Journal of Psychology* 102, no. 2 (2011): 147–60; Marcella L. Wood, Doeschka J. Anschutz, Tatjana Van Strien, and Eni S. Becker, "Measuring Thinspiration and Fear of Fat Indirectly: A Matter of Approach and Avoidance," *Appetite* 56, no. 2 (2011): 451–55.

29. Brenda Major, Jeffrey M. Hunger, Debra P. Bunyan, and Carol T. Miller, "The Ironic Effects of Weight Stigma," *Journal of Experimental Social Psychology* 51 (2014): 74–80.

30. Samar Noureddine and Bonnie Metzger, "Do Health-Related Feared Possible Selves Motivate Healthy Eating?" *Health Psychology Research* 2, no. 1 (2014): 1043.

31. Michelle J. Pearce, Julie Boergers, and Mitchell J. Prinstein, "Adolescent Obesity, Overt and Relational Peer Victimization, and Romantic Relationships," *Obesity Research* 10, no. 5 (2002): 386–93.

32. Mark V. Roehling, Patricia V. Roehling, and Shaun Pichler, "The Relationship Between Body Weight and Perceived Weight-Related Employment Discrimination: The Role of Sex and Race," *Journal of Vocational Behavior* 71, no. 2 (2007): 300–18.

33. Jeannine A. Gailey, "Fat Shame to Fat Pride: Fat Women's Sexual and Dating Experiences," *Fat Studies* 1, no. 1 (2012): 114–27.

34. Satinsky, Dennis, Reece, Sanders, and Bardzell, "My 'Fat Girl Complex,'" 710–25.

35. Jeannine A. Gailey, *The Hyper (In)Visible Fat Woman: Weight and Gender Discourse in Contemporary Society* (New York: Palgrave, 2014); Cat Pausé, "Human Nature: On Fat Sexual Identity and Agency," in *Fat Sex: New Directions in Theory and Activism*, eds. Helen Hester and Caroline Walters (Surrey: Ashgate, 2015), 37–48.

36. Mimi Nichter and Nancy Vuckovic, "Fat Talk: Body Image Among Adolescent Girls," in *Many Mirrors: Body Image and Social Relations*, ed. Nicole Sault (New Brunswick, NJ: Rutgers University Press, 1994), 109–31.

37. Rachel Hannah Salk and Renee Engeln-Maddox, "Fat Talk Among College Women Is Both Contagious and Harmful," *Sex Roles* 66, no. 9 (2012): 636–45.

38. Chon Man Chow, Holly Ruhl, Cin Tan, and Lilian Ellis, "Fear of Fat and Restrained Eating: Negative Body Talk Between Female Friends as a Moderator," *Eating and Weight Disorders-Studies on Anorexia, Bulimia and Obesity* 24, no. 6 (2019): 1181–88.

39. Salk and Engeln-Maddox, "Fat Talk Among College Women Is Both Contagious and Harmful," 636–45.

40. Beatrice "Bean" E. Robinson, Lane C. Bacon, and Julia O'Reilly, "Fat Phobia: Measuring, Understanding, and Changing Anti-Fat Attitudes," *International Journal of Eating Disorders* 14, no. 4 (1993): 467–80.

41. Robinson, Bacon, and O'Reilly, "Fat Phobia," 467–80.

42. Alexandra A. Brewis, Daniel J. Hruschka, and Amber Wutich, "Vulnerability to Fat-Stigma in Women's Everyday Relationships," *Social Science & Medicine* 73, no. 4 (2011): 491–97; Chong Man Chow and Cin Tan, "The Role of Fat Talk in Eating Pathology and Depressive Symptoms Among Mother-Daughter Dyads," *Body Image* 24 (2018): 36–43.

43. Amy Barwick, Doris Bazzini, Denise Martz, Courtney Rocheleau, and Lisa Curtin, "Testing the Norm to Fat Talk for Women of Varying Size: What's Weight Got to Do with It?" *Body Image* 9, no. 1 (2012): 176–79.

44. Leonore Tiefer, *Sex Is Not a Natural Act and Other Essays* (Boulder, CO: Westview, 2004), 11.

45. This study utilized qualitative data from twenty women (mean age = 35.35, SD = 12.01) recruited in 2014 in Phoenix, Arizona, selected only for gender, racial/ethnic background, sexual identity, and age; no other prescreening questions were asked. All but one weighed under two hundred pounds. A purposive sample provided greater demographic diversity: sexual minority women and racial/ethnic minority women were intentionally oversampled and a range of ages was represented—eighteen to thirty-one (seven), thirty-two to forty-five (eight), and forty-six to fifty-nine (five). The sample included twelve white women and eight women of color (four Mexican Americans, two African Americans, and two Asian Americans). Sexual identity was self-reported (twelve heterosexual women, four bisexual women, and four lesbian women, though sexual behavior did not always overlap with sexual identity). All participants consented to audiotaped and fully transcribed interviews and received $20 compensation. Identifying data were removed; each participant received a pseudonym to ensure anonymity.

46. Stuart Hall and Tony Jefferson, eds., *Resistance Through Rituals: Youth Subcultures in Post-War Britain* (East Sussex: Psychology Press, 1993); James C. Scott, *Domination and the Arts of Resistance: Hidden Transcripts* (New Haven, CT: Yale University Press, 2008).

47. Cheryl A. Hyde and Betty J. Ruth, "Multicultural Content and Class Participation: Do Students Self-Censor?" *Journal of Social Work Education* 38, no. 2 (2002): 241–56.

48. Heather Lynne Talley, *Saving Face: Disfigurement and the Politics of Appearance* (New York: New York University Press, 2014), 4.
49. Simone Schnall, Jonathan Haidt, Gerald L. Clore, and Alexander H. Jordan, "Disgust as Embodied Moral Judgment," *Personality and Social Psychology Bulletin* 34, no. 8 (2008): 1096–1109; Jonathan Haidt, Silvia Helena Koller, and Maria G. Dias, "Affect, Culture, and Morality, or Is it Wrong to Eat Your Dog?" *Journal of Personality and Social Psychology* 65, no. 4 (1993): 613–28.
50. Cathy J. Cohen, "Punks, Bulldaggers, and Welfare Queens: The Radical Potential of Queer Politics?" *GLQ* 3, no. 4 (1997): 437–65; Debra Merskin, "The Construction of Arabs as Enemies: Post-September 11 Discourse of George W. Bush," *Mass Communication & Society* 7, no. 2 (2004): 157–75; Ellen Reese, *Backlash Against Welfare Mothers: Past and Present* (Berkeley: University of California Press, 2005).
51. Simone Schnall, Jennifer Benton, and Sophie Harvey, "With a Clean Conscience: Cleanliness Reduces the Severity of Moral Judgments," *Psychological Science* 19, no. 12 (2008): 1219–22; Michelle Meagher, "Jenny Saville and a Feminist Aesthetics of Disgust," *Hypatia* 18, no. 4 (2003): 23–41; Kathleen Taylor, "Disgust Is a Factor in Extreme Prejudice," *British Journal of Social Psychology* 46, no. 3 (2007): 597–617.
52. Lenny R. Vartanian, "Disgust and Perceived Control in Attitudes Toward Obese People," *International Journal of Obesity* 34, no. 8 (2010): 1302–7.
53. Laura Smith, Kim Baranowski, Alizah Allen, and Rashidah Bowen, "Poverty, Crime Seriousness, and the 'Politics of Disgust,'" *Journal of Poverty* 17, no. 4 (2013): 375–93.
54. Karen Soldatic and Helen Meekosha, "The Place of Disgust: Disability, Class, and Gender in Spaces of Workfare," *Societies* 2, no. 3 (2012): 139–56.
55. David A. Snow and Leon Anderson, *Down on Their Luck: A Study of Homeless Street People* (Berkeley: University of California Press, 1993).
56. Ellen K. Feder, "Tilting the Ethical Lens: Shame, Disgust, and the Body in Question," *Hypatia* 23, no. 3 (2011): 632–50.
57. Sara Rodrigues and Ela Przybylo, "Introduction: On the Politics of Ugliness," in *On the Politics of Ugliness*, ed. Sara Rodrigues and Ela Przybylo (London: Palgrave, 2018), 1–31, 5.
58. The people in this sample had a range of identities and demographic backgrounds: 50 percent white and 50 percent people of color (six Asian Americans, two Mexican Americans, one African American, and two biracial women) and 41 percent heterosexual, 32 percent bisexual, 18 percent lesbian, and 9 percent queer. Their ages were twenty-one to sixty-three (mean age = 34.05, SD = 13.11). Their geographical locations ranged across the US: six from the San Francisco Bay area; three from New York City; one from Los Angeles; one from Portland, Oregon; five from small towns in Pennsylvania, Mississippi, Texas, and North Carolina; two from suburban cities in Colorado and Illinois; one from a large college town in Wisconsin; and one from Santa Fe, New Mexico. Political viewpoints included three moderately conservative, three moderate, nine moderately liberal/progressive, and seven very liberal/progressive. Only three women in the sample had fat or fatter bodies over two hundred pounds. I include here only data from the seventeen women under two hundred pounds.

59. I use the term "women" to refer to the twenty-two study participants. The two non-binary participants said that they prefer they/them pronouns and that, as AFAB (assigned female at birth) people, they do not object to being included in an aggregate group called "women." This use is done consciously and with permission of participants.

60. Lisa Blackman, "The Subject of Affect: Bodies, Process, Becoming," in *Immaterial Bodies: Affect, Embodiment, Mediation*, ed. Lisa Blackman (London: Sage, 2012), 1–25, 4.

61. Blackman, "The Subject of Affect," 4.

62. Jeanette Winterson, *Lighthousekeeping* (New York: Harcourt, 2004), 175.

CHAPTER 2: "LAZY, UNMOTIVATED, DEPRESSED, SEXLESS, OVEREATING, AND EMOTIONAL"

1. Tessa E. S. Charlesworth and Mahzarin R. Banaji, "Patterns of Implicit and Explicit Attitudes: Long-Term Change and Stability from 2006–2016," *Psychological Science* 30, no. 2 (2019): 174–92.

2. Rheanna N. Ata and J. Kevin Thompson, "Weight Bias in the Media: A Review of Recent Research," *Obesity Facts* 3, no. 1 (2010): 41–46.

3. Centers for Disease Control and Prevention, "Healthystyles Survey Executive Summary: Prime Time Viewers and Health Information," 2000, http://www.cdc.gov/healthmarketing/entertainment_education/2000Survey.htm; Shaniece Criss, Jennifer A. Woo Baidal, Roberta E. Goldman, Meghan Perkins, Courtney Cunningham, and Elsie M. Taveras, "The Role of Health Information Sources in Decision-Making Among Hispanic Mothers During Their Children's First 1000 Days of Life," *Maternal and Child Health Journal* 19 (2015): 2536–43.

4. Kristen Harrison and Joanne Cantor, "The Relationship Between Media Consumption and Eating Disorders," *Journal of Communication* 47, no. 1 (1997): 40–67.

5. Kathrin Karsay and Desirée Schmuck, "'Weak, Sad, and Lazy Fatties': Adolescents' Explicit and Implicit Weight Bias Following Exposure to Weight Loss Reality TV Shows," *Media Psychology* 22, no. 1 (2019): 60–81; Sarah E. Domoff, Nova G. Hinman, Afton M. Koball, Amy Storfer-Isser, Victoria L. Carhart, Kyoung D. Baik, and Robert A. Carels, "The Effects of Reality Television on Weight Bias: An Examination of *The Biggest Loser*," *Obesity* 20, no. 5 (2012): 993–98.

6. Jina H. Yoo, "No Clear Winner: Effects of *The Biggest Loser* on the Stigmatization of Obese Persons," *Health Communication* 28, no. 3 (2013): 294–303.

7. Michael L. Silk, Jessica Francombe, and Faye Bachelor, "*The Biggest Loser*: The Discursive Constitution of Fatness," *Interactions: Studies in Communication & Culture* 1, no. 3 (2011): 369–89.

8. Marla E. Eisenberg, Ashley Carlson-McGuire, Sarah E. Gollust, and Dianne Neumark-Sztainer, "A Content Analysis of Weight Stigmatization in Popular Television Programming for Adolescents," *International Journal of Eating Disorders* 48, no. 6 (2015): 759–66.

9. Bradley S. Greenberg, Matthew Eastin, Linda Hofschire, Ken Lachlan, and Kelly D. Brownell, "Portrayals of Overweight and Obese Individuals on Commercial Television," *American Journal of Public Health* 93, no. 8 (2003): 1342–48.

10. Jacob M. Burmeister and Robert A. Carels, "Weight-Related Humor in the Media: Appreciation, Distaste, and Anti-Fat Attitudes," *Psychology of Popular Media Culture* 3, no. 4 (2014): 223–38.

11. Susan M. Himes and J. Kevin Thompson, "Fat Stigmatization in Television Shows and Movies: A Content Analysis," *Obesity* 15, no. 3 (2007): 712–18.

12. Gregory Fouts and Kimberley Vaughan, "Television Situation Comedies: Male Weight, Negative References, and Audience Reactions," *Sex Roles* 46, no. 11 (2002): 439–42.

13. Gregory Fouts and Kimberley Burggraf, "Television Situation Comedies: Female Weight, Male Negative Comments, and Audience Reactions," *Sex Roles* 42, no. 9 (2000): 925–32.

14. Lauren Bosc, "'Where Everything Round Is Good': Exploring and Reimagining Fatness in Fairy-Tale Media," in *The Routledge Companion to Media and Fairy-Tale Cultures*, ed. Pauline Greenhill, Jill Terry Rudy, Naomi Hamer, and Lauren Bosc (New York: Routledge, 2018), 252–62.

15. Melissa Zimdars, "*American Housewife* and *Super Fun Night*: Fat Ambiguity and Televised Bodily Comedy," *Fat Studies* 10, no. 1 (2021): 50–63; Laura Major, "'She Was Proud of Her Build': Fat and Tradition in the *No 1. Ladies' Detective Agency* Series," *Fat Studies* 10, no. 1 (2021): 21–33; Melissa Zimdars, "Fat Acceptance TV?: Rethinking Reality Television with TLC's *Big Sexy* and the Carnivalesque," *Popular Communication* 13, no. 3 (2015): 232–46; Anna Kurowicka and Marta Usiekniewicz, "Fat Girl's Wet Dream: Girl Sexuality, Fatness, and Mental Disability in *My Mad Fat Diary*," *Fat Studies* 10, no. 1 (2021): 7–20.

16. Gillian Brown, "Demanding Our Stories Be Told: We Are Ready for Authentic Representations of Fat Folks' Stories," *The Body Is Not An Apology: Radical Self-Love for Everybody and Every Body*, September 13, 2018, https://thebodyisnotanapology.com /magazine/demanding-our-stories-be-told-we-are-ready-for-authentic-representations -of-fat-folks-stories.

17. Layla Cameron, "The 'Good Fatty' Is a Dancing Fatty: Fat Archetypes in Reality Television," *Fat Studies* 8, no. 3 (2019): 259–78.

18. Hannah Taylor and Jeannine A. Gailey, "Fiction Meets Reality: A Comparison of *Dietland* and the Experiences of North American Fat Women," *Fat Studies* 10, no. 1 (2021): 34–49; Lyla E. E. Byers and Heidi M. Williams, "Hollywood's Slim Pickings for Fat Characters: A Textual Analysis of *Gilmore Girls, Sweet Magnolias, This is Us, Shrill*, and *Dietland*," *Fat Studies* 12, no. 2 (2022): 273–85.

19. Jenelle Riley, "A Fat Girl's Take on 'Shrill,'" *Variety*, March 15, 2019, https://variety .com/2019/tv/columns/shrill-aidy-bryant-fat-girl-review-1203164161; Carlos Valladares, "Review: 'Shrill' Aims to Show Us That Fat Is Beautiful, But the Message Is Muddled," *Datebook*, March 12, 2019, https://datebook.sfchronicle.com/entertainment /review-shrill-aims-to-show-us-that-fat-is-beautiful-but-the-message-is-muddled.

20. Barbara Plotz, *Fat on Film: Gender, Race and Body Size in Contemporary Hollywood Cinema* (London: Bloomsbury, 2020), 5.

21. Plotz, *Fat on Film*.

22. Jackie Wykes, "'I Saw a Knock-Out': Fatness, (In)visibility, and Desire in *Shallow Hal*," *Somatechnics* 2, no. 1 (2012): 60–79.

23. Kathleen LeBesco, "Situating Fat Suits: Blackface, Drag, and the Politics of Performance," *Women & Performance* 15, no. 2 (2005): 231–42.

24. Megan Garber, "*Shallow Hal* and the Never-Ending Fat Joke," *The Atlantic*, November 9, 2021, https://www.theatlantic.com/culture/archive/2021/11/shallow-hal-20th-anniversary-never-ending-fat-joke/620637.

25. Sylvia Herbozo, Stacey Tantleff-Dunn, Jessica Gokee-Larose, and J. Kevin Thompson, "Beauty and Thinness Messages in Children's Media: A Content Analysis," *Eating Disorders* 12, no. 1 (2004): 21–34.

26. Jennifer A. Harriger, Kelsey N. Serier, Madeline Luedke, Sienna Robertson, and Ashley Bojorquez, "Appearance-Related Themes in Children's Animated Movies Released Between 2004 and 2016: A Content Analysis," *Body Image* 26 (2018): 78–82; Temple Northup and Carol M. Liebler, "The Good, the Bad, and the Beautiful: Beauty Ideals on the Disney and Nickelodeon Channels," *Journal of Children and Media* 4, no. 3 (2010): 265–82.

27. Elizabeth M. Throop, Asheley Cockrell Skinner, Andrew J. Perrin, Michael J. Steiner, Adebowale Odulana, and Eliana M. Perrin, "Pass the Popcorn: 'Obesogenic' Behaviors and Stigma in Children's Movies," *Obesity* 22, no. 7 (2014): 1694–1700.

28. Courtney C. Simpson, Melissa A. Kwitowski, Rachel L. Boutte, R. Gow, and S. Mazzeo, "Messages About Appearance, Food, Weight and Exercise in 'Tween' Television," *Eating Behaviors* 23 (2016): 70–75.

29. Jolien Trekels and Steven Eggermont, "Beauty Is Good: The Appearance Culture, the Internalization of Appearance Ideals, and Dysfunctional Appearance Beliefs Among Tweens," *Human Communication Research* 43, no. 2 (2017): 173–92.

30. Amy Slater, Marika Tiggemann, Kimberley Hawkins, and Douglas Werchon, "Just One Click: A Content Analysis of Advertisements on Teen Web Sites," *Journal of Adolescent Health* 50, no. 4 (2012): 339–45.

31. Renee Hobbs, Sharon Broder, Holly Pope, and Jonelle Rowe, "How Adolescent Girls Interpret Weight-Loss Advertising," *Health Education Research* 21, no. 5 (2006): 719–30.

32. Marika Tiggemann and Jessica Miller, "The Internet and Adolescent Girls' Weight Satisfaction and Drive for Thinness," *Sex Roles* 63, no. 1 (2010): 79–90.

33. Katherine N. Balantekin, Leann L. Birch, and Jennifer S. Savage, "Family, Friend, and Media Factors are Associated with Patterns of Weight-Control Behavior Among Adolescent Girls," *Eating and Weight Disorders-Studies on Anorexia, Bulimia and Obesity* 23, no. 2 (2018): 215–23.

34. Dina L. G. Borzekowski, Thomas N. Robinson, and Joel D. Killen, "Does the Camera Add 10 Pounds? Media Use, Perceived Importance of Appearance, and Weight Concerns Among Teenage Girls," *Journal of Adolescent Health* 26, no. 1 (2000): 36–41.

35. Jasmine Fardouly and Lenny R. Vartanian, "Social Media and Body Image Concerns: Current Research and Future Directions," *Current Opinion in Psychology* 9 (2016): 1–5.

36. Stefan Stieger, Hannah M. Graf, Stella P. Riegler, Sophie Biebl, and Viren Swami, "Engagement with Social Media Content Results in Lower Appearance Satisfaction: An Experience Sampling Using a Wrist-Worn Wearable and a Physical Analogue Scale," *Body Image* 43 (2022): 232–43.

37. Marisa Minadeo, "Weight-Normative Messaging Predominates on TikTok: A Qualitative Content Analysis," *PLOS One* 17, no. 11 (2022): e0267997.

38. Leah M. Lessard and Rebecca M. Puhl, "Adolescents' Exposure to and Experiences of Weight Stigma During the COVID-19 Pandemic," *Journal of Pediatric Psychology* 46, no. 8 (2021): 950–59.

39. Chelly Maes and Laura Vandenbosch, "Adolescent Girls' Instagram and TikTok Use: Examining Relations with Body Image-Related Constructs Over Time Using Random Intercept Cross-Lagged Panel Models," *Body Image* 41 (2022): 453–59.

40. Alison E. Field, Lilian Cheung, Anne M. Wolf, David B. Herzog, Steven L. Gortmaker, and Graham A. Colditz, "Exposure to the Mass Media and Weight Concerns Among Girls," *Pediatrics* 103, no. 3 (1999): e36.

41. Elizabeth M. Cameron and F. Richard Ferraro, "Body Satisfaction in College Women After Brief Exposure to Magazine Images," *Perceptual and Motor Skills* 98, no. 3 (2004): 1093–99.

42. Tina B. Eskes, Margaret Carlisle Duncan, and Eleanor M. Miller, "The Discourse of Empowerment: Foucault, Marcuse, and Women's Fitness Texts," *Journal of Sport and Social Issues* 22, no. 3 (1998): 317–44.

43. Katie Cook and Ciann L. Wilson, "Representations of Fatness in *Parents* magazine: A Critical Discourse Analysis," *Fat Studies* 8, no. 3 (2019): 320–33.

44. Natalie Boero, "All the News That's Fat to Print: The American 'Obesity Epidemic' and the Media," *Qualitative Sociology* 30, no. 1 (2007): 41–60.

45. "Study: Obesity Linked to Headlessness," Reddit, February 9, 2011, https://www .reddit.com/r/BodyAcceptance/comments/fiky9/study_obesity_linked_to _headlessness.

46. Josephine Previte and Lauren Gurrieri, "Who Is the Biggest Loser? Fat News Coverage Is a Barrier to Healthy Lifestyle Promotion," *Health Marketing Quarterly* 32, no. 4 (2015): 330–49.

47. Rebecca M. Puhl, Joerg Luedicke, and Chelsea A. Heuer, "The Stigmatizing Effect of Visual Media Portrayals of Obese Persons on Public Attitudes: Does Race or Gender Matter?" *Journal of Health Communication* 18, no. 7 (2013): 805–26.

48. Patricia Cain, Ngaire Donaghue, and Graeme Ditchburn, "Concerns, Culprits, Counsel, and Conflict: A Thematic Analysis of 'Obesity' and Fat Discourse in Digital News Media," *Fat Studies* 6, no. 2 (2017): 170–88.

49. Kathleen LeBesco, "Neoliberalism, Public Health, and the Moral Perils of Fatness," *Critical Public Health* 21 (2011): 153–64.

50. Annemarie Jutel, "The Emergence of Overweight as a Disease Entity: Measuring Up Normality," *Social Science & Medicine* 63, no. 9 (2006): 2268–76.

51. Emma Rich and John Evans, "'Fat Ethics'—The Obesity Discourse and Body Politics," *Social Theory & Health* 3, no. 4 (2005): 341–58.

52. Edith Bracho-Sanchez and John Rausch, "The COVID-19 Pandemic Worsened an Already Dire Childhood Obesity Epidemic," CNN, January 8, 2021, https://www .cnn.com/2021/01/08/health/childhood-obesity-covid-19-pandemic-wellness/index .html; Sandee LaMotte, "For Millennials, Cancers Fueled by Obesity Are On Rise, Study Says," CNN, February 4, 2019, https://www.cnn.com/2019/02/04/health /obesity-cancer-increase-millennials-study/index.html; Jen Christensen, "To Fix

Climate Change, Fix the Obesity and Starvation Epidemics, Reports Say," CNN, January 27, 2019, https://www.cnn.com/2019/01/27/health/obesity-climate -change-undernutrition/index.html.

53. J. Eric Oliver, "The Politics of Pathology: How Obesity Became an Epidemic Disease," *Perspectives in Biology and Medicine* 49, no. 4 (2006): 611–27.

54. J. Eric Oliver, *Fat Politics: The Real Story Behind America's Obesity Epidemic* (New York: Oxford University Press, 2006).

55. Jacqueline Howard, "Childhood Obesity: America's 'True National Crisis' Measured State by State," CNN, October 24, 2018, https://www.cnn.com/2018/10/24 /health/childhood-obesity-state-rates-study/index.html.

56. Ariana Eunjung Cha, "Standing Desks at Schools: The Solution to the Childhood Obesity Epidemic?" *Washington Post*, July 21, 2015, https://www.washingtonpost .com/news/to-your-health/wp/2015/07/21/standing-desks-at-schools-the-solution -to-the-childhood-obesity-epidemic.

57. Matthew Hutson, "'A Big Fat Crisis' by Deborah Cohen," *Washington Post*, January 10, 2014, https://www.washingtonpost.com/opinions/a-big-fat-crisis-by-deborah -cohen/2014/01/10/197ba200-6bf5-11e3-b405-7e360f7e9fd2_story.html; "Obesity Is Too Dangerous to Normalize," *Washington Post*, December 2, 2018, https://www .washingtonpost.com/opinions/obesity-is-too-dangerous-to-normalize/2018/12 /02/e5468f12-f421-11e8-99c2-cfca6fcf610c_story.html; Danielle Paquette, "The Growth of Wal-Mart May Have Made America's Obesity Epidemic Worse," *Washington Post*, January 26, 2015, https://www.washingtonpost.com/news/wonk/wp /2015/01/26/did-the-growth-of-wal-mart-make-americas-obesity-epidemic-worse; Tara Parker-Pope, "In Obesity Epidemic, What's One Cookie?" *New York Times*, March 1, 2010, https://archive.nytimes.com/well.blogs.nytimes.com/2010/03/01 /in-obesity-epidemic-whats-one-cookie/; Anahad O'Connor, "Can Home Cooking Reverse the Obesity Epidemic?" *New York Times*, June 12, 2019, https://www.nytimes .com/2019/06/12/well/eat/can-home-cooking-reverse-the-obesity-epidemic.html.

58. Richard Bernstein, "There's Blame to Go Around in US Obesity Epidemic," *New York Times*, June 4, 2008, https://www.nytimes.com/2008/06/04/world/americas /04iht-letter.1.13453139.html; Jane E. Brody, "Attacking the Obesity Epidemic by First Figuring Out Its Cause," *New York Times*, September 12, 2011, https://www .nytimes.com/2011/09/13/health/13brody.html.

59. Linda Clare Tapsell, Vanessa Brenninger, and Janelle Barnard, "Applying Conversation Analysis to Foster Accurate Reporting in the Diet History Interview," *Journal of the American Dietetic Association* 100, no. 7 (2000): 818–24.

60. Emma Bedor and Atsushi Tajima, "No Fat Moms! Celebrity Mothers' Weight-Loss Narratives in *People* Magazine," *Journal of Magazine Media* 13, no. 2 (2012), https:// muse.jhu.edu/article/773720/pdf.

61. "True Life: What Diet Culture Did to My Mental Health," *House of Dorough*, August 26, 2019, https://www.houseofdorough.com/home/2019/8/25/true-life-what -dietculture-did-to-my-mental-health-your-anonymous-stories.

62. Alejandro Magallares, "Right Wing Autoritharism, Social Dominance Orientation, Controllability of the Weight and Their Relationship with Antifat Attitudes,"

Universitas Psychologica 13, no. 2 (2014): 771–79; Christian Crandall and Monica Biernat, "The Ideology of Anti-Fat Attitudes," *Journal of Applied Social Psychology* 20, no. 3 (1990): 227–43.

63. Terace Garnier, "Newest Device to Help Combat Obesity Epidemic," Fox News, February 2, 2017, https://www.foxnews.com/health/newest-device-to-help-combat -obesity-epidemic; Sandra E. Garcia, "Organizations Strive to Solve the Latino Childhood Obesity Epidemic," Fox News, January 4, 2017, https://www.foxnews .com/health/organizations-strive-to-solve-the-latino-childhood-obesity-epidemic; Deborah Cohen, "Snack Attack: It's Time to Kick Vending Machines Out of the Workplace," Fox News, June 29, 2018, https://www.foxnews.com/opinion/snack -attack-its-time-to-kick-vending-machines-out-of-the-workplace; Shaun Wooller, "Yogurt Contributing to Obesity Epidemic, Study Claims," Fox News, September 19, 2018, https://www.foxnews.com/food-drink/yogurt-contributing-to-obesity -epidemic-study-claims.

64. "Anti-Hunger Smells Could Battle Obesity," Fox News, January 13, 2015, https:// www.foxnews.com/science/anti-hunger-smells-could-battle-obesity; "Obesity Epidemic Propels Fitness as Career," Fox News, October 24, 2015, https://www.fox news.com/health/obesity-epidemic-propels-fitness-as-career; "Overweight Is the New Normal," Fox News, October 27, 2015, https://www.foxnews.com/health /overweight-is-the-new-normal-weight.

65. Robert Schmad, "Stop Being Fat," *Washington Examiner*, June 3, 2021, https://www .washingtonexaminer.com/opinion/stop-being-fat.

66. Ryan Girdsky, "Milo Yiannopoulos Dressed in Drag: 'Fat Shaming Works,'" *Washington Examiner*, September 26, 2016, https://www.washingtonexaminer.com/red -alert-politics/rap-interview-milo-yiannopoulos-college-tour-greatest-show-on -earth.

67. Lucas Nolan, "Milo: '100% of Fat People Are Fucking Gross," *Breitbart*, September 22, 2016, https://www.breitbart.com/social-justice/2016/09/22/milo-explains-fat -shaming-good.

68. Alexandra A. Brewis, Amber Wutich, Ashlan Falletta-Cowden, and Isa Rodriguez-Soto, "Body Norms and Fat Stigma in Global Perspective," *Current Anthropology* 52, no. 2 (2011): 269–76.

69. Tara Margrét Vilhjálmsdóttir, "Fat Hatred and Body Respect: The Curious Case of Iceland," in *The Routledge International Handbook of Fat Studies*, ed. Cat Pausé and Sonya Renee Taylor (New York: Routledge, 2021), 199–204.

70. Samantha Murray, "Marked as 'Pathological': 'Fat' Bodies as Virtual Confessors," in *Biopolitics and 'Obesity' Epidemic: Governing Bodies*, ed. Jan Wright and Valerie Harwood (New York: Routledge, 2012), 86–98.

71. Paula M. Brochu and Victoria M. Esses, "What's in a Name? The Effects of the Labels 'Fat' Versus 'Overweight' on Weight Bias," *Journal of Applied Social Psychology* 41, no. 8 (2011): 1981–2008.

72. Rebecca Puhl, Jamie L. Peterson, and Joerg Luedicke, "Motivating or Stigmatizing? Public Perceptions of Weight-Related Language Used by Health Providers," *International Journal of Obesity* 37, no. 4 (2013): 612–19.

73. Jeffrey M. Hunger, Alison Blodorn, Carol T. Miller, and Brenda Major, "The Psychological and Physiological Effects of Interacting with an Anti-Fat Peer," *Body Image* 27 (2018): 148–55.

74. Priscila Lopes Cardozo and Suzete Chiviacowsky, "Overweight Stereotype Threat Negatively Impacts the Learning of a Balance Task," *Journal of Motor Learning and Development* 3, no. 2 (2015): 140–50; Veronica Guardabassi and Carlo Tomasetto, "Does Weight Stigma Reduce Working Memory? Evidence of Stereotype Threat Susceptibility in Adults with Obesity," *International Journal of Obesity* 42, no. 8 (2018): 1500–1507.

75. Robert A. Carels, Sarah E. Domoff, Jacob M. Burmeister, Afton M. Koball, Nova G. Hinman, Alan K. Davis, Marissa Wagner Oehlhof, Michelle Leroy, Erin Bannon, and Debra A. Hoffmann, "Examining Perceived Stereotype Threat Among Overweight/Obese Adults Using a Multi-Threat Framework," *Obesity Facts* 6, no. 3 (2013): 258–68.

76. Brenda Major, Dina Eliezer, and Heather Rieck, "The Psychological Weight of Weight Stigma," *Social Psychological and Personality Science* 3, no. 6 (2012): 651–58.

77. Benjamin J. Li, May O. Lwin, and Younbo Jung, "Wii, Myself, and Size: The Influence of Proteus Effect and Stereotype Threat on Overweight Children's Exercise Motivation and Behavior in Exergames," *Games for Health: Research, Development, and Clinical Applications* 3, no. 1 (2014): 40–48.

78. Angela Meadows and Andrea E. Bombak, "Yes, We Can (No, You Can't): Weight Stigma, Exercise Self-Efficacy, and Active Fat Identity Development," *Fat Studies* 8, no. 2 (2019): 135–53.

79. Jason D. Seacat and Kristin D. Mickelson, "Stereotype Threat and the Exercise/Dietary Health Intentions of Overweight Women," *Journal of Health Psychology* 14, no. 4 (2009): 556–67; Ashley M. Araiza and Joseph D. Wellman, "Weight Stigma Predicts Inhibitory Control and Food Selection in Response to the Salience of Weight Discrimination," *Appetite* 114 (2017): 382–90.

80. Natasha Schvey, Rebecca M. Puhl, and Kelly D. Brownell, "The Impact of Weight Stigma on Caloric Consumption," *Obesity* 19, no. 10 (2011): 1957–62.

81. Jeffrey M. Hunger, Brenda Major, Alison Blodorn, and Carol T. Miller, "Weighed Down by Stigma: How Weight-Based Social Identity Threat Contributes to Weight Gain and Poor Health," *Social and Personality Psychology Compass* 9, no. 6 (2015): 255–68; Lawrence J. Nolan and Amy Eshleman, "Paved with Good Intentions: Paradoxical Eating Responses to Weight Stigma," *Appetite* 102 (2016): 15–24.

82. Aubrey Gordon, *"You Just Need to Lose Weight" and 19 Other Myths About Fat People* (Boston: Beacon Press, 2023).

83. Jean Kim and Josée L Jarry, "Holding Fat Stereotypes Is Associated with Lower Body Dissatisfaction in Normal Weight Caucasian Women Who Engage in Body Surveillance," *Body Image* 11, no. 4 (2014): 331–36.

84. Peggy Chin Evans, "'If Only I Were Thin Like Her, Maybe I Could Be Happy Like Her': The Self-Implications of Associating a Thin Female Ideal with Life Success," *Psychology of Women Quarterly* 27, no. 3 (2003): 209–14.

85. Jill A. Cattarin, J. Kevin Thompson, Carmen Thomas, and Robyn Williams, "Body Image, Mood, and Televised Images of Attractiveness: The Role of Social Comparison," *Journal of Social and Clinical Psychology* 19, no. 2 (2000): 220–39; Kathryn

Trottier, Janet Polivy, and C. Peter Herman, "Effects of Exposure to Thin and Overweight Peers: Evidence of Social Comparison in Restrained and Unrestrained Eaters," *Journal of Social and Clinical Psychology* 26, no. 2 (2007): 155–72.

86. Anna S. Mueller, Jennifer Pearson, Chandra Muller, Kenneth Frank, and Alyn Turner, "Sizing Up Peers: Adolescent Girls' Weight Control and Social Comparison in the School Context," *Journal of Health and Social Behavior* 51, no. 1 (2010): 64–78; Marla E. Eisenberg, Dianne Neumark-Sztainer, Mary Story, and Cheryl Perry, "The Role of Social Norms and Friends' Influences on Unhealthy Weight-Control Behaviors Among Adolescent Girls," *Social Science & Medicine* 60, no. 6 (2005): 1165–73.

87. Eleanor H. Wertheim, Susan J. Paxton, Helena K. Schutz, and Sharryn L. Muir, "Why Do Adolescent Girls Watch Their Weight? An Interview Study Examining Sociocultural Pressures to Be Thin," *Journal of Psychosomatic Research* 42, no. 4 (1997): 345–55.

88. Stacy Bias, "12 Good Fatty Archetypes," June 2014, http://stacybias.net/2014/06/12 -good-fatty-archetypes.

89. Zoë Meleo-Erwin, "Disrupting Normal: Toward the 'Ordinary and Familiar' in Fat Politics," *Feminism & Psychology* 22, no. 3 (2012): 388–402.

90. Maria Elvira De Caroli and Elisabetta Sagone, "Anti-Fat Prejudice and Stereotypes in Psychology University Students," *Procedia-Social and Behavioral Sciences* 84 (2013): 1184–89.

91. Cat Pausé, "Rebel Heart: Performing Fatness Wrong Online," *MC Journal* 18, no. 3 (2015), https://journal.media-culture.org.au/index.php/mcjournal/article/view/977.

92. The group of women I recruited was diverse: ten white women and ten women of color (five African Americans, three Asian American and Pacific Islanders, one Mexican American, and one Native American). Twelve were heterosexual, five were bisexual, and three were lesbian women. Their ages ranged from twenty-seven to sixty-six (mean age = 40.4, SD = 11.83). There was an array of sizes within the category of "fat," including three women under 200 pounds, ten women between 200 and 250 pounds, four women between 250 and 300 pounds, and three women over 300 pounds. All names are pseudonyms in order to protect participants' identities.

93. Elizabeth Grosz, *Volatile Bodies: Toward a Corporeal Feminism* (New York: Routledge, 2020), xi.

CHAPTER 3: FINDING A "BETTER YOU"

1. "Wellness Economy Statistics & Facts," Global Wellness Institute, https://global wellnessinstitute.org/press-room/statistics-and-facts, accessed February 3, 2023.

2. "Wellness Economy Statistics & Facts."

3. "Wellness Economy Statistics & Facts."

4. Nita Mary McKinley, "Ideal Weight/Ideal Women: Society Constructs the Female," in *Weighty Issues: Fatness and Thinness as Social Problems*, ed. Jeffery Sobal (New York: Routledge, 2017), 97–115.

5. Sabrina Strings, *Fearing the Black Body: The Racial Origins of Fat Phobia* (New York: New York University Press, 2019); Da'Shaun L. Harrison, *Belly of the Beast: The Politics of Anti-Fatness as Anti-Blackness* (Berkeley: North Atlantic Books, 2021).

6. Strings, *Fearing the Black Body*.

7. Strings, *Fearing the Black Body*, 6.

8. Robert W. Jeffery and Simone A. French, "Socioeconomic Status and Weight Control Practices Among 20-to-45-Year-Old Women," *American Journal of Public Health* 86, no. 7 (1996): 1005–10.

9. Lauren Merklin via Change.org started a petition to the Federal Trade Commission to limit the false advertising practices of Noom, see Jay Allen, "How Noom Is Harming Its Customers," *Gaia's Last Laugh*, September 23, 2021, https://gaiaslastlaugh .medium.com/how-noom-is-harming-its-customers-ec6bf560480b.

10. "Noom's False Advertising Is Causing Harm," Change.org, February 2021, https:// www.change.org/p/federal-trade-commission-noom-s-false-advertising-is-causing -harm.

11. Allyson Chiu, "The New Weight Watchers Is All About 'Wellness.' Critics Say It's 'Diet Culture' in Disguise," *Washington Post*, September 25, 2018, https://www .washingtonpost.com/news/morning-mix/wp/2018/09/25/weight-watchers -rebrands-critics-say-its-another-disguise-for-the-diet-culture.

12. Chiu, "The New Weight Watchers Is All About 'Wellness.'"

13. Chiu, "The New Weight Watchers Is All About 'Wellness.'"

14. Samantha Cassetty, as quoted by Kraig Becker, "The 7 Best Diet and Weight Loss Apps of 2021, According to a Dietician," *Insider*, October 15, 2021, https://www .insider.com/guides/health/fitness/best-weight-loss-apps#faqs-8.

15. Traci Mann, Janet A. Tomiyama, Erika Westling, Ann-Marie Lew, Barbra Samuels, and Jason Chatman, "Medicare's Search for Effective Obesity Treatments: Diets Are Not the Answer," *American Psychologist* 62, no. 3 (2007): 220–33; Tianying Wu, Xiang Gao, Ming Chen, and Rob M. Van Dam, "Long-Term Effectiveness of Diet-Plus-Exercise Interventions vs. Diet-Only Interventions for Weight Loss: A Meta-Analysis," *Obesity Reviews* 10, no. 3 (2009): 313–23; Simone A. French, Robert W. Jeffery, and David Murray, "Is Dieting Good for You? Prevalence, Duration and Associated Weight and Behaviour Changes for Specific Weight Loss Strategies over Four Years in US Adults," *International Journal of Obesity* 23, no. 3 (1999): 320–27.

16. Robyn L. Osborn, Kelly L. Forys, Tricia L. Psota, and Tracy Sbrocco, "Yo-Yo Dieting in African American Women: Weight Cycling and Health," *Ethnicity & Disease* 21, no. 3 (2011): 274–80.

17. Huda I. A. Qazi and Harshad Keval, "At War with Their Bodies or at War with Their Minds? A Glimpse into the Lives and Minds of Female Yo-Yo Dieters—the Curtain Has Lifted in UK?" *Journal of International Women's Studies* 14, no. 1 (2013): 311–32.

18. Dani Blum, "Ozempic Can Cause Major Weight Loss. What Happens If You Stop Taking It?" *New York Times*, February 4, 2023, https://www.nytimes.com/2023/02 /03/well/live/ozempic-wegovy-weight-loss.html.

19. Chiu, "The New Weight Watchers Is All About 'Wellness.'"

20. Tia Ghose, "Counting Steps: Are You Walking More, But Enjoying It Less?" *Live Science*, January 7, 2016, https://www.livescience.com/53297-fitness-trackers-may -reduce-activity.html.

21. Mary Louise Adams, "Step-Counting in the 'Health-Society': Phenomenological Reflections on Walking in the Era of the Fitbit," *Social Theory & Health* 17, no. 1 (2019): 109–24.

22. Brittany Wong, "PSA: You Probably Don't Need to Be Weighed at the Doctor's Office," *Huffington Post*, January 19, 2022, https://www.huffpost.com/entry/you-dont-need-to-get-weighed-at-the-doctors-office_l_61e72664e4b05645a6ed73ce.

23. Virgie Tovar, "Athleta to Train Employees on Body Positive Language and Plus-Size Fit," *Forbes*, January 21, 2021, https://www.forbes.com/sites/virgietovar/2021/01/21/athleta-to-train-employees-on-body-positive-language--plus-size-fit/?sh=1a8ef2796f98.

24. Lindsay Schallon, "The Fashion Industry Has a Plus-Size Problem. These Women Want to Fix It," *Glamour*, August 26, 2019, https://www.glamour.com/story/what-its-like-to-be-plus-size-and-work-in-fashion.

25. Rachel Colls, "Outsize/Outside: Bodily Bignesses and the Emotional Experiences of British Women Shopping for Clothes," *Gender, Place & Culture* 13, no. 5 (2006): 529–45.

26. Stacy Bias, "Examining 12 'Good Fatty' Archetypes We Depend On," *Everyday Feminism*, March 4, 2015, https://everydayfeminism.com/2015/03/12-good-fatty-archetypes.

27. Stacy Bias, "12 Good Fatty Archetypes," self-published zine, June 4, 2014, http://stacybias.net/2014/06/12-good-fatty-archetypes.

28. Bias, "12 Good Fatty Archetypes."

29. Bias, "12 Good Fatty Archetypes."

30. Bias, "12 Good Fatty Archetypes."

31. Bias, "12 Good Fatty Archetypes."

32. Bias, "12 Good Fatty Archetypes."

33. Bias, "12 Good Fatty Archetypes."

34. Bias, "12 Good Fatty Archetypes."

35. Tarra L. Penney and Sara F. L. Kirk, "The Health at Every Size Paradigm and Obesity: Missing Empirical Evidence May Help Push the Reframing Obesity Debate Forward," *American Journal of Public Health* 105, no. 5 (2015): e38–e42.

36. Michael G. Perri, "The Maintenance of Treatment Effects in the Long-Term Management of Obesity," *Clinical Psychology: Science and Practice* 5, no. 4 (1998): 526–43.

37. Penney and Kirk, "The Health at Every Size Paradigm and Obesity," e38–e42.

38. Penney and Kirk, "The Health at Every Size Paradigm and Obesity," e38–e42.

39. Penney and Kirk, "The Health at Every Size Paradigm and Obesity," e38–e42.

40. M. D. Ulian et al., "Effects of Health at Every Size Interventions on Health-Related Outcomes of People with Overweight and Obesity: A Systematic Review," *Obesity Reviews* 19, no. 12 (2018): 1659–66.

41. Penney and Kirk, "The Health at Every Size Paradigm and Obesity," e38–e42.

42. Gemma Gibson, "Health(ism) at Every Size: The Duties of the 'Good Fatty,'" *Fat Studies* 11, no. 1 (2022): 22–35.

43. Deborah Harris-Moore, *Media and the Rhetoric of Body Perfection: Cosmetic Surgery, Weight Loss and Beauty in Popular Culture* (New York: Routledge, 2016); Feona

Attwood, *Porn.com: Making Sense of Online Pornography* (New York: Peter Lang, 2010); Elizabeth M. Matelski, *Reducing Bodies: Mass Culture and the Female Figure in Postwar America* (New York: Routledge, 2017).

44. Joan C. Chrisler, "Leaks, Lumps, and Lines: Stigma and Women's Bodies," *Psychology of Women Quarterly* 35, no. 2 (2011): 202–14; Margaret L. Hunter, *Race, Gender, and the Politics of Skin Tone* (New York: Routledge, 2013); Sherry Dingman, Maria E. Melilli Otte, and Christopher Foster, "Cosmetic Surgery: Feminist Perspectives," *Women & Therapy* 35, no. 3–4 (2012): 181–92.

45. Karen Synne Groven, "'They Think Surgery Is Just a Quick Fix,'" *International Journal of Qualitative Studies on Health and Well-Being* 9, no. 1 (2014).

46. "Bariatric Surgery Market Growth—at a CAGR of 9.0%," *BioSpace*, May 6, 2022, https://www.biospace.com/article/bariatric-surgery-market-growth-at-a-cagr-of -9-0-percent-emergen-research.

47. Arendse Tange Larsen, Betina Højgaard, Rikke Ibsen, and Jakob Kjellberg, "The Socio-Economic Impact of Bariatric Surgery," *Obesity Surgery* 28 (2018): 338–48; Raquel Sanchez-Santos et al., "Is the Morbid Obesity Surgery Profitable in Times of Crisis? A Cost-Benefit Analysis of Bariatric Surgery," *Cirugía Española (English Edition)* 91, no. 8 (2013): 476–84.

48. Sarah Trainer and Tonya Benjamin, "Elective Surgery to Save My Life: Rethinking the 'Choice' in Bariatric Surgery," *Journal of Advanced Nursing* 73, no. 4 (2017): 894–904.

49. Katherine A. Elder and Bruce M. Wolfe, "Bariatric Surgery: A Review of Procedures and Outcomes," *Gastroenterology* 132, no. 6 (2007): 2253–71.

50. Marie-Eve Piche, Audrey Auclair, Jany Harvey, Simon Marceau, and Paul Poirier, "How to Choose and Use Bariatric Surgery in 2015," *Canadian Journal of Cardiology* 31, no. 2 (2015): 153–66; Daniel Cottam, Jeffrey Lord, Ramsey M. Dallal, Bruce Wolfe, Kelvin Higa, Kathleen McCauley, and Philip Schauer, "Medicolegal Analysis of 100 Malpractice Claims Against Bariatric Surgeons," *Surgery for Obesity and Related Diseases* 3, no. 1 (2007): 60–66.

51. William E. Encinosa, Didem M. Bernard, Dongyi Du, and Claudia A. Steiner, "Recent Improvements in Bariatric Surgery Outcomes," *Medical Care* (2009): 531–35; "Bariatric Surgery Procedures," *American Society for Metabolic and Bariatric Surgery*, May 2021, https://asmbs.org/patients/bariatric-surgery-procedures.

52. M. Christopher Eagan, "Article Commentary: Bariatric Surgery: Malpractice Risks and Risk Management Guidelines," *American Surgeon* 71, no. 5 (2005): 369–75; Asad J. Choudhry, Nadeem N. Haddad, Matthew Martin, Cornelius A. Thiels, Elizabeth B. Habermann, and Martin D. Zielinski, "Medical Malpractice in Bariatric Surgery: A Review of 140 Medicolegal Claims," *Journal of Gastrointestinal Surgery* 21 (2017): 146–54.

53. Daniel Cottam, Jeffrey Lord, Ramsey M. Dallal, Bruce Wolfe, Kelvin Higa, Kathleen McCauley, and Philip Schauer, "Medicolegal Analysis of 100 Malpractice Claims Against Bariatric Surgeons," *Surgery for Obesity and Related Diseases* 3, no. 1 (2007): 60–66.

54. Jane Ogden, Cecilia Clementi, and Simon Aylwin, "The Impact of Obesity Surgery and the Paradox of Control: A Qualitative Study," *Psychology & Health* 21, no. 2 (2006): 273–93.

55. Karen Synne Groven, Gunn Engelsrud, and Målfrid Råheim, "Living with Bodily Changes After Weight Loss Surgery: Women's Experiences of Food and 'Dumping,'" *Phenomenology & Practice* 6, no. 1 (2012), https://journals.library.ualberta.ca/pandpr/index.php/pandpr/article/view/19853/15379.

56. Sarah Trainer, Amber Wutich, and Alexandra Brewis, "Eating in the Panopticon: Surveillance of Food and Weight Before and After Bariatric Surgery," *Medical Anthropology* 36, no. 5 (2017): 500–514.

57. Ingrid Ruud Knutsen, Laura Terragni, and Christina Foss, "Empowerment and Bariatric Surgery: Negotiations of Credibility and Control," *Qualitative Health Research* 23, no. 1 (2013): 66–77.

58. Kathryn Pauly Morgan, "Foucault, Ugly Ducklings, and Technoswans: Analyzing Fat Hatred, Weight-Loss Surgery, and Compulsory Biomedicalized Aesthetics in America," *International Journal of Feminist Approaches to Bioethics (IJFAB)* 4, no. 1 (2011): 188–220, 188.

59. Morgan, "Foucault, Ugly Ducklings, and Technoswans," 188–220.

60. Whether these weight-loss patterns could change, with the recent emergence of semaglutide medications that help to reduce appetite, such as Ozempic and Wegovy, remains to be seen. As fatness is reframed as a continuum rather than a dichotomy and as people lose smaller amounts of weight without drastic, irreversible measures like surgeries, the framing of bariatric surgery may shift.

61. Sonmoon Mohapatra, Keerthana Gangadharan, and Capecomorin S. Pitchumoni, "Malnutrition in Obesity Before and After Bariatric Surgery," *Disease-a-month* 66, no. 2 (2020): 100866; Nana Gletsu-Miller and Breanne N. Wright, "Mineral Malnutrition Following Bariatric Surgery," *Advances in Nutrition* 4, no. 5 (2013): 506–17.

62. Melissa A. Kalarchian, Marsha D. Marcus, Anita P. Courcoulas, Yu Cheng, and Michele D. Levine, "Self-Report of Gastrointestinal Side Effects After Bariatric Surgery," *Surgery for Obesity and Related Diseases* 10, no. 6 (2014): 1202–7; Emily M. Stein and Shonni J. Silverberg, "Bone Loss After Bariatric Surgery: Causes, Consequences, and Management," *Lancet Diabetes & Endocrinology* 2, no. 2 (2014): 165–74; Cindy L. Marihart, Ardith R. Brunt, and Angela A. Geraci, "Older Adults Fighting Obesity with Bariatric Surgery: Benefits, Side Effects, and Outcomes," *SAGE Open Medicine* 2 (2014): 2050312114530917.

63. Karen Synne Groven, Målfrid Råheim, and Gunn Engelsrud, "'My Quality of Life Is Worse Compared to My Earlier Life': Living with Chronic Problems After Weight Loss Surgery," *International Journal of Qualitative Studies on Health and Well-Being* 5, no. 4 (2010): article 5553.

64. Daniéla Oliveira Magro, Bruno Geloneze, Regis Delfini, Bruna Contini Pareja, Francisco Callejas, and José Carlos Pareja, "Long-Term Weight Regain After Gastric Bypass: A 5-Year Prospective Study," *Obesity Surgery* 18, no. 6 (2008): 648–51.

65. David B. Sarwer and Anthony N. Fabricatore, "Psychiatric Considerations of the Massive Weight Loss Patient," *Clinics in Plastic Surgery* 35, no. 1 (2008): 1–10; John B. Dixon, Maureen E. Dixon, and Paul E. O'Brien, "Body Image: Appearance Orientation and Evaluation in the Severely Obese: Changes with Weight Loss," *Obesity Surgery* 12, no. 1 (2002): 65–71.

66. Bennet I. Omalu, Diane G. Ives, Alhaji M. Buhari, Jennifer L. Lindner, Philip R. Schauer, Cyril H. Wecht, and Lewis H. Kuller, "Death Rates and Causes of Death After Bariatric Surgery for Pennsylvania Residents, 1995 to 2004," *Archives of Surgery* 142, no. 10 (2007): 923–28.

67. Hilary A. Tindle, Bennet Omalu, Anita Courcoulas, Marsha Marcus, Jennifer Hammers, and Lewis H. Kuller, "Risk of Suicide After Long-Term Follow-Up from Bariatric Surgery," *American Journal of Medicine* 123, no. 11 (2010): 1036–42.

68. Karen D. Coulman, Fiona MacKichan, Jane M. Blazeby, and Amanda Owen-Smith, "Patient Experiences of Outcomes of Bariatric Surgery: A Systematic Review and Qualitative Synthesis," *Obesity Reviews* 18, no. 5 (2017): 547–559; Karen D. Coulman, Fiona MacKichan, Jane M. Blazeby, Jenny L. Donovan, and Amanda Owen-Smith, "Patients' Experiences of Life After Bariatric Surgery and Follow-Up Care: A Qualitative Study," *BMJ open* 10, no. 2 (2020): e035013.

69. "10 FAQ About Bariatric Surgery," *Baristic*, July 15, 2019, https://bariatric-surgery -tijuana.com/10-faq-about-bariatric-surgery.

CHAPTER 4: HEAVY LIFTING

1. Christy M. Glass, Steven A. Haas, and Eric N. Reither, "The Skinny on Success: Body Mass, Gender and Occupational Standing Across the Life Course," *Social Forces* 88, no. 4 (2010): 1777–1806; Katherine Haskins and Edward Ransford, "The Relationship Between Weight and Career Payoffs Among Women," *Sociological Forum* 14, no. 2 (1999): 295–318; John Cawley, "The Impact of Obesity on Wages," *Journal of Human Resources* 39, no. 2 (2004): 451–74; Sirpa Sarlio-Lähteenkorva, Karri Silventoinen, and Eero Lahelma, "Relative Weight and Income at Different Levels of Socioeconomic Status," *American Journal of Public Health* 94, no. 3 (2004): 468–72.

2. Michael Hobbes, "Everything You Know About Obesity Is Wrong," *Huffington Post*, September 19, 2018, https://highline.huffingtonpost.com/articles/en/everything -you-know-about-obesity-is-wrong.

3. Angelina R. Sutin, Yannick Stephan, and Antonio Terracciano, "Weight Discrimination and Risk of Mortality," *Psychological Science* 26, no. 11 (2015): 1803–11.

4. Rebecca Puhl and Kelly D. Brownell, "Bias, Discrimination, and Obesity," *Obesity Research* 9, no. 12 (2001): 788–805.

5. Puhl and Brownell, "Bias, Discrimination, and Obesity," 788–805.

6. Esther D. Rothblum, Pamela A. Brand, Carol T. Miller, and Helen A. Oetjen, "The Relationship Between Obesity, Employment Discrimination, and Employment-Related Victimization," *Journal of Vocational Behavior* 37, no. 3 (1990): 251–66.

7. Kaela S. Singleton, De-Shaine R. K. Murray, Angeline J. Dukes, and Lietsel N. S. Richardson, "A Year in Review: Are Diversity, Equity, and Inclusion Initiatives Fixing Systemic Barriers?" *Neuron* 109, no. 21 (2021): 3365–67; Stephanie J. Creary, Nancy Rothbard, and Jared Scruggs, *Improving Workplace Culture Through Evidence-Based Diversity, Equity and Inclusion Practices*, report, Wharton School of the University of Pennsylvania (May 2021), https://www.wharton.upenn.edu/wp-content /uploads/2021/05/Applied-Insights-Lab-Report.pdf.

8. William J. Scarborough, Danny L. Lambouths III, and Allyson L. Holbrook, "Support of Workplace Diversity Policies: The Role of Race, Gender, and Beliefs About Inequality," *Social Science Research* 79 (2019): 194–210.

9. Flora Oswald, Samantha Stevens, Mary Kruk, Catherine Murphy, and Jes L. Matsick, "Signaling Sizeism: An Assessment of Body Size-Based Threat and Safety Cues," *Analyses of Social Issues and Public Policy* 22, no. 1 (2022): 378–407.

10. Lesleigh Owen, "Living Fat in a Thin-Centric World: Effects of Spatial Discrimination on Fat Bodies and Selves," *Feminism & Psychology* 22, no. 3 (August 2012): 290–306; Lora A. Cavuoto and Maury A. Nussbaum, "Influences of Obesity on Job Demands and Worker Capacity," *Current Obesity Reports* 3, no. 3 (2014): 341–47.

11. Lucy Aphramor, "Disability and the Anti-Obesity Offensive," *Disability & Society* 24, no. 7 (2009): 897–909.

12. Gwen Moran, "5 Ways Your Workplace Isn't Accommodating to Fat People," *Fast Company*, July 12, 2021, https://www.fastcompany.com/90474839/5-ways-your -workplace-isnt-accommodating-to-fat-people.

13. Stephen Bevan, "50% of All Employers Are Less Likely to Hire Obese Candidates," World Economic Forum, February 2, 2019, https://www.weforum.org/agenda /2019/02/half-of-employers-say-they-are-less-inclined-to-recruit-obese-candidates -its-not-ok.

14. Mark V. Roehling, Patricia V. Roehling, and L. Maureen Odland, "Investigating the Validity of Stereotypes About Overweight Employees: The Relationship Between Body Weight and Normal Personality Traits," *Group & Organization Management* 33, no. 4 (2008): 392–424.

15. "Employers' Attitude to Obese Candidates," *Crossland*, April 11, 2015, https://www .crosslandsolicitors.com/site/crossland_news/Employer_survey_obese_candidates _2015_html.

16. Marco Caliendo and Wang-Sheng Lee, "Fat Chance! Obesity and the Transition from Unemployment to Employment," *Economics & Human Biology* 11, no. 2 (2013): 121–33.

17. Mark V. Roehling, Shaun Pichler, Fred Oswald, and Tamara A. Bruce, "The Effects of Weight Bias on Job-Related Outcomes: A Meta-Analysis of Experimental Studies," paper presented to the Annual Meeting of the Academy of Management, Anaheim, CA, 2008.

18. Jens Agerström and Dan-Olof Rooth, "The Role of Automatic Obesity Stereotypes in Real Hiring Discrimination," *Journal of Applied Psychology* 96, no. 4 (2011): 790–805.

19. Dan-Olof Rooth, "Obesity, Attractiveness, and Differential Treatment in Hiring: A Field Experiment," *Journal of Human Resources* 44, no. 3 (2009): 710–35.

20. Reed Alexander, "Only 15% of Hiring Managers Would Consider Hiring an Overweight Woman," *Market Watch*, December 11, 2017, https://www.marketwatch.com /story/only-15-of-hiring-managers-would-consider-hiring-an-overweight-woman -2017-12-11.

21. Regina Pingitore, Bernard L. Dugoni, R. Scott Tindale, and Bonnie Spring, "Bias Against Overweight Job Applicants in a Simulated Employment Interview," *Journal of Applied Psychology* 79, no. 6 (1994): 909–17.

22. Pingitore, Dugoni, Tindale, and Spring, "Bias Against Overweight Job Applicants in a Simulated Employment Interview," 909–17.
23. Paula M. Popovich, Wendi J. Everton, Karin L. Campbell, Rhonda M. Godinho, Kevin M. Kramer, and Michael R. Mangan, "Criteria Used to Judge Obese Persons in the Workplace," *Perceptual and Motor Skills* 85, no. 3 (1997): 859–66; Stuart W. Flint, Martin Čadek, Sonia C. Codreanu, Vanja Ivić, Colene Zomer, and Amalia Gomoiu, "Obesity Discrimination in the Recruitment Process: 'You're Not Hired!'" *Frontiers in Psychology* 7 (2016): article 647.
24. Michelle R. Hebl and Robert E. Kleck, "Acknowledging One's Stigma in the Interview Setting: Effective Strategy or Liability?" *Journal of Applied Social Psychology* 32, no. 2 (2002): 223–49.
25. Lynn K. Bartels, "Fat Women Need Not Apply: Employment Weight Discrimination Against Women," in *Handbook on Well-Being of Working Women*, ed. Mary L. Connerley and Jiyun Wu (Dordrecht: Springer, 2016), 33–46.
26. Kerry S. O'Brien, Janet D. Latner, Daria Ebneter, and Jackie A. Hunter, "Obesity Discrimination: The Role of Physical Appearance, Personal Ideology, and Anti-Fat Prejudice," *International Journal of Obesity* 37, no. 3 (2013): 455–60.
27. Mark Lacter, "In the Skinny-Is-Best Workplace, Fat Is Not Where It's At," *South Florida Sun Sentinel*, October 6, 1993, https://www.sun-sentinel.com/news/fl-xpm-1993-10-07-9310060289-story.html.
28. Charles L. Baum and William F. Ford, "The Wage Effects of Obesity: A Longitudinal Study," *Health Economics* 13, no. 9 (2004): 885–99.
29. John Cawley, "The Impact of Obesity on Wages," *Journal of Human Resources* 39, no. 2 (2004): 451–74.
30. Lindsay Dodgson, "People Who Are Overweight Get Paid Less, According to a New Study," *Insider*, November 1, 2018, https://www.insider.com/overweight-people-earn-less-money-study-shows-2018-11.
31. Cheryl L. Maranto and Ann Fraedrich Stenoien, "Weight Discrimination: A Multidisciplinary Analysis," *Employee Responsibilities and Rights Journal* 12 (2000): 9–24.
32. Sirpa Sarlio-Lähteenkorva, Karri Silventoinen, and Eero Lahelma, "Relative Weight and Income at Different Levels of Socioeconomic Status," *American Journal of Public Health* 94, no. 3 (2004): 468–72.
33. Jacob M. Burmeister, Allison E. Kiefner, Robert A. Carels, and Dara R. Musher-Eizenman, "Weight Bias in Graduate School Admissions," *Obesity* 21, no. 5 (2013): 918–20.
34. James Burford, "'Dear Obese PhD Applicants': Twitter, Tumblr, and the Contested Affective Politics of Fat Doctoral Embodiment," *M/C Journal* 18, no. 3 (2015), https://journal.media-culture.org.au/index.php/mcjournal/article/view/969.
35. Katherine Mason, "The Unequal Weight of Discrimination: Gender, Body Size, and Income Inequality," *Social Problems* 59, no. 3 (2012): 411–35.
36. Scott Klarenbach, Raj Padwal, Anderson Chuck, and Philip Jacobs, "Population-Based Analysis of Obesity and Workforce Participation," *Obesity* 14, no. 5 (2006): 920–27; Kaan Tunceli, Kemeng Li, and L. Keoki Williams, "Long-Term Effects of Obesity on Employment and Work Limitations Among US Adults, 1986 to 1999," *Obesity* 14, no. 9 (2006): 1637–46.

37. Rebecca M. Puhl and Chelsea A. Heuer, "The Stigma of Obesity: A Review and Update," *Obesity* 17, no. 5 (2009): 941–64.
38. Lindsay Dodgson, "People Who Are Overweight Get Paid Less, According to a New Study," *Insider*, November 1, 2018, https://www.insider.com/overweight-people-earn -less-money-study-shows-2018-11.
39. Bevan, "50% of All Employers Are Less Likely to Hire Obese Candidates."
40. Malgorzata Obara-Golebiowska, "Employment Discrimination Against Obese Women in Obesity Clinic's Patients Perspective," *Roczniki Państwowego Zakładu Higieny* 67, no. 2 (2016): 147–53.
41. Bevan, "50% of All Employers are Less Likely to Hire Obese Candidates."
42. Cheryl L. Maranto and Ann Fraedrich Stenoien, "Weight Discrimination: A Multi-disciplinary Analysis," *Employee Responsibilities and Rights Journal* 12 (2000): 9–24.
43. Puhl and Heuer, "The Stigma of Obesity," 941–64; Mark V. Roehling, Patricia V. Roehling, and Shaun Pichler, "The Relationship Between Body Weight and Per-ceived Weight-Related Employment Discrimination: The Role of Sex and Race," *Journal of Vocational Behavior* 71, no. 2 (2007): 300–318.
44. Roehling, Roehling, and Pichler, "The Relationship Between Body Weight and Perceived Weight-Related Employment Discrimination," 300–318.
45. Julia Carpenter, "One Type of Diversity We Don't Talk About at Work: Body Size," CNN, January 3, 2019, https://www.cnn.com/2019/01/03/success/weight-bias -work/index.html.
46. Renate van der Zee, "Demoted or Dismissed Because of Your Weight? The Reality of the Size Ceiling," *The Guardian*, August 30, 2017, https://www.theguardian .com/inequality/2017/aug/30/demoted-dismissed-weight-size-ceiling-work -discrimination.
47. Rebecca M. Puhl, Tatiana Andreyeva, and Kelly D. Brownell, "Perceptions of Weight Discrimination: Prevalence and Comparison to Race and Gender Discrimi-nation in America," *International Journal of Obesity* 32, no. 6 (2008): 992–1000.
48. Deborah Carr and Michael A. Friedman, "Is Obesity Stigmatizing? Body Weight, Perceived Discrimination, and Psychological Well-Being in the United States," *Journal of Health and Social Behavior* 46, no. 3 (2005): 244–59.
49. Patricia V. Roehling, Mark V. Roehling, Jeffrey D. Vandlen, Justin Blazek, and Wil-liam C. Guy, "Weight Discrimination and the Glass Ceiling Effect Among Top US CEOs," *Equal Opportunities International* 28, no. 2 (2009): 179–96.
50. Mark V. Roehling, Patricia V. Roehling, and Maria Fernanda Wagstaff, "Sex Differ-ences in Perceived Weight-Based Employment Discrimination When Weight Dis-crimination Is Illegal," *Employee Responsibilities and Rights Journal* 25 (2013): 159–76.
51. Yueting Ji, Qianyao Huang, Haiyang Liu, and Caleb Phillips, "Weight Bias 2.0: The Effect of Perceived Weight Change on Performance Evaluation and the Moderat-ing Role of Anti-Fat Bias," *Frontiers in Psychology* 12 (2021).
52. Michael Addison Johnson and Matthew D. Griffith, "Heavy Is the Head That Wears the Crown? Employee Reactions to a Supervisor's Adiposity," *Academy of Management Proceedings* 1 (2016): article 16289.
53. Van der Zee, "Demoted or Dismissed Because of Your Weight? The Reality of the Size Ceiling."

54. Stuart W. Flint and Jeremé Snook, "Obesity and Discrimination: The Next 'Big Issue'?" *International Journal of Discrimination and the Law* 14, no. 3 (2014): 183–93.

55. Moran, "5 Ways Your Workplace Isn't Accommodating to Fat People."

56. Joseph A. Bellizzi and Ronald W. Hasty, "The Effects of a Stated Organizational Policy on Inconsistent Disciplinary Action Based on Salesperson Gender and Weight," *Journal of Personal Selling & Sales Management* 21, no. 3 (2001): 189–98; Janna Fikkan and Esther Rothblum, "Weight Bias in Employment," in *Weight Bias: Nature, Consequences, and Remedies*, ed. Kelly D. Brownell, Rebecca M. Puhl, Marlene B. Schwartz, and Leslie Ed Rudd (New York: Guilford, 2005), 15–28.

57. Rachel Gaines and Vinod Vincent, "Weight Discrimination: Implications to the Workplace," *Strategic HR Review* 21, no. 2 (2022): 54–58.

58. Noortje van Amsterdam and Dide van Eck, "In the Flesh: A Poetic Inquiry into How Fat Female Employees Manage Weight-Related Stigma," *Culture and Organization* 25, no. 4 (2019): 300–316.

59. Noortje van Amsterdam and Dide van Eck, "'I Have to Go the Extra Mile': How Fat Female Employees Manage Their Stigmatized Identity at Work," *Scandinavian Journal of Management* 35, no. 1 (2019): 46–55.

60. Esther D. Rothblum, Pamela A. Brand, Carol T. Miller, and Helen A. Oetjen, "The Relationship Between Obesity, Employment Discrimination, and Employment-Related Victimization," *Journal of Vocational Behavior* 37, no. 3 (1990): 251–66; Van Amsterdam and van Eck, "'I Have to Go the Extra Mile,'" 46–55.

61. Andrea N. Hunt and Tammy Rhodes, "Fat Pedagogy and Microaggressions: Experiences of Professionals Working in Higher Education Settings," *Fat Studies* 7, no. 1 (2018): 21–32; Christina Fisanick, "'They Are Weighted with Authority': Fat Female Professors in Academic and Popular Cultures," *Feminist Teacher* 17, no. 3 (2007): 237–55.

62. Christina Fisanick, "Evaluating the Absent Presence: The Professor's Body at Tenure and Promotion," *Review of Education, Pedagogy, and Cultural Studies* 28, no. 3–4 (2006): 325–38.

63. Beatrice Venturini, Luigi Castelli, and Silvia Tomelleri, "Not All Jobs Are Suitable for Fat People: Experimental Evidence of a Link Between Being Fat and 'Out-of-Sight' Jobs," *Social Behavior and Personality* 34, no. 4 (2006): 389–98.

64. Bridget Miller, "Accommodation Options for Overweight Employees," *HR Advisor*, April 26, 2019, https://hrdailyadvisor.blr.com/2019/04/26/accommodation-options -for-overweight-employees.

65. Moran, "5 Ways Your Workplace Isn't Accommodating to Fat People."

66. Suzanne Lucas, "Your Employees Are Fat. Make Your Office Accommodating," *Inc.*, June 15, 2021, https://www.inc.com/suzanne-lucas/your-employees-are-fat-make -your-office-accommodating.html.

67. Mikki Hebl, Cassandra N. Phetmisy, Ivy Watson, and Felix Y. Wu, "Reducing Weight Stigma in the Workplace," in *Innovative Stigma and Discrimination Reduction Programs Across the World*, ed. Alicia H. Nordstrom and Wind Goodfriend (New York: Routledge, 2021), 203–15.

68. Erika Edwards, "As Weight Loss Drugs Soar in Popularity, Many Who Benefit Can't Get Them," NBC News, February 2, 2023, https://www.nbcnews.com/health /health-news/ozempic-wegovy-weight-loss-drugs-demand-soars-rcna68425.

69. Karen M. Powroznik, "Healthism and Weight-Based Discrimination: The Unintended Consequences of Health Promotion in the Workplace," *Work and Occupations* 44, no. 2 (2017): 139–70.
70. Emily Douglas, "Should Overweight Staff Be Allowed to Start Work Late?" *Human Resources Director*, May 28, 2018, https://www.hcamag.com/ca/specialization /benefits/should-overweight-staff-be-allowed-to-start-work-late/120775.
71. Heidi M. Blanck, Amy L. Yaroch, Audie A. Atienza, Sarah L. Yi, Jian Zhang, and Louise C. Mâsse, "Factors Influencing Lunchtime Food Choices Among Working Americans," *Health Education & Behavior* 36, no. 2 (2009): 289–301.
72. Nicole Maestas, Kathleen J. Mullen, and Stephanie Rennane, "Unmet Need for Workplace Accommodation," *Journal of Policy Analysis and Management* 38, no. 4 (2019): 1004–27.
73. Chris Ceplenski, "Reasonable Accommodations for Obesity as a Disability," *HR Daily Advisor*, May 18, 2015, https://hrdailyadvisor.blr.com/2014/03/03/reasonable -accommodations-for-obesity-as-a-disability; Mark V. Roehling and Mevan Jayasinghe, "One Size Does Not Fit All: Accommodating Obesity-Related Disabilities in the Workplace," *Employee Responsibilities and Rights Journal* 31, no. 1 (2019): 1–27.
74. Jessica Marinelli and Jim Paretti, "Risky Business: EEOC Interprets ADA Coverage for Individuals at Higher Risk of Contracting COVID-19," *Littler*, May 8, 2020, https://www.littler.com/publication-press/publication/risky-business-eeoc-interprets -ada-coverage-individuals-higher-risk; Frank Griffin, "Covid-19 and the Americans with Disabilities Act: Balancing Fear, Safety, and Risk as America Goes Back to Work," *Seton Hall Law Review* 51 (2020): 383–429.
75. Tom Usher, "Obese Employees Should Be Able to Work from Home, Government Advisor Says," *Metro*, May 26, 2018, https://metro.co.uk/2018/05/26/obese -employees-should-be-able-to-work-from-home-government-adviser-says -7579664.
76. Stuart W. Flint and Jeremé Snook, "Obesity and Discrimination: The Next 'Big Issue'?" *International Journal of Discrimination and the Law* 14, no. 3 (2014): 183–93.
77. Anna Kirkland, *Fat Rights: Dilemmas of Difference and Personhood* (New York: New York University Press, 2008), 26.
78. Kirkland, *Fat Rights*.
79. Noortje Van Amsterdam, "Big Fat Inequalities, Thin Privilege: An Intersectional Perspective on 'Body Size,'" *European Journal of Women's Studies* 20, no. 2 (2013): 155–69.
80. Anwyn Crawford, "Fat, Privilege, and Resistance," *Overland* 208 (Spring 2012): 15–19, https://overland.org.au/previous-issues/issue-208/feature-anwyn-crawford.
81. Meredith Nash and Megan Warin, "Squeezed Between Identity Politics and Intersectionality: A Critique of 'Thin Privilege' in Fat Studies," *Feminist Theory* 18, no. 1 (2017): 69–87.
82. Peggy McIntosh, "White Privilege: Unpacking the Invisible Knapsack," *Peace & Freedom* (1989), https://psychology.umbc.edu/wp-content/uploads/sites/57/2016 /10/White-Privilege_McIntosh-1989.pdf.
83. Crawford, "Fat, Privilege, and Resistance," 15–19.

CHAPTER 5: THE SPECTER OF FAT DEATH

1. Freda Mold and Angus Forbes, "Patients' and Professionals' Experiences and Perspectives of Obesity in Health-Care Settings: A Synthesis of Current Research," *Health Expectations* 16, no. 2 (2013): 119–42.

2. Angela S. Alberga, Iyoma Y. Edache, Mary Forhan, and Shelly Russell-Mayhew, "Weight Bias and Health Care Utilization: A Scoping Review," *Primary Health Care Research & Development* 20 (2019): 1–14.

3. Michael Hobbes, "Everything You Know About Obesity Is Wrong," *Huffington Post*, September 19, 2018, https://highline.huffingtonpost.com/articles/en/everything -you-know-about-obesity-is-wrong.

4. Hobbes, "Everything You Know About Obesity Is Wrong."

5. Joy Wilke, "Nearly Half in U.S. Remain Worried About Their Weight," *Gallup*, July 25, 2014, https://news.gallup.com/poll/174089/nearly-half-remain-worried-weight .aspx; Hobbes, "Everything You Know About Obesity Is Wrong."

6. Kaitlin Sullivan, "New Guidelines for Treating Childhood Obesity Include Medications and Surgery for First Time," NBC News, January 9, 2023, https://www.nbc news.com/health/kids-health/new-guidelines-treating-childhood-obesity-include -medications-surgery-rcna64651.

7. Hobbes, "Everything You Know About Obesity Is Wrong."

8. Fangjian Guo and W. Timothy Garvey, "Cardiometabolic Disease Risk in Metabolically Healthy and Unhealthy Obesity: Stability of Metabolic Health Status in Adults," *Obesity* 24, no. 2 (2016): 516–25.

9. Hobbes, "Everything You Know About Obesity Is Wrong."

10. David P. Miller Jr., John G. Spangler, Mara Z. Vitolins, Mr Stephen W. Davis, Edward H. Ip, Gail S. Marion, and Sonia J. Crandall, "Are Medical Students Aware of Their Anti-Obesity Bias?" *Academic Medicine: Journal of the Association of American Medical Colleges* 88, no. 7 (2013): 978–82; Sean M. Phelan et al., "The Mixed Impact of Medical School on Medical Students' Implicit and Explicit Weight Bias," *Medical Education* 49, no. 10 (2015): 983–92.

11. Cat Pausé, "Die Another Day: The Obstacles Facing Fat People in Accessing Quality Healthcare," *Narrative Inquiry in Bioethics* 4, no. 2 (2014): 135–41; Janice A. Sabin, Maddalena Marini, and Brian A. Nosek, "Implicit and Explicit Anti-Fat Bias Among a Large Sample of Medical Doctors by BMI, Race/Ethnicity and Gender," *PloS One* 7, no. 11 (2012): e48448.

12. Kate Siber, "'You Don't Look Anorexic': New Research Shows That Our Assumptions About Eating Disorders Are Often Wrong—And That Many Larger-Bodied People Are Starving Themselves," *New York Times*, November 10, 2022, https:// www.nytimes.com/2022/10/18/magazine/anorexia-obesity-eating-disorder.html; Deborah L. Reas and Carlos M. Grilo, "Timing and Sequence of the Onset of Overweight, Dieting, and Binge Eating in Overweight Patients with Binge Eating Disorder," *International Journal of Eating Disorders* 40, no. 2 (2007): 165–70.

13. Ian Brown and Stuart W. Flint, "Weight Bias and the Training of Health Professionals to Better Manage Obesity: What Do We Know and What Should We Do?" *Current Obesity Reports* 2 (2013): 333–40.

14. Justine Seymour, Jennifer L. Barnes, Julie Schumacher, and Rachel L. Vollmer, "A Qualitative Exploration of Weight Bias and Quality of Health Care Among Health Care Professionals Using Hypothetical Patient Scenarios," *Inquiry: The Journal of Health Care Organization, Provision, and Financing* 55 (2018): 0046958018774171.

15. Laura Pengelly, John Cousins, Andrew McKechnie, "Communicating Risks of Obesity Before Anaesthesia from the Patient's Perspective: Informed Consent or Fat-Shaming?" *Anaesthesia* 76, no. 2 (2021): 282–83.

16. Michelle R. Hebl and Jie Xu, "Weighing the Care: Physicians' Reactions to the Size of a Patient," *International Journal of Obesity* 25, no. 8 (2001): 1246–52.

17. Bob LaMendola and Sun Sentinel, "Some OB-GYNs in South Florida Turn Away Overweight Women," *Sun Sentinel*, May 15, 2011, https://www.sun-sentinel.com/fl-xpm-2011-05-16-fl-hk-no-obesity-doc-20110516-story.html; J. Firger, "Doctor Turns Away Obese Patients," *Everyday Health*, August 29, 2012, http://www.everydayhealth.com/weight/0829/doctor-turns-away-obese-patients.aspx.

18. Nir Eyal, "Denial of Treatment to Obese Patients: The Wrong Policy on Personal Responsibility for Health," *International Journal of Health Policy and Management* 1, no. 2 (2013): 107–10.

19. Emma Austen and Scott Griffiths, "Weight Stigma Predicts Reduced Psychological Wellbeing and Weight Gain Among Sexual Minority Men: A 12-Month Longitudinal Cohort Study Using Random Intercept Cross-Lagged Panel Models," *Body Image* 40 (2022): 19–29; Jeffrey M. Hunger, Brenda Major, Alison Blodorn, and Carol T. Miller, "Weighed Down by Stigma: How Weight-Based Social Identity Threat Contributes to Weight Gain and Poor Health," *Social and Personality Psychology Compass* 9, no. 6 (2015): 255–68.

20. Adeline L. Goss, Leah Rethy, Rebecca L. Pearl, and Horace M. DeLisser, "The 'Difficult' Cadaver: Weight Bias in the Gross Anatomy Lab," *Medical Education Online* 25, no. 1 (2020): 1742966.

21. Hobbes, "Everything You Know About Obesity Is Wrong."

22. Jeanne M. Ferrante, Eric K. Seaman, Alicja Bator, Pamela Ohman-Strickland, Daniel Gundersen, Lynn Clemow, and Rebecca Puhl, "Impact of Perceived Weight Stigma Among Underserved Women on Doctor-Patient Relationships," *Obesity Science & Practice* 2, no. 2 (2016): 128–35.

23. Tasha M. Hughes et al., "Practices and Perceptions Among Surgical Oncologists in the Perioperative Care of Obese Cancer Patients," *Annals of Surgical Oncology* 25 (2018): 2513–19.

24. Maria C. Cusimano, Andrea N. Simpson, Angela Han, Robin Hayeems, Marcus Q. Bernardini, Deborah Robertson, Sari L. Kives, Abheha Satkunaratnam, Nancy N. Baxter, and Sarah E. Ferguson, "Barriers to Care for Women with Low-Grade Endometrial Cancer and Morbid Obesity: A Qualitative Study," *BMJ Open* 9, no. 6 (2019): e026872.

25. Henri Azaïs, Gaby Moawad, Catherine Uzan, Geoffroy Canlorbe, and Jérémie Belghiti, "Perceptions, Relationship, and Management of Morbidly Obese Patients and the Role of Robotic Surgery," *Obesity Surgery* 29 (2019): 4062–63.

26. Pausé, "Die Another Day," 135–41.

27. Pausé, "Die Another Day," 135–41.

28. Pausé, "Die Another Day," 135–41, 138.

29. Hobbes, "Everything You Know About Obesity Is Wrong."

30. Siber, "'You Don't Look Anorexic.'"

31. Siber, "'You Don't Look Anorexic.'"

32. Hobbes, "Everything You Know About Obesity Is Wrong."

33. "People of Color and Eating Disorders," National Eating Disorders Association, https://www.nationaleatingdisorders.org/people-color-and-eating-disorders.

34. Blake J. Lawrence, Deborah Kerr, Christina M. Pollard, Mary Theophilus, Elise Alexander, Darren Haywood, and Moira O'Connor, "Weight Bias Among Health Care Professionals: A Systematic Review and Meta-Analysis," *Obesity* 29, no. 11 (2021): 1802–12.

35. American Psychological Association, "Fat Shaming in the Doctor's Office Can Be Mentally and Physically Harmful," press release, August 3, 2017.

36. Astrid van Huisstede, Manuel Castro Cabezas, Gert-Jan M. van de Geijn, Guido H. Mannaerts, Tjin L. Njo, Christian Taube, Pieter S. Hiemstra, and Gert-Jan Braunstahl, "Underdiagnosis and Overdiagnosis of Asthma in the Morbidly Obese," *Respiratory Medicine* 107, no. 9 (2013): 1356–64; Bruce Jancin, "Knee Osteoarthritis Often Overlooked in the Obese," *Family Practice News* 43, no. 19 (2013): 5–10; Frits M. E. Franssen, "Overweight and Obesity Are Risk Factors for COPD Misdiagnosis and Overtreatment," *Chest* 146, no. 6 (2014): 1426–28.

37. Virginie Borgès Da Silva, Roxane Borgès Da Silva, Jean Michel Azorin, and Raoul Belzeaux, "Mood Disorders Are Highly Prevalent but Underdiagnosed Among Patients Seeking Bariatric Surgery," *Obesity Surgery* 25, no. 3 (2015): 543–44.

38. Joan C. Chrisler and Angela Barney, "Sizeism Is a Health Hazard," *Fat Studies* 6, no. 1 (2017): 38–53.

39. Stewart C. Alexander, Mary E. Cox, Christy L. Boling Turer, Pauline Lyna, Truls Østbye, James A. Tulsky, Rowena J. Dolor, and Kathryn I. Pollak, "Do the Five A's Work When Physicians Counsel About Weight Loss?" *Family Medicine* 43, no. 3 (2011): 179–184.

40. Kimberly A. Gudzune, Mary Catherine Beach, Debra L. Roter, and Lisa A. Cooper, "Physicians Build Less Rapport with Obese Patients," *Obesity* 21, no. 10 (2013): 2146–52.

41. Jenny Carryer, "Embodied Largeness: A Significant Women's Health Issue," *Nursing Inquiry* 8, no. 2 (2001): 90–97; Christine Aramburu Alegria Drury and Margaret Louis, "Exploring the Association Between Body Weight, Stigma of Obesity, and Health Care Avoidance," *Journal of the American Academy of Nurse Practitioners* 14, no. 12 (2002): 554–561.

42. Chrisler and Barney, "Sizeism Is a Health Hazard," 38–53.

43. Emily Allen Paine, "'Fat Broken Arm Syndrome': Negotiating Risk, Stigma, and Weight Bias in LGBTQ Healthcare," *Social Science & Medicine* 270 (2021): article 113609.

44. Kelso Harper, "'That Could Have Killed Me': How Anti-Fat Bias Can Be Dangerous, Even Deadly, for Heavier Patients," (master's thesis, MIT, 2021), https://dspace.mit.edu/handle/1721.1/139976?show=full; Jennifer Adaeze Okwerekwu, "In

Treating Obese Patients, Too Often Doctors Can't See Past Weight," *STAT*, June 3, 2016, https://www.statnews.com/2016/06/03/weight-obese-doctors-patients.

45. Caroline Hallen Moore, Tracy L. Oliver, Justus Randolph, and Elizabeth B. Dowdell, "Interventions for Reducing Weight Bias in Healthcare Providers: An Interprofessional Systematic Review and Meta-Analysis," *Clinical Obesity* 12, no. 6 (2022): e12545.

46. Charlotte Cooper, "Fat Studies: Mapping the Field," *Sociology Compass* 4, no. 12 (2010): 1020–34; Paul Campos, "Does Fat Kill? A Critique of the Epidemiological Evidence," in *Debating Obesity: Critical Perspectives*, ed. Emma Rich, Lee F. Monaghan, and Lucy Aphramor (London: Palgrave, 2011), 36–59.

47. Hobbes, "Everything You Know About Obesity Is Wrong."

48. Sandee LaMotte, "Half of America Will Be Obese Within 10 Years, Study Says, Unless We Work Together," CNN, December 19, 2019, https://www.cnn.com/2019/12/18/health/american-obesity-trends-wellness/index.html.

49. Tamar Haspel, "6 Ideas for Curbing Our Obesity Epidemic," *Washington Post*, September 21, 2018, https://www.washingtonpost.com/lifestyle/food/6-ideas-for-curbing-our-obesity-epidemic/2018/09/20/e959a3c2-bb74-11e8-bdc0-90f81cc58c5d_story.html.

50. Sameer Mohammad, Rafia Aziz, Saeed Al Mahri, Shuja Shafi Malik, Esraa Haji, Altaf Husain Khan, Tanvir Saleem Khatlani, and Abderrezak Bouchama, "Obesity and COVID-19: What Makes Obese Host So Vulnerable?" *Immunity & Ageing* 18, no. 1 (2021): article 1.

51. Rebecca L. Pearl, "Weight Stigma and the 'Quarantine-15,'" *Obesity*, 28, no. 7 (2020): 1180–81.

52. "Now that I've lived through a plague …," iFunny, April 19, 2020, https://ifunny.co/meme/now-that-i-ve-lived-during-a-plague-i-understand-TSdlhDza7.

53. Madeline Ward, "Fatphobia, Women, and COVID-19," *Blog of the APA: Women in Philosophy*, July 15, 2020, https://blog.apaonline.org/2020/07/15/fatphobia-women-and-covid-19.

54. Renee Cafaro, "My Body Should Not Be Your New Favorite Coronavirus Quarantine Punchline," *Huffington Post*, April 26, 2020, https://www.huffpost.com/entry/fat-shaming-memes-coronavirus_n_5ea2f6d5c5b6f9639813b568.

55. Leah M. Lessard and Rebecca M. Puhl, "Adolescents' Exposure to and Experiences of Weight Stigma During the COVID-19 Pandemic," *Journal of Pediatric Psychology* 46, no. 8 (2021): 950–59.

56. Kirsten Weir, "The Extra Weight of COVID-19," *Monitor on Psychology*, July 2021, https://www.apa.org/monitor/2021/07/extra-weight-covid.

57. Pearl, "Weight Stigma and the 'Quarantine-15,'" 1180–81.

58. A. Janet Tomiyama, "Weight Stigma Is Stressful. A Review of Evidence for the Cyclic Obesity/Weight-Based Stigma Model," *Appetite* 82 (2014): 8–15.

59. Joseph D. Wellman, Ashley M. Araiza, Ellen E. Newell, and Shannon K. McCoy, "Weight Stigma Facilitates Unhealthy Eating and Weight Gain Via Fear of Fat," *Stigma and Health* 3, no. 3 (2018): 186–94.

60. Oli Williams and Ellen Annandale, "Obesity, Stigma and Reflexive Embodiment: Feeling the 'Weight' of Expectation," *Health* 24, no. 4 (2020): 421–41.

61. William Dietz and Carlos Santos-Burgoa, "Obesity and Its Implications for COVID-19 Mortality," *Obesity* 28, no. 6 (2020): 1.

62. Sara Y. Tartof et al., "Obesity and Mortality Among Patients Diagnosed with COVID-19: Results from an Integrated Health Care Organization," *Annals of Internal Medicine* 173, no. 10 (2020): 773–81.

63. Fengqin Zhang et al., "Obesity Predisposes to the Risk of Higher Mortality in Young COVID-19 Patients," *Journal of Medical Virology* 92, no. 11 (2020): 2536–42.

64. Zhang et al., "Obesity Predisposes to the Risk of Higher Mortality in Young COVID-19 Patients," 2536–42; Gianluca Iacobellis, Alexis Elias Malavazos, and Tanira Ferreira, "COVID-19 Rise in Younger Adults with Obesity: Visceral Adiposity Can Predict the Risk," *Obesity* 28, no. 10 (2020): 1795.

65. Amany Magdy Beshbishy, Helal F. Hetta, Diaa E. Hussein, Abdullah A. Saati, Christian C. Uba, Nallely Rivero-Perez, Adrian Zaragoza-Bastida, Muhammad Ajmal Shah, Tapan Behl, and Gaber El-Saber Batiha, "Factors Associated with Increased Morbidity and Mortality of Obese and Overweight COVID-19 Patients," *Biology* 9, no. 9 (2020): 280–304.

66. Meridith Wadman, "Why COVID-19 Is More Deadly in People with Obesity— Even If They're Young," *Science*, September 8, 2020, https://www.sciencemag.org/news/2020/09/why-covid-19-more-deadly-people-obesity-even-if-theyre-young.

67. Matteo Rottoli et al., "Obesity Is One of the Strongest Risk Factor for Respiratory Failure and Death in COVID-19 Patients: A Retrospective Multicentric Cohort Study," *The Lancet* (2020), https://papers.ssrn.com/sol3/papers.cfm?abstract_id=3578779.

68. Andrea P. Rossi, Leonardo Gottin, Katia Donadello, Vittorio Schweiger, Riccardo Nocini, Matteo Taiana, Mauro Zamboni, and Enrico Polati, "Obesity as a Risk Factor for Unfavourable Outcomes in Critically Ill Patients Affected by Covid 19," *Nutrition, Metabolism, and Cardiovascular Diseases* 31, no. 3 (2021): 762–68.

69. Barry M. Popkin, Shufa Du, William D. Green, Melinda A. Beck, Taghred Algaith, Christopher H. Herbst, Reem F. Alsukait, Mohammed Alluhidan, Nahar Alazemi, and Meera Shekar, "Individuals with Obesity and COVID-19: A Global Perspective on the Epidemiology and Biological Relationships," *Obesity Reviews* 21, no. 11 (2020): e13128.

70. Eyal Klang, Gassan Kassim, Shelly Soffer, Robert Freeman, Matthew A. Levin, and David L. Reich, "Severe Obesity as an Independent Risk Factor for COVID-19 Mortality in Hospitalized Patients Younger Than 50," *Obesity* 28, no. 9 (2020): 1595–99.

71. Sarah Boseley, "Covid Deaths High in Countries with More Overweight People, Says Report," *The Guardian*, March 3, 2021, https://www.theguardian.com/world/2021/mar/03/covid-deaths-high-in-countries-with-more-overweight-people-says-report.

72. Kevin M. Curtin, Lisa R. Pawloski, Penelope Mitchell, and Jillian Dunbar, "COVID-19 and Morbid Obesity: Associations and Consequences for Policy and Practice," *World Medical and Health Policy* 12, no. 4 (2020): 512–32.

73. Nicolas S. Hendren et al., "Association of Body Mass Index and Age with Morbidity and Mortality in Patients Hospitalized with COVID-19: Results from the American Heart Association COVID-19 Cardiovascular Disease Registry," *Circulation* 143, no. 2 (2021): 135–44.

74. Maura Judkis, "People Are Getting Vaccinated Due to Their BMI. They Have Mixed Feelings About It," *Washington Post*, March 9, 2021, https://www.washington post.com/lifestyle/style/vaccine-obesity-bmi-covid/2021/03/08/dd795fea-7c4a -11eb-a976-c028a4215c78_story.html.

75. Sarah Varney, "High Obesity Rates in Southern States Magnify COVID-19's Threat," NPR, March 11, 2021, https://www.npr.org/sections/health-shots/2021/03 /11/975486163/high-obesity-rates-in-southern-states-magnify-covid-19-s-threat.

76. Anna Maria Rychter, Agnieszka Zawada, Alicja Ewa Ratajczak, Agnieszka Dobro-wolska, and Iwona Krela-Kaźmierczak, "Should Patients with Obesity Be More Afraid of COVID-19?" *Obesity Reviews* 21, no. 9 (2020): e13083.

77. Alice Tamara and Dicky L. Tahapary, "Obesity as a Predictor for a Poor Prognosis of COVID-19: A Systematic Review," *Diabetes & Metabolic Syndrome: Clinical Research & Reviews* 14, no. 4 (2020): 655–59.

78. "Prioritization of Anti-SARS-CoV-2 Monoclonal Antibodies and Oral Antivirals for the Treatment of COVID-19 During Times of Resource Limitations," New York Department of Health, December 29, 2021, https://coronavirus.health.ny .gov/system/files/documents/2021/12/prioritization_of_mabs_during_resource _shortages_20211229.pdf.

79. Carole H. Sudre et al., "Attributes and Predictors of Long COVID," *Nature Medicine* 27, no. 4 (2021): 626–31.

80. Abigail Saguy, "Why Fat Is a Feminist Issue," *Sex Roles* 66 (2012): 600–607.

81. Ying Sun, Quanyi Wang, Guoyan Yang, Changying Lin, Yi Zhang, and Peng Yang, "Weight and Prognosis for Influenza A (H1N1) Infection During the Pandemic Period Between 2009 and 2011: A Systematic Review of Observational Studies with Meta-Analysis," *Infectious Diseases* 48, no. 11–12 (2016): 813–22.

82. Nikhil V. Dhurandhar, Dylan Bailey, and Diana Thomas, "Interaction of Obesity and Infections," *Obesity Reviews* 16, no. 12 (2015): 1017–29; Raul Pellini et al., "Obesity May Hamper SARS-CoV-2 Vaccine Immunogenicity," *MedRXiv* (2021), https:// www.medrxiv.org/content/10.1101/2021.02.24.21251664v1.full.pdf.

83. Scott D. Painter, Inna G. Ovsyannikova, and Gregory A. Poland, "The Weight of Obesity on the Human Immune Response to Vaccination," *Vaccine* 33, no. 36 (2015): 4422–29.

84. Painter, Ovsyannikova, and Poland, "The Weight of Obesity on the Human Immune Response to Vaccination," 4422–29.

85. Sarah Varney, "America's Obesity Epidemic Threatens Effectiveness of Any COVID Vaccine," KHN, August 6, 2020, https://khn.org/news/americas-obesity-epidemic -threatens-effectiveness-of-any-covid-vaccine/.

86. Scott D. Neidich, William D. Green, Jennifer Rebeles, Erik A. Karlsson, Stacey Schultz-Cherry, Terry L. Noah, Sujatro Chakladar, Michael G. Hudgens, Sam S. Weir, and Melinda A. Beck, "Increased Risk of Influenza Among Vaccinated Adults Who Are Obese," *International Journal of Obesity* 41, no. 9 (2017): 1324–30.

87. Wei Fan, Xiao-fang Chen, Chao Shen, Zhi-rong Guo, and Chen Dong, "Hepatitis B Vaccine Response in Obesity: A Meta-Analysis," *Vaccine* 34, no. 40 (2016): 4835–41.

88. Miriam E. Tucker, "Diabetes, Obesity Weaken COVID-19 Vaccine Response," *Univadis*, February 7, 2023, https://www.univadis.com/viewarticle/diabetes-obesity -weaken-covid-19-vaccine-response-2023a10002hg; Arwa A. Faizo et al., "A Potential

Association Between Obesity and Reduced Effectiveness of COVID-19 Vaccine–Induced Neutralizing Humoral Immunity," *Journal of Medical Virology* 95, no. 1 (2023): e28130.

89. Sara Palma and Pamela Strohfus, "Are IM Injections IM in Obese and Overweight Females? A Study in Injection Technique," *Applied Nursing Research* 26, no. 4 (2013): e1–e4.

90. Shradha Chhabria and Fatima Cody Stanford, "A Long Shot: The Importance of Needle Length in Vaccinating Patients with Obesity Against COVID-19," *Vaccine* 40, no. 1 (2022): 9–10; Ronnie Sebro, "Statistical Estimation of Deltoid Subcutaneous Fat Pad Thickness: Implications for Needle Length for Vaccination," *Scientific Reports* 12, no. 1 (2022): 1–8; David J. Weber, William A. Rutala, Gregory P. Samsa, Jane E. Santimaw, and Stanley M. Lemon, "Obesity as a Predictor of Poor Antibody Response to Hepatitis B Plasma Vaccine," *JAMA* 254, no. 22 (1985): 3187–89; Gregory A. Poland, Aleta Borrud, Robert M. Jacobson, Kristina McDermott, Peter C. Wollan, Duane Brakke, and J. William Charboneau, "Determination of Deltoid Fat Pad Thickness: Implications for Needle Length in Adult Immunization," *JAMA* 277, no. 21 (1997): 1709–11.

91. Mette Gyldenløve, Lone Skov, Cecilie B. Hansen, and Peter Garred, "Recurrent Injection-Site Reactions After Incorrect Subcutaneous Administration of a COVID-19 Vaccine," *Journal of the European Academy of Dermatology and Venereology* 35, no. 9 (2021): e545.

92. Amy B. Middleman, Roberta Anding, and Celestine Tung, "Effect of Needle Length When Immunizing Obese Adolescents with Hepatitis B Vaccine," *Pediatrics* 125, no. 3 (2010): e508–e512.

93. Maria K. Poirier, Gregory A. Poland, and Robert M. Jacobson, "Parameters Potentially Affecting Interpretation of Immunogenicity and Efficacy Data in Vaccine Trials: Are They Adequately Reported?" *Vaccine* 14, no. 1 (1996): 25–27.

94. Chhabria and Stanford, "A Long Shot," 9–10.

95. Kimberly Dark, "Fat Activism," interview by Breanne Fahs, Zoom, April 8, 2022.

96. "Know Your Rights Guide to Surviving COVID-19 Triage Protocols," *#NoBodyIs Disposable*, accessed February 24, 2023, https://nobodyisdisposable.org/know-your-rights.

97. "Know Your Rights Guide to Surviving COVID-19 Triage Protocols."

98. Cat Pausé and Sonya Renee Taylor, "Fattening Up Scholarship," in *The Routledge International Handbook of Fat Studies*, eds. Cat Pausé and Sonya Renee Taylor (New York: Routledge, 2021), 1–18; Cat J. Pausé, "Ray of Light: Standpoint Theory, Fat Studies, and a New Fat Ethics," *Fat Studies* 9, no. 2. (2020): 42–56; Cat J. Pausé, "Living to Tell: Coming Out as Fat," *Somatechnics* 2, no. 1 (2012): 42–56; Cat Pausé, Jackie Wykes, and Samantha Murray, eds., *Queering Fat Embodiment* (New York: Routledge, 2016).

99. "Massey University 'Fat Studies' Professor Cat Pause Dies Suddenly," Reddit, March 26, 2022, https://www.reddit.com/r/Conservative/comments/tp9ppr/massey_university_fat_studies_professor_cat_pause.

100. "(Not a Meme) Fat Acceptance Feminist 'Healthy at Any Size,' Lecturer and One of My Inspirations Dr. Cat Pause PhD Died This Week of a Heart Attack, Aged

36. Please Take a Moment to Send Your Respects," Reddit, April 3, 2022, https://
www.reddit.com/r/LouderWithCrowder/comments/tv5zau/not_a_meme_fat
_acceptance_feminist_healthy_at_any.

101. "Crowder Responds to Cat Pausé Tragedy," *Louder with Crowder*, April 3, 2022,
https://www.youtube.com/watch?v=wOo9Gp3hOqQ.

102. Mikey Mercedes, "Fat Activism," interview by Breanne Fahs, Zoom, May 12, 2022.

103. Aubrey Gordon, "Fat Activism," interview by Breanne Fahs, Zoom, August 29,
2022.

104. Tigress Osborn, "Fat Activism," interview by Breanne Fahs, Zoom, May 12, 2022.

105. Osborn, interview.

CHAPTER 6: ON FAT VULNERABILITY

1. Peter Blanck, "Disability and Aging: Historical and Contemporary Views," in *Disability and Aging Discrimination*, ed. Richard L. Wiener and Steven L. Willborn
(New York: Springer, 2011), 49–70.

2. Jan-Ocko Heuer and Katharina Zimmermann, "Unravelling Deservingness: Which
Criteria Do People Use to Judge the Relative Deservingness of Welfare Target
Groups? A Vignette-Based Focus Group Study," *Journal of European Social Policy* 30,
no. 4 (2020): 389–403.

3. Alison Kafer, *Feminist Queer Crip* (Bloomington: Indiana University Press, 2013), 5.

4. Kafer, *Feminist Queer Crip*, 6.

5. Kafer, *Feminist Queer Crip*, 9.

6. Thomas Shakespeare, "The Social Model of Disability," in *The Disability Studies
Reader*, ed. Lennard Davis (New York: Routledge, 2010), 266–73.

7. Claire Edwards and Rob Imrie, "Disability and Bodies as Bearers of Value," *Sociology*
37, no. 2 (2003): 239–56.

8. Doron Dorfman, "Fear of the Disability Con: Perceptions of Fraud and Special
Rights Discourse," *Law & Society Review* 53, no. 4 (2019): 1051–91.

9. Dorfman, "Fear of the Disability Con," 1051–91.

10. Doron Dorfman, "[Un] Usual Suspects: Deservingness, Scarcity, and Disability
Rights," *UC Irvine Law Review* 10 (2019): 557–618.

11. Karen Soldatic and Barbara Pini, "The Three Ds of Welfare Reform: Disability, Disgust and Deservingness," *Australian Journal of Human Rights* 15, no. 1 (2009): 77–95.

12. Marjolein Jeene, Wim Van Oorschot, and Wilfred Uunk, "Popular Criteria for the
Welfare Deservingness of Disability Pensioners: The Influence of Structural and
Cultural Factors," *Social Indicators Research* 110, no. 3 (2013): 1103–17.

13. Ben Baumberg Geiger, "Disabled but Not Deserving? The Perceived Deservingness of Disability Welfare Benefit Claimants," *Journal of European Social Policy* 31,
no. 3 (2021): 337–51.

14. Nancy Lapid, "Economists Warn of Costs If Medicare Covers New Obesity
Drugs," Reuters, March 11, 2023, https://www.reuters.com/world/us/economists
-warn-costs-if-us-medicare-covers-new-obesity-drugs-2023-03-11; Elaine Chen,
"Covering New Weight Loss Drugs Could Strain Medicare, Policy Experts Warn,"
STAT, March 11, 2023, https://www.statnews.com/2023/03/11/new-weight-loss
-drugs-wegovy-medicare.

15. Julie Guthman, "Teaching the Politics of Obesity: Insights into Neoliberal Embodiment and Contemporary Biopolitics," *Antipode* 41, no. 5 (2009): 1110–33.

16. Christian S. Crandall, Silvana D'Anello, Nuray Sakalli, Eleana Lazarus, Grazyna Wieczorkowska Nejtardt, and N. T. Feather, "An Attribution-Value Model of Prejudice: Anti-Fat Attitudes in Six Nations," *Personality and Social Psychology Bulletin* 27, no. 1 (2001): 30–37.

17. Kathleen LeBesco, "Neoliberalism, Public Health, and the Moral Perils of Fatness," *Critical Public Health* 21, no. 2 (2011): 153–64.

18. Andrea Elizabeth Shaw, *The Embodiment of Disobedience: Fat Black Women's Unruly Political Bodies* (New York: Lexington Books, 2006), 9.

19. Sabrina Strings, *Fearing the Black Body: The Racial Origins of Fat Phobia* (New York: New York University Press, 2019), 210.

20. Leticia Sabsay, "The Political Aesthetics of Vulnerability and the Feminist Revolt," *Critical Times* 3, no. 2 (2020): 179–99.

21. Judith Butler, "Judith Butler on Rethinking Vulnerability, Violence, Resistance," *Verso Blog*, March 6, 2020, https://www.versobooks.com/blogs/4583-judith-butler -on-rethinking-vulnerability-violence-resistance.

22. Georg Frerks, Jeroen Warner, and Bart Weijs, "The Politics of Vulnerability and Resilience," *Ambiente & Sociedade* 14, no. 2 (2011): 105–22.

23. Peter Glick and Susan T. Fiske, "An Ambivalent Alliance: Hostile and Benevolent Sexism as Complementary Justifications for Gender Inequality," *American Psychologist* 56, no. 2 (2001): 109–18.

24. Judith Butler, "Rethinking Vulnerability and Resistance," in *Vulnerability in Resistance*, ed. Judith Butler, Zeynep Gambetti, and Leticia Sabsay (Durham, NC: Duke University Press, 2016), 12–27.

25. Butler, "Judith Butler on Rethinking Vulnerability, Violence, Resistance."

26. Butler, "Judith Butler on Rethinking Vulnerability, Violence, Resistance."

27. Butler, "Judith Butler on Rethinking Vulnerability, Violence, Resistance."

28. Butler, "Judith Butler on Rethinking Vulnerability, Violence, Resistance."

29. For more details on the group of fat activists I interviewed, see the book's introduction.

30. Martijn Van Zomeren, "Building a Tower of Babel? Integrating Core Motivations and Features of Social Structure into the Political Psychology of Political Action," *Political Psychology* 37 (2016): 87–114; Robert D. Benford and David A. Snow, "Framing Processes and Social Movements: An Overview and Assessment," *Annual Review of Sociology* 26, no. 1 (2000): 611–39.

31. This group was highly diverse: Six people were of color (two Black, one biracial, one Afro-Latina, one Latinx/mixed, and one Latinx). Three were nonbinary and seven were cisgender women. Three were heterosexual and seven were sexual minorities (five queer-identified, one lesbian-identified, and one pansexual-identified). Ages ranged from twenty-five to seventy-five (mean age = 45.2, SD = 16.52). Class backgrounds were also diverse, with incomes ranging from $15,000 to $190,000 (mean income = $67,333, SD = $52,680).

32. Aubrey Gordon, "Fat Activism," interview by Breanne Fahs, Zoom, August 29, 2022.

33. Mikey Mercedes, "Fat Activism," interview by Breanne Fahs, Zoom, May 12, 2022.

34. Da'Shaun L. Harrison, "Fat Activism," interview by Breanne Fahs, Zoom, May 6, 2022.

35. Caleb Luna, "Fat Activism," interview by Breanne Fahs, Zoom, May 27, 2022.

36. Esther Rothblum, "Fat Activism," interview by Breanne Fahs, Zoom, April 29, 2022.

37. Kimberly Dark, "Fat Activism," interview by Breanne Fahs, Zoom, April 8, 2022.

38. Dark, interview.

39. Tigress Osborn, "Fat Activism," interview by Breanne Fahs, Zoom, May 12, 2022.

40. Stacy Bias, "Fat Activism," interview by Breanne Fahs, Zoom, April 25, 2022.

41. Bias, interview.

42. Virgie Tovar, "Fat Activism," interview by Breanne Fahs, Zoom, April 18, 2022.

43. Harrison, interview.

44. Harrison, interview.

45. Dark, interview.

46. Rothblum, interview.

47. Luna, interview.

48. Mercedes, interview.

49. Gordon, interview.

50. Bias, interview.

51. Tovar, interview.

52. Tovar, interview.

53. Osborn, interview.

54. Barbara Bruno, "Fat Activism," interview by Breanne Fahs, Zoom, May 7, 2022.

55. Luna, interview.

56. Judith Butler, Zeynep Gambetti, and Leticia Sabsay, "Introduction," in Butler, Gambetti, and Sabsay, *Vulnerability in Resistance*, 5–6.

57. Breanne Fahs, *Firebrand Feminism: The Radical Lives of Ti-Grace Atkinson, Kathie Sarachild, Roxanne Dunbar-Ortiz, and Dana Densmore* (Seattle: University of Washington Press, 2018).

58. Butler, Gambetti, and Sabsay, "Introduction," 5.

CHAPTER 7: GUTTURAL RESISTANCE

1. Rebecca Traister, *Good and Mad: The Revolutionary Power of Women's Anger* (New York: Simon & Schuster, 2018), xxi.

2. Traister, *Good and Mad*, xxvii.

3. Traister, *Good and Mad*, xxiii.

4. Traister, *Good and Mad*, xxiv.

5. Traister, *Good and Mad*, xxvii.

6. Audre Lorde, "The Uses of Anger: Women Responding to Racism," in *Sister Outsider: Essays and Speeches* (Trumansburg, NY: Crossing Press, 1984), 127.

7. Stacy Bias, "Fat Activism," interview by Breanne Fahs, Zoom, April 25, 2022.

8. Mikey Mercedes, "Fat Activism," interview by Breanne Fahs, Zoom, May 12, 2022.

9. Esther Rothblum, "Fat Activism," interview by Breanne Fahs, Zoom, April 9, 2022.

10. Caleb Luna, "Fat Activism," interview by Breanne Fahs, Zoom, May 27, 2022.

11. Kimberly Dark, "Fat Activism," interview by Breanne Fahs, Zoom, April 8, 2022.

12. Aubrey Gordon, "Fat Activism," interview by Breanne Fahs, Zoom, August 29, 2022.

13. Da'Shaun L. Harrison, *Belly of the Beast: The Politics of Anti-Fatness as Anti-Blackness* (Berkeley, CA: North Atlantic Books, 2021), 5.

14. Luna, interview.

15. Barbara Bruno, "Fat Activism," interview by Breanne Fahs, Zoom, May 7, 2022.

16. Bias, interview.

17. Mercedes, interview.

18. Da'Shaun L. Harrison, "Fat Activism," interview by Breanne Fahs, Zoom, May 6, 2022.

19. For a more thorough examination of these tensions, see Breanne Fahs, *Firebrand Feminism: The Radical Lives of Ti-Grace Atkinson, Kathie Sarachild, Roxanne Dunbar-Ortiz, and Dana Densmore* (Seattle: University of Washington Press, 2018).

20. Bias, interview.

21. Rothblum, interview.

22. Dark, interview.

23. Luna, interview.

24. Sabrina Strings, *Fearing the Black Body: The Racial Origins of Fat Phobia* (New York: New York University Press, 2019), 211–12.

25. Harrison, interview.

26. Harrison, interview.

27. Virgie Tovar, "Fat Activism," interview by Breanne Fahs, Zoom, April 18, 2022.

28. Tigress Osborn, "Fat Activism," interview by Breanne Fahs, Zoom, May 12, 2022.

29. Jackie Wykes, "Introduction: Why Queering Fat Embodiment?" in *Queering Fat Embodiment*, ed. Cat Pausé, Jackie Wykes, and Samantha Murray (London: Routledge, 2016), 2.

30. Wykes, "Introduction: Why Queering Fat Embodiment?"; Charlotte Cooper, "Fat Studies: Mapping the Field," *Sociology Compass* 4, no. 12 (2010): 1020–34.

31. Leslie Feinberg, *Transgender Warriors: Making History from Joan of Arc to Dennis Rodman* (Boston: Beacon Press, 1996), 92.

32. Luna, interview.

33. Luna, interview.

34. Bias, interview.

35. Bias, interview.

36. Gordon, interview.

37. Mercedes, interview.

38. Osborn, interview.

39. Chris Bobel and Breanne Fahs, "From Bloodless Respectability to Radical Menstrual Embodiment: Shifting Menstrual Politics from Private to Public," *Signs: Journal of Women in Culture and Society* 45, no. 4 (2020): 955–83.

CHAPTER 8: FAT FURY

1. Soraya Chemaly, *Rage Becomes Her: The Power of Women's Anger* (New York: Atria, 2018), 295–96.

2. Michel Foucault, *Discipline and Punish: The Birth of the Prison* (London: Penguin, 1991).

3. Chemaly, *Rage Becomes Her*, xx (emphasis hers).

4. Jody L. Newman, Elizabeth A. Gray, and Dale R. Fuqua, "Sex Differences in the Relationship of Anger and Depression: An Empirical Study," *Journal of Counseling & Development* 77, no. 2 (1999): 198–203; Elizabeth D. Sperberg and Sally D. Stabb, "Depression in Women as Related to Anger and Mutuality in Relationships," *Psychology of Women Quarterly* 22, no. 2 (1998): 223–38; Phyllis Chesler, *Women and Madness* (Chicago: Chicago Review Press, 2018).

5. Virgie Tovar, "Fat Activism," interview by Breanne Fahs, Zoom, April 18, 2022.

6. Tigress Osborn, "Fat Activism," interview by Breanne Fahs, Zoom, May 12, 2022.

7. Caleb Luna, "Fat Activism," interview by Breanne Fahs, Zoom, May 27, 2022.

8. Luna, interview.

9. Da'Shaun L. Harrison, "Fat Activism," interview by Breanne Fahs, Zoom, May 6, 2022.

10. Stacy Bias, "Fat Activism," interview by Breanne Fahs, Zoom, April 25, 2022.

11. Esther Rothblum, "Fat Activism," interview by Breanne Fahs, Zoom, April 29, 2022.

12. Aubrey Gordon, "Fat Activism," interview by Breanne Fahs, Zoom, August 29, 2022.

13. Stefan Stürmer, Bernd Simon, Michael Loewy, and Heike Jörger, "The Dual-Pathway Model of Social Movement Participation: The Case of the Fat Acceptance Movement," *Social Psychology Quarterly* 66, no. 1 (2003): 71–82.

14. Tovar, interview.

15. Tovar, interview.

16. Osborn, interview.

17. Bias, interview.

18. Bias, interview.

19. Rothblum, interview.

20. Mikey Mercedes, "Fat Activism," interview by Breanne Fahs, Zoom, May 12, 2022.

21. Gordon, interview.

22. Luna, interview.

23. Luna, interview.

24. Harrison, interview.

25. Kimberly Dark, "Fat Activism," interview by Breanne Fahs, Zoom, April 8, 2022.

26. Dark, interview.

27. Barbara Bruno, "Fat Activism," interview by Breanne Fahs, Zoom, May 7, 2022.

28. Rothblum, interview.

29. Tovar, interview.

30. Dark, interview.

31. Bias, interview.

32. Gordon, interview.

33. Osborn, interview.

34. Harrison, interview.

35. Luna, interview.

36. Mercedes, interview.

37. Bias, interview.

38. Gordon, interview.

39. Rothblum, interview.
40. Dark, interview.
41. Luna, interview.
42. Tovar, interview.
43. Mercedes, interview.
44. Osborn, interview.
45. Harrison, interview.
46. Salman Rushdie, *Fury* (New York: Random House, 2002), 30–31.

INDEX

ableism, xiii, 18, 107, 132, 139, 145, 153,
    173. *See also* disabilities; healthiness,
    rhetoric of
abortion, xiv, 137, 168
academia, xii, 64, 69, 76, 130, 163
accommodating fatness in the work-
    place, xi, 72–76. *See also* workplace
    stigma
activism: anger and defiance in, 155–60;
    call for guttural resistance, 148–50;
    for civil rights of Black people, 129;
    future of, 172–77; on healthiness,
    55; manifesting, 160–67; solidarity
    among movements in, 143–48; for
    systemic change, xi, 167–72. *See also*
    intersectionality; solidarity
ADA (Americans with Disabilities Act),
    74–75
Adele, xii, 38, 39
Ahmed, Sara, 4
air travel. *See* travel and fat bodies
American Academy of Pediatrics, 86. *See*
    also children
American Housewife (television series), 27
American Medical Association (AMA),
    175. *See also* medical failures and fat
    bodies
anger, 129–31, 152, 155–60. *See also* fat
    fury; rage
anorexia, 90. *See also* diet culture
anti-Blackness, xix, 119, 140–41. *See also*
    racism

antidiscrimination laws, 168–72
anti-fatness, 79–81; as anti-Blackness,
    xix, 140–41; during COVID-19,
    94–102; fat women's response to,
    92–94; in mainstream discourse,
    xi, xiv; roots of, 137–43; through
    stereotyping, 25–30, 33–36. *See also*
    fatness; fearmongering; healthiness,
    rhetoric of
anxiety, 8, 16, 18, 19, 46, 121, 154. *See*
    also mental health
apple cider vinegar consumption, 50. *See*
    also weight-loss programs
asthma, 90, 109
Athleta, 50
Atkins diet, 50, 87. *See also* weight-loss
    programs
author positionality, ix–xiv, xx–xxi

bariatric surgery, 57–63, 90. *See also*
    gastric bypass surgery
becoming, ix–x, 5–6, 19
beet diet, 50. *See also* weight-loss
    programs
Belly of the Beast (Harrison), 114, 134,
    165
Bias, Stacy: on activism, 146, 158, 162,
    172; on anti-fatness, 122, 138; on
    body positivity, 131–32; *Flying
    While Fat* animation by, 117, 146,
    162; on "good fatty," 36, 52–54;
    on medical discrimination, 169;

primal scream, 150
Przybylo, Ela, 19
public policies and legislation on fatness,
168–71

quarantine 15, 21, 95. *See also* COVID-19

racial identity, 10, 114
racism, xiii, xix, 7, 18, 20, 100, 119,
140–42. *See also* anti-Blackness; civil
rights movement
Rad Fatty archetype, 54
rage, 112, 132. *See also* anger; fat fury
Rasmussen, Nicolas, 8
Reddit, 31
relationships and fatness, 12, 13, 124
research methods, xviii–xix, 10, 20, 186,
187, 195, 214
restrictive eating disorder, 90. *See also*
diet culture
Revenge Body (Luna), 115
Rodrigues, Sara, 19
Roe v. Wade, 168
Roseanne (television series), 27
Rothblum, Esther, xviii, 115, 133, 138,
159, 163, 167, 173
Rushdie, Salman, 178

San Francisco, California, 101
Seat Act (proposed), 169
self-care rhetoric, 45, 48
self-censorship, 15
self-control, 7–8
sexual desirability, 9, 17–18
sexual economy, 4
shame. *See* fat shame and fat-shaming
Shaw, Andrea Elizabeth, 110
Shallow Hal (film), 28
Shrill (television series), xii, 27
slavery, 142. *See also* racism
SlimFast, 50. *See also* weight-loss
programs
smoothie dieting, 50. *See also* weight-
loss programs

social media, 30, 95
solidarity, 111–12, 134–37, 143–48. *See
also* activism
Somebody Somewhere (television series),
25
specters, 4–5, 85–92
starvation, 50. *See also* weight-loss
programs
stereotyping, 25–30, 33–36. *See also*
media portrayals of fatness
stigma, 64–70. *See also* anti-fatness; fat
stereotypes; workplace stigma
Strings, Sabrina, xix, 47, 110, 139–40
suicide, 61
Super Fun Night (television series), 27
Sweat (app), 49
systemic change, 167–72

Talley, Heather Laine, 15–16
Taylor, Sonya Renee, 85
TechnoDyke.com, 162
terrorization, xi, xiii, xx, 41, 63, 118–22,
154
terror of fatness, overview, xi–xii
thinness and health discourse, xv, 134
thin privilege, 76–79
thin women: dominance and, xvi–xvii;
fat future of, 3–10; fear of weight
gain by, 10–15, 20–23; privilege of,
76–79
This is Us (television series), xii, 25
Thore, Whitney Way, 55
Tiefer, Leonore, 10
TikTok, 30
Tovar, Virgie: on anti-fatness, 141–42;
on fat activist work, 160–61, 168,
174; on fat embodiment, 123, 155,
156; *You Have the Right to Remain
Fat*, 118
Traister, Rebecca, 129–30
trans people, xviii, xix, 4, 17, 19, 111
trauma, xii, 12, 113–14, 118–22
travel and fat bodies, xi, xvi, 117, 146,
169

ABOUT THE AUTHOR

Breanne Fahs is a professor of women's and gender studies at Arizona State University and a practicing clinical psychologist with over twenty years of clinical experience. Her writing on feminism, women's sexuality, critical body studies, and political activism amongst other topics has been published and reviewed widely including in the *New York Times*, the *Boston Review*, *Dissent*, the *Paris Review*, *The Guardian*, and the *Los Angeles Review of Books*. She has published over eighty articles in feminist, social science, and humanities journals, and is the author of six books, including *Performing Sex: The Making and Unmaking of Women's Erotic Lives* (2011), *Valerie Solanas: The Defiant Life of the Woman Who Wrote SCUM (and Shot Andy Warhol)* (2014), *Out for Blood: Essays on Menstruation and Resistance* (2016), *Firebrand Feminism: The Radical Lives of Ti-Grace Atkinson, Kathie Sarachild, Roxanne Dunbar-Ortiz, and Dana Densmore* (2018), *Women, Sex, and Madness: Notes from the Edge* (2019), and, most recently, *Unshaved: Resistance and Revolution in Women's Body Hair Politics* (2022). She has also edited or coedited four books: *The Moral Panics of Sexuality* (2013), *Transforming Contagion: Risky Contacts Among Bodies, Disciplines, and Nations* (2018), *The Palgrave Handbook of Critical Menstruation Studies* (2020), and *Burn It Down! Feminist Manifestos for the Revolution* (2020), which was a *New York Times* notable book. She is also the founder and director of the Feminist Research on Gender and Sexuality Group at Arizona State University.